D1537184

# Alcoholism

Other Books in the Current Controversies Series:

The Abortion Controversy
Assisted Suicide
Capital Punishment
Computers and Society
Conserving the Environment
Crime
The Disabled
Drug Trafficking
Ethics
Europe
Family Violence
Free Speech
Gambling
Garbage and Waste
Gay Rights
Genetics and Intelligence
Gun Control
Guns and Violence
Hate Crimes
Hunger
Illegal Drugs
Illegal Immigration
The Information Highway

Interventionism
Iraq
Marriage and Divorce
Medical Ethics
Mental Health
Minorities
Nationalism and Ethnic
    Conflict
Native American Rights
Police Brutality
Politicians and Ethics
Pollution
Prisons
Racism
Reproductive Technologies
The Rights of Animals
Sexual Harassment
Smoking
Teen Addiction
Urban Terrorism
Violence Against Women
Violence in the Media
Women in the Military

# Alcoholism

**James D. Torr**, *Book Editor*

**David Bender**, *Publisher*
**Bruno Leone**, *Executive Editor*

**Bonnie Szumski**, *Editorial Director*
**David M. Haugen**, *Managing Editor*

CURRENT CONTROVERSIES

Cover photo: © Super Stock

Library of Congress Cataloging-in-Publication Data

Alcoholism / James D. Torr, book editor.
    p.  cm. — (Current controversies)
    Includes bibliographical references and index.
    ISBN 0-7377-0139-0 (lib. : alk. paper). — ISBN 0-7377-0138-2
(pbk. : alk. paper)
    1. Alcoholism—United States. I. Torr, James D., 1974–      .
II. Series.
HV5292.A3855   2000
362.292—dc21                                                      99-37265
                                                                        CIP

©2000 by Greenhaven Press, Inc., PO Box 289009, San Diego, CA 92198-9009
Printed in the U.S.A.

# Contents

Foreword                                                    12

Introduction                                                14

## Chapter 1: How Serious Are the Problems of Alcoholism and Alcohol Abuse?

Chapter Preface                                             18

### Alcoholism and Alcohol Abuse Are Serious Problems

Alcoholism Is a Serious Problem *by Well-Connected*         19

Alcoholism is a chronic, progressive disease that affects millions of
Americans. It can cause a large number of medical problems and is
associated with violence and child abuse. Alcoholism can be hard to
detect because there is no clear point at which problem drinking becomes alcohol dependence. Recovering alcoholics can learn abstinence but must constantly guard against the possibility of relapse.

Children of Alcoholics Face Many Problems

*by the American Academy of Child and Adolescent Psychiatry*   30

The people harmed most by alcoholism are often not the alcoholics
themselves, but their families. Children raised in alcoholic homes
are more likely to abuse alcohol or other drugs later in life and often
develop serious emotional problems as a means of coping with their
parent's drinking problem.

Alcohol Abuse Is a Serious Problem for Teenagers

*by Center for Science in the Public Interest*              32

Alcohol is the most widely abused drug among youth. Alcohol
abuse among young people is associated with health problems, teen
suicide, traffic accidents, crime, sexually transmitted diseases, and
problems in school. In addition, underage drinking is often the first
step toward other types of drug abuse.

Binge Drinking on College Campuses Is a Serious Problem

*by J.J. Thompson*                                          38

Most college administrators are not aware of the frequency with
which college students abuse alcohol. Binge drinking is a widespread problem on college campuses, one that is associated with low
grades, unsafe sexual practices, and violence. Colleges that restrict
the use of alcohol on campus and provide students with nonalcoholic activities and events have lower rates of binge drinking.

## The Problems of Alcoholism and Alcohol Abuse Are Exaggerated

The Dangers of Alcohol Are Exaggerated *by Stanton Peele*                     44
For decades the temperance movement has exaggerated the dangers
of alcohol and the risk of alcoholism. This has led to irrational alcohol policies, such as raising the legal drinking age to 21, that have
not helped to reduce alcohol-related problems. There are some indications that the strong anti-alcohol sentiment in America is beginning to recede, in part because of the government's admission that
moderate drinking can help prevent heart disease. However, Americans still retain a very negatively biased view of alcohol.

Alcohol Consumption Is Unfairly Condemned *by Colman Andrews*                  50
Drinking can be a very pleasurable activity, and even drinking to the
point of intoxication is not wrong if it is done responsibly and in the
appropriate setting. However, it is becoming increasingly unacceptable to drink alcohol at all, and those who do drink frequently or
heavily are often erroneously regarded as alcoholics. This negative
view of alcohol is unjustified; alcohol misuse, not alcohol itself,
should be the target of public disapproval.

The Extent of Binge Drinking Among Young People Is Exaggerated
*by David J. Hanson*                                                          59
The term "binge drinking" describes an extended period of heavy
drinking in which the drinker gives up his or her usual obligations in
order to become intoxicated. However, some researchers have defined bingeing simply as the consumption of five or more drinks in
one day. This has led to deceptive statistics that make it seem as
though most teenagers and college students are heavy drinkers. In
reality, binge drinking among young people has been declining for
years.

# Chapter 2: Is Alcoholism a Disease?

Chapter Preface                                                               64

## Yes: Alcoholism Is a Disease

Physicians Should Treat Alcoholism as a Disease *by Thomas R. Hobbs*          65
For decades the medical community has recognized that alcoholism
is a progressive, often fatal disease that is influenced by genetic,
psychosocial, and environmental factors. Yet studies indicate that
many doctors still view alcoholism as merely a behavioral problem,
and consequently often fail to detect or treat the disease. Hospitals
and medical schools must help physicians understand that alcoholism is a preventable, treatable disease.

Addiction Is a Disease *by Greg Skipper*                                      69
The medical concept of disease is often misunderstood by the general public. Many people think that diseases indiscriminately attack
healthy bodies, whereas alcoholism or other drug addictions are
brought on by substance abuse. In fact, many diseases, such as heart

disease or lung cancer, are brought on by unhealthy behaviors. The disease model of addiction is compatible with the idea that addicts are responsible for their behavior.

Alcoholism Has a Genetic Basis *by Marc Alan Schuckit*    73
Just as individuals have different genetic susceptibilities for heart disease or cancer, they also have different genetic risks for developing alcoholism. Studies have shown that children of alcoholics are more likely to develop alcoholism, even when they are raised in adoptive families where alcohol is not prevalent. However, no one is predestined by their genes to become an alcoholic; individuals who are aware of a family history of alcoholism can always choose not to drink.

Alcoholics Should Not Be Blamed for Their Disease *by W. Waldo*    76
Alcoholism is a brain disease that occurs in people who have a genetic susceptibility to this type of addiction. Alcoholism has a biological basis, just like cancer or diabetes, and telling alcoholics that their disease is a result of weak character or insufficient willpower is just as wrong as telling cancer patients or diabetics that they are responsible for their diseases. When someone is diagnosed with alcoholism, they should receive treatment, not moral criticism.

## No: Alcoholism Is Not a Disease

The Genetic Basis of Alcoholism Has Been Exaggerated
*by Stanton Peele*    78
There is little evidence to support the idea that alcoholism is an inherited disease. Studies purporting to show the link between alcoholism and genetics often have conflicting or ambiguous results. Moreover, even the scientists conducting such research acknowledge that genetics can explain only part of the problem, and that cultural and social factors play a large role in the development of alcoholism.

Treating Alcoholism as a Disease Harms Alcoholics
*by Edward A. Dreyfus*    83
Alcoholism was originally termed a disease in order to help people understand that it was a serious problem for which they should seek help. However, the disease metaphor is being overused and applied to all manner of individuals, from "workaholics" to smokers. As the use of the term "disease" increases, alcoholics and other emotionally disturbed people are coming to believe they are "sick," and need medical rather than psychological help to overcome their addictions.

# Chapter 3: How Effective Is Alcoholics Anonymous?

Chapter Preface    90

## Alcoholics Anonymous Is Effective

Alcoholics Anonymous Is Effective *by Robert Zimmerman*    91
Alcoholics Anonymous has over 2 million members worldwide, all

of whom attend regular meetings where they help each other stay sober. The organization has helped thousands of alcoholics overcome their disease, and AA teachings have also been used to treat other types of addiction. Alcoholics Anonymous is over 60 years old, but its original twelve-step philosophy has not changed at all in that time.

AA's Emphasis on Spirituality Benefits Alcoholics *by William W. May*      95
In order to achieve long-term sobriety, alcoholics must undergo a "moment of clarity"—a spiritual awakening through which individuals are able to find the inner strength to overcome alcoholism. Alcoholics Anonymous works because it teaches people how to achieve this spiritual experience and use it to stay sober.

## Alcoholics Anonymous Is Ineffective

Alcoholics Anonymous Is Ineffective *by Michael J. Lemanski*      101
When Alcoholics Anonymous was developed, no other treatments for alcoholism existed. Thus it was embraced by the medical and psychological communities only by default. Unfortunately, AA has since become entrenched in the treatment field—even though only a very small percentage of AA participants maintain sobriety—because the few people that AA does help become obsessed with spreading their quasi-religious beliefs to others.

AA's Methods Harm Many Alcoholics *by Ursula Kenny*      110
Many former members of Alcoholics Anonymous say that the organization is nothing more than a cult that brainwashes and bullies its members into staying sober. They charge that, in AA, alcoholics merely replace their compulsive drinking with another unhealthy behavior: allowing other AA members to control their lives. Still others find AA's teaching that alcoholism is a lifelong, incurable disease disempowering.

# Chapter 4: Does the Alcohol Industry Market Its Products Responsibly?

Chapter Preface      115

## Yes: Industry Self-Regulation Has Been Effective

The Government Should Not Regulate Alcohol Advertising
*by Thomas A. Hemphill*      116
Government regulation of alcohol advertising is unnecessary. Alcohol companies that use irresponsible marketing practices quickly become the target of public scorn, and advertising outlets, such as television broadcasters, refuse to carry the offending advertisements. This is why the alcohol industry voluntarily follows self-imposed marketing codes which ensure that alcohol advertising is socially responsible.

Alcohol Advertising Does Not Promote Underage Drinking
   *by Morris E. Chafetz*                                                126
   There is no evidence linking alcohol advertising to increased consumption among youth. In contrast to the claims of child protection
   advocates, teenagers make their own decisions about drinking: They
   do not blindly follow what either pro-alcohol advertisements or anti-
   alcohol groups tell them. Young people, like adults, regard alcohol
   advertisements as a mundane part of daily life; limiting young
   people's access to them could backfire and increase their allure.

The Alcohol Industry Should Be Permitted to Advertise the Health
   Benefits of Moderate Drinking *by Stephen Chapman*                   130
   Overzealous public health advocates believe that it is the government's job to discourage people from engaging in any potentially
   harmful behavior. This is why the government prohibits winemakers
   from telling consumers about the health benefits of moderate drinking. In trying to protect people from themselves, the government un-
   justly curtails free speech and treats its citizens like children.

## No: The Government Should Regulate the Alcohol Industry

The Government Should Combat the Influence of Alcohol Advertising
   on Youth *by George A. Hacker*                                       133
   Ironically, the decision by the liquor industry to advertise on television has called attention to the harm that beer and wine advertising
   have already caused: All alcohol advertising has a harmful effect on
   society because it encourages people—especially children and teenagers—to drink. There are a variety of steps that the government
   should take to curb the effects of this advertising, including restricting it to late-night programming and funding public health messages
   that stress the negative aspects of alcohol use.

The Alcohol Industry Should Not Be Permitted to Advertise the Health
   Benefits of Moderate Drinking *by Robert Zimmerman*                  141
   The wine industry wants the government to amend warning labels
   on wine bottles to include information about the health effects of
   moderate drinking, but Congress should allow no such thing. The
   health benefits of alcohol are often exaggerated, and any amount of
   alcohol is dangerous to recovering alcoholics. Moreover, most
   Americans have a poor understanding of what "moderate" drinking
   actually means.

The Alcohol Industry Has Too Much Political Influence
   *by Michael Massing*                                                 144
   The alcohol industry wields an enormous amount of political power
   at the national, state, and local levels, and this is the primary reason
   that, even as tobacco companies have become the target of lawsuits
   and increased government regulation, alcohol companies remain
   free to advertise on television. Alcohol lobbyists' many government
   connections, along with the millions of dollars at their disposal, prevent public health advocates from raising awareness about the dangers of alcohol.

# Chapter 5: How Can Alcohol-Related Problems Be Prevented?

Chapter Preface                                                                 156

## More Restrictive Policies Toward Alcohol Are Needed

Raising Taxes on Alcoholic Beverages Would Reduce Alcohol-Related
  Problems *by Center for Science in the Public Interest*          157
  Raising taxes on alcoholic beverages would raise the final price of
  such products, and consequently people would buy fewer of them.
  This would benefit public health because when people drink less,
  alcohol-related problems are reduced. Raising taxes is fair because
  alcohol-related problems cost state governments billions of dollars
  in the form of property damage, medical expenses, and lost productivity, yet the revenue currently generated from alcohol taxes is not
  nearly enough to offset these costs.

Law Enforcement Strategies Can Help Reduce Underage Drinking
  *by Bobby Little and Mike Bishop*                                      162
  Underage drinking is a very serious problem, one that the police
  should address. There are a variety of methods that police can use to
  catch underage drinkers, and states that have increased the number
  of arrests for underage drinking show a corresponding decrease in
  drunk driving and other problems.

The Government Should Lower the Legal Threshold for Drunk
  Driving *by the National Highway Traffic Safety Administration*       167
  States can help reduce the number of alcohol-related motor vehicle
  fatalities by adopting .08 percent blood-alcohol content, rather than
  .10, as the legal limit at which a driver is considered to be under the
  influence of alcohol. Research shows that drivers at .08 BAC should
  certainly not be driving. Most other industrialized nations use the
  .08 standard, and states that have already adopted the .08 standard
  have had fewer fatal crashes as a result.

## Less Restrictive Policies Toward Alcohol Are Needed

Restrictive Alcohol Policies Are Ineffective *by David J. Hanson*       172
  Nationwide alcohol prohibition failed in America, but many "neo-
  prohibitionists" still believe that alcohol-related problems can be
  solved by limiting people's access to alcohol. However, research
  shows that restrictive alcohol policies, such as raising alcohol taxes,
  are ultimately ineffective and usually cause more harm than good. A
  more moderate approach that stresses responsible drinking while
  still not condoning alcohol abuse would be much more effective.

Age-21 Drinking Laws Exacerbate Alcohol-Related Problems
  *by Ruth Engs*                                                        179
  Because society forbids young people to drink until they are 21,
  they see alcohol as a "forbidden fruit" and a symbol of adulthood
  and consider underage drinking to be an act of rebellion. Lowering
  the drinking age to 18 or 19 would be the most effective way to

reduce alcohol abuse among youth, because it would allow them to begin moderate drinking, in controlled environments such as restaurants, at an earlier age.

The Government Should Not Lower the Legal Threshold for Drunk Driving *by Richard Berman*     182

It is wrong to try to reduce drunk driving simply by redefining drunkenness as a .08 percent blood-alcohol content rather than .10. Awareness about drunk driving is at an all-time high, and the people who cause drunk driving fatalities today are usually reckless, irresponsible individuals with BAC levels as high as .18 percent. Yet groups like Mothers Against Drunk Driving, in their zeal, want to criminalize even moderate drinking, thus trivializing the very real problem of drunk driving.

Bibliography     187

Organizations to Contact     191

Index     196

# Foreword

By definition, controversies are "discussions of questions in which opposing opinions clash" (Webster's Twentieth Century Dictionary Unabridged). Few would deny that controversies are a pervasive part of the human condition and exist on virtually every level of human enterprise. Controversies transpire between individuals and among groups, within nations and between nations. Controversies supply the grist necessary for progress by providing challenges and challengers to the status quo. They also create atmospheres where strife and warfare can flourish. A world without controversies would be a peaceful world; but it also would be, by and large, static and prosaic.

## The Series' Purpose

The purpose of the Current Controversies series is to explore many of the social, political, and economic controversies dominating the national and international scenes today. Titles selected for inclusion in the series are highly focused and specific. For example, from the larger category of criminal justice, Current Controversies deals with specific topics such as police brutality, gun control, white collar crime, and others. The debates in Current Controversies also are presented in a useful, timeless fashion. Articles and book excerpts included in each title are selected if they contribute valuable, long-range ideas to the overall debate. And wherever possible, current information is enhanced with historical documents and other relevant materials. Thus, while individual titles are current in focus, every effort is made to ensure that they will not become quickly outdated. Books in the Current Controversies series will remain important resources for librarians, teachers, and students for many years.

In addition to keeping the titles focused and specific, great care is taken in the editorial format of each book in the series. Book introductions and chapter prefaces are offered to provide background material for readers. Chapters are organized around several key questions that are answered with diverse opinions representing all points on the political spectrum. Materials in each chapter include opinions in which authors clearly disagree as well as alternative opinions in which authors may agree on a broader issue but disagree on the possible solutions. In this way, the content of each volume in Current Controversies mirrors the mosaic of opinions encountered in society. Readers will quickly realize that there are many viable answers to these complex issues. By questioning each author's conclusions, students and casual readers can begin to develop the critical thinking skills so important to evaluating opinionated material.

Current Controversies is also ideal for controlled research. Each anthology in the series is composed of primary sources taken from a wide gamut of informational categories including periodicals, newspapers, books, United States and foreign government documents, and the publications of private and public organizations. Readers will find factual support for reports, debates, and research papers covering all areas of important issues. In addition, an annotated table of contents, an index, a book and periodical bibliography, and a list of organizations to contact are included in each book to expedite further research.

Perhaps more than ever before in history, people are confronted with diverse and contradictory information. During the Persian Gulf War, for example, the public was not only treated to minute-to-minute coverage of the war, it was also inundated with critiques of the coverage and countless analyses of the factors motivating U.S. involvement. Being able to sort through the plethora of opinions accompanying today's major issues, and to draw one's own conclusions, can be a complicated and frustrating struggle. It is the editors' hope that Current Controversies will help readers with this struggle.

Greenhaven Press anthologies primarily consist of previously published material taken from a variety of sources, including periodicals, books, scholarly journals, newspapers, government documents, and position papers from private and public organizations. These original sources are often edited for length and to ensure their accessibility for a young adult audience. The anthology editors also change the original titles of these works in order to clearly present the main thesis of each viewpoint and to explicitly indicate the opinion presented in the viewpoint. These alterations are made in consideration of both the reading and comprehension levels of a young adult audience. Every effort is made to ensure that Greenhaven Press accurately reflects the original intent of the authors included in this anthology.

*"Historically, controversy over compulsive drinking has dealt not with what causes it, but rather with how to prevent it."*

# Introduction

Before recorded history, human beings discovered that grape juice, when exposed to naturally occurring yeasts, becomes wine. Scientists would eventually describe this process as fermentation, thousands of years after wine and other alcoholic beverages had become an integral part of many cultures' meals, celebrations, and religious ceremonies.

Unfortunately, alcoholic beverages have also contributed to a considerable portion of human misery. Data from the National Center for Health Statistics indicate that excessive alcohol consumption causes more than 100,000 deaths per year in the United States alone, primarily through cirrhosis of the liver, drunk driving, and alcohol-related homicide and suicide. According to *The Columbia University College of Physicians and Surgeons Complete Home Medical Guide*, alcohol use is involved in half of all murders, accidental deaths, and suicides; half of all crimes; and almost half of all fatal automobile accidents.

The problem most often associated with heavy drinking, however, is alcoholism. Simply put, alcoholism is addiction to alcohol, but beyond this basic definition the symptoms of alcoholism can be difficult to pinpoint. They include a craving for alcohol, lack of self-control when drinking, a high tolerance for the effects of alcohol, and physical withdrawal symptoms, such as sweating, shakiness, and anxiety, when alcohol use ceases. Alcoholics often continue drinking despite repeated alcohol-related problems, such as losing a job, harming friends or family, or getting into trouble with the law.

There are approximately 14 million people with alcohol problems in America alone, somewhat less than half of whom are alcoholics. Such estimates are very rough because many people who drink heavily do not develop the physical and psychological dependence on alcohol that characterizes true alcoholics. The terms "problem drinking" or "alcohol abuse" are used to describe these drinking patterns, which may not lead to alcoholism but are nonetheless often destructive both to the drinker and to others.

In fact, nine out of ten people who drink do not become alcoholics. Researchers posit many explanations for why some people seem prone to alcoholism, while others are able to drink responsibly—or even to habitually abuse alcohol—without becoming dependent on it. Yet, despite decades of research, the exact mechanisms behind alcoholism remain poorly understood. Most scientists agree that alcoholism has at least some genetic basis, but they are also quick to warn that biology only explains part of the problem. Psychologists point out that while alcoholism does tend to run in families, this may be because children learn harmful drinking behaviors from their parents. Other researchers point to cultural influences, arguing that people from certain religious, ethnic, or socioeconomic backgrounds are more prone to alcoholism than others.

Controversy over the causes of alcoholism, however, is a relatively recent phenomenon: The term "alcoholism" itself was not coined until 1860, and the theory that it is a medical disease was only postulated in 1930. Historically, controversy over compulsive drinking has dealt not with what causes it, but rather with how to prevent it; those most concerned about alcoholism have not sought to study the condition, but instead to reduce alcohol consumption. This is especially true of the United States.

In colonial times, the states imposed fines on citizens for drunken behavior, or for selling alcohol to known drunks. Alcoholic beverages themselves, however, were not frowned upon until the end of the 18th century, when the temperance movement began in earnest. Led by religious leaders such as Cotton Mather and John Wesley, the temperance movement first preached against the evils of "ardent spirits," or hard liquor. But by the early 19th century, leaders like the Irish priest Theobald Matthew and groups such as the American Temperance Society began advocating complete abstinence from alcohol. At the end of the Civil War in 1865, there was a clear conflict between "drys," who favored the banning of alcoholic beverages, and "wets," who did not. Groups such as the Woman's Christian Temperance Union, founded in 1874, and the Anti-Saloon League of America, founded in 1895, steadily gained political influence. By 1913, nine states had instituted complete prohibition of alcohol, and many other states had severely restricted alcohol availability.

Finally, in 1917, temperance groups persuaded Congress to adopt national prohibition. In 1919 the 18th Amendment was ratified by the states, and the National Prohibition Act, also known as the Volstead Act, went into effect on January 27, 1920. Prohibition lasted for thirteen years, during which time the manufacture, sale, transportation, or importation of alcoholic beverages was illegal in America.

Prohibition, sometimes called "the noble experiment," was a failure. Rather than eliminating alcohol consumption, it forced it underground into illegal speakeasies; by the late 1920s there were more speakeasies than there had been saloons. Bootlegging liquor became a lucrative practice, controlled by gangsters who bribed local police and public officials. Violence and corruption soared, while the problem of alcohol abuse only worsened. Prohibition was finally repealed on December 5, 1933, with the passage of the 21st Amendment.

The government's attempt to solve alcohol problems through law alone had failed. But the problems remained, and, after the repeal of Prohibition, other types of strategies were developed to deal with alcoholism. The most famous of these is Alcoholics Anonymous. Founded in the 1930s, it still strives today to teach alcoholics how to overcome their addiction and stay sober. More recently, psychological counseling techniques have been developed and organizations besides AA have formed to help people overcome alcoholism. Moreover, public awareness of the problem has increased substantially; rather than being seen simply as sinful or irresponsible behavior, as it was prior to Prohibition, since the 1930s more and more people have begun to view alcoholism as a medical problem rather than as a vice.

Although compassion for alcoholics has increased, the problem of alcoholism has not gone away, and Americans' views toward alcoholic beverages remain mixed. After Prohibition was repealed, most states maintained laws that restricted alcohol availability. In the 1970s many of these laws were strengthened: Taxes on alcoholic beverages were increased and the legal drinking age was raised to 21. Many observers speculated that America was entering an era of "neo-prohibitionism"—a shift in public policy back to temperance ideals. Then, in the mid-1990s, widespread media coverage of the possible health benefits of moderate drinking led many to theorize that attitudes had shifted once again, and that the United States was beginning a renewed "love affair" with alcohol. Whatever Americans' current attitudes toward alcohol may be, one thing is certain: Millions of them continue to become alcoholics, while countless more experience the devastating problems associated with alcohol abuse.

The authors in *Alcoholism: Current Controversies* debate the nature of alcoholism and the extent of alcohol-related problems, as well as what should be done to prevent them, in the following chapters: How Serious Are the Problems of Alcoholism and Alcohol Abuse? Is Alcoholism a Disease? How Effective Is Alcoholics Anonymous? Does the Alcohol Industry Market Its Products Responsibly? How Can Alcohol-Related Problems Be Prevented? It is hoped that by exploring the issues surrounding alcoholism and alcohol abuse, readers will better understand why, despite thousands of years of experience with the effects of alcoholic beverages, these problems continue to plague human society.

# Chapter 1

# How Serious Are the Problems of Alcoholism and Alcohol Abuse?

# Chapter Preface

Few people dispute that alcohol abuse can be dangerous or that regular drinking poses the risk of developing alcoholism. Yet some believe that warnings about these problems too often overshadow the positive aspects of drinking. These two views of alcohol are apparent in the recent controversy over the health benefits of moderate drinking.

The traditional medical wisdom regarding alcohol—that abstinence was the best policy—began to be questioned in 1991 after *60 Minutes* aired "The French Paradox," a segment which suggested that the French may have a lower incidence of heart disease, even though they eat more fat than Americans, because of their high per capita consumption of wine. Since then, numerous studies have confirmed that moderate alcohol consumption—no more than one drink a day for women, two for men—reduces the risk of heart disease for most people. This was surprising news to most Americans, even though many doctors had long suspected the link between alcohol and heart disease.

In 1979 the Framingham Heart Study found that drinkers were less prone to heart disease than abstainers. But William Castelli, director of the study, expressed his reluctance to publicize this finding in an editorial in the *Journal of the American Medical Association*: "With 17 million alcoholics in this country we perhaps have a message for which this country is not ready." Less than twenty years later, physicians' attitudes had changed: In 1997, another *JAMA* editorial estimated that if Americans stopped drinking altogether, an additional eighty-one thousand people a year would die from heart disease.

Still, many doctors believe Castelli was right, and that the thousands of headlines proclaiming the health benefits of alcohol hurt more people than they help. "If you make broad generalizations about the benefits of drinking, you're going to raise the average consumption of society and get more people abusing alcohol," writes physician Michael Criqui. Dr. Albert B. Lowenfels explains that most adults already drink some alcohol, and that those who abstain are often recovering alcoholics, have a family history of alcoholism, or have moral objections to drinking. "Clearly," writes Lowenfels, "it would be unwise to recommend light or moderate drinking to patients in any of these categories."

In order to educate people about responsible drinking, teachers, parents, and policy makers must decide how to portray the positive and negative aspects of alcohol use. And in making decisions about alcohol, individuals must, like the authors in the following chapter, weigh the benefits of moderate drinking against the disastrous consequences of alcoholism and alcohol abuse.

# Alcoholism Is a Serious Problem

## by Well-Connected

**About the author:** *Well-Connected reports are written and updated by medical writers and reviewed by a board of physicians at Harvard Medical School and Massachusetts General Hospital.*

*What Is Alcoholism?*

Alcoholism is a chronic disease, progressive and often fatal; it is a primary disorder and not a symptom of other diseases or emotional problems. The chemistry of alcohol allows it to affect nearly every type of cell in the body, including those in the central nervous system. In the brain, alcohol interacts with centers responsible for pleasure and other desirable sensations. After prolonged exposure to alcohol, the brain adapts to the changes alcohol makes and becomes dependent on it. For people with alcoholism, drinking becomes the primary medium through which they can deal with people, work, and life. Alcohol dominates their thinking, emotions, and actions. The severity of this disease is influenced by factors such as genetics, psychology, culture, and response to physical pain.

## Loss of Control

Alcoholism can develop insidiously; often there is no clear line between problem drinking and alcoholism. The only early indications of alcoholism may be the unpleasant physical responses to withdrawal that occur during even brief periods of abstinence. Sometimes people experience long-term depression or anxiety, insomnia, chronic pain, or personal or work stress that lead to the use of alcohol for relief, but often no extraordinary events have occurred that account for the drinking problem.

Alcoholics have little or no control over the quantity they drink or the duration or frequency of their drinking. They are preoccupied with drinking, deny their own addiction, and continue to drink even though they are aware of the dangers. Over time, some people become tolerant to the effects of drinking and require more alcohol to become intoxicated, creating the illusion that they can "hold their liquor." They have blackouts after drinking and frequent hangovers that cause them to miss work and other normal activities. Alcoholics might drink alone and start early in the day. They periodically quit drinking or switch from hard liquor to beer or wine, but these periods rarely last. Severe alcoholics often have a history of accidents, marital and work instability, and alcohol-related health problems. Episodic violent and abusive incidents involving spouses and children and a history of unexplained or frequent accidents are often signs of drug or alcohol abuse.

> *"For people with alcoholism, drinking becomes the primary medium through which they can deal with people, work, and life."*

*What Causes Alcoholism?*

People have been drinking alcohol for perhaps 15,000 years. Just drinking steadily and consistently over time can cause a sense of dependence and withdrawal symptoms during periods of abstinence; this physical dependence, however, is not the sole cause of alcoholism. To develop alcoholism, other factors usually come into play, including biology and genetics, culture, and psychology.

## Brain Chemistry and Genetic Factors

The craving for alcohol during abstinence, the pain of withdrawal, and the high rate of relapse are due to the brain's adaptation to and dependence on the changes in its own chemistry caused by long term use of alcohol. Alcohol causes relaxation and euphoria but also acts as a depressant on the central nervous system. Even after years of research, experts still do not know exactly how alcohol affects the brain or how the brain affects alcoholism. Alcohol appears to have major effects upon the hippocampus, an area in the brain associated with learning and memory and the regulation of emotion, sensory processing, appetite, and stress. Alcohol breaks down into products called fatty acid ethyl esters, which appear to inhibit important neurotransmitters (chemical messengers in the brain) in the hippocampus. Of particular importance to researchers of alcoholism are the neurotransmitters gamma aminobutyric acid (GABA), dopamine, and serotonin, which are strongly associated with emotional behavior and cravings. Research indicates that dopamine transmission, particularly, is strongly associated with the rewarding properties of alcohol, nicotine, opiates, and cocaine. Investigators have focused on nerve-cell structures known as dopamine D2 receptors (DRD2), which influence the activity of dopamine. Mice with few of these receptors show low interest in and even aversion to alcohol.

In people with severe alcoholism, researchers have located a gene that alters the function of DRD2. This gene is also found in people with attention deficit disorder, who have an increased risk for alcoholism, and in people with

Tourette's syndrome and autism. One major study, however, found no connection at all between the DRD2 gene and alcoholism. More work in this area is needed. Researchers are also investigating genes that regulate certain enzymes known as kinases that affect alcohol uptake in the brain as well as genes that affect serotonin. Even if genetic factors can be identified, however, they are unlikely to explain all cases of alcoholism. In fact, lack of genetic protection may play a role in alcoholism. Because alcohol is not found easily in nature, genetic mechanisms to protect against excessive consumption may not have evolved in humans as they frequently have for protection against natural threats.

## Risk Factors for Alcoholism

*Who Becomes an Alcoholic?*

*General Risks and Age.* Some population studies indicate that in a single year, between 7.4% and 9.7% of the population are dependent on alcohol, and between 13.7% and 23.5% of Americans are alcohol-dependent at some point in their lives. A 1996 national survey reported that 11 million Americans are heavy drinkers (five or more drinks per occasion on five or more days in a month) and 32 million engaged in binge drinking (five or more drinks on one occasion) in the month previous to the survey. People with a family history of alcoholism are more likely to begin drinking before the age of 20 and to become alcoholic. But *anyone* who begins drinking in adolescence is at higher risk. Currently 1.9 mil-

*"In a single year, between 7.4% and 9.7% of the population are dependent on alcohol."*

lion young people between the ages of 12 and 20 are considered heavy drinkers and 4.4 million are binge drinkers. Although alcoholism usually develops in early adulthood, the elderly are not exempt. In fact, in one study, 15% of men and 12% of women over age 60 drank more than the national standard for excess alcohol consumption. Alcohol also affects the older body differently; people who maintain the same drinking patterns as they age can easily develop alcohol dependency without realizing it. Physicians may overlook alcoholism when evaluating elderly patients, mistakenly attributing the signs of alcohol abuse to the normal effects of the aging process.

*Gender.* Most alcoholics are men, but the incidence of alcoholism in women has been increasing over the past 30 years. About 9.3% of men and 1.9% of women are heavy drinkers, and 22.8% of men are binge drinkers compared to 8.7% of women. In general, young women problem drinkers follow the drinking patterns of their partners, although they tend to engage in heavier drinking during the premenstrual period. Women tend to become alcoholic later in life than men, and it is estimated that 1.8 million older women suffer from alcohol addiction. Even though heavy drinking in women usually occurs later in life, the medical problems women develop because of the disorder occur at about the same age as men, suggesting that women are more susceptible to the physical toxicity of alcohol.

*Family History and Ethnicity.* The risk for alcoholism in sons of alcoholic fathers is 25%. The familial link is weaker for women, but genetic factors contribute to this disease in both genders. In one study, women with alcoholism tended to have parents who drank. Women who came from families with a history of emotional disorders, rejecting parents, or early family disruption had no higher risk for drinking than women without such backgrounds. A stable family and psychological health were not protective in people with a genetic risk. Unfortunately, there is no way to predict which members of alcoholic families are most at risk for alcoholism.

Irish and Native Americans are at increased risk for alcoholism; Jewish and Asian Americans are at decreased risk. Overall, there is no difference in alcoholic prevalence between African Americans, whites, and Hispanic people. Although the biological causes of such different risks are not known, certain people in these population groups may be at higher or lower risk because of the way they metabolize alcohol. One study of Native Americans, for instance, found that they are less sensitive to the intoxicating effects of alcohol. This confirms other studies, in which young men with alcoholic fathers exhibited fewer signs of drunkenness and had lower levels of stress hormones than those without a family history. In other words, they "held their liquor" better. Experts suggest such people may inherit a lack of those warning signals that ordinarily make people stop drinking. Many Asians, on the other hand, are less likely to become alcoholic because of a genetic factor that makes them deficient in aldehyde dehydrogenase, a chemical used by the body to metabolize ethyl alcohol. In its absence, toxic substances build up after drinking alcohol and rapidly lead to flushing, dizziness, and nausea. People with this genetic susceptibility, then, are likely to experience adverse reactions to alcohol and therefore *not* become alcoholic. This deficiency is not completely protective against drinking, however, particularly if there is added social pressure, such as among college fraternity members. It is important to understand that, whether it is inherited or not, people with alcoholism are still legally responsible for their actions.

*Emotional Disorders.* Severely depressed or anxious people are at high risk for alcoholism, smoking, and other forms of addiction. Major depression, in fact, accompanies about one-third of all cases of alcoholism. It is more common among alcoholic women (and women in general) than men. Interestingly, one study indicated that

> *"Alcoholism can kill in many different ways."*

depression in alcoholic women may cause them to drink less than nondepressed alcoholic women, while in alcoholic men, depression has the opposite effect. Depression and anxiety may play a major role in the development of alcoholism in the elderly, who are often subject to dramatic life changes, such as re-

22

tirement, the loss of a spouse or friends, and medical problems. Problem drinking in these cases may be due to self-medication of the anxiety or depression. It should be noted, however, that in all adults with alcoholism these mood disorders may be actually caused *by* alcoholism and often abate after withdrawal from alcohol.

*"Alcohol is implicated in 67% of all murders."*

*Personality Traits.* Studies are finding that alcoholism is strongly related to impulsive, excitable, and novelty-seeking behavior, and such patterns are established early on, if not inherited. People with attention deficit hyperactivity disorder, a condition that shares these behaviors, have a higher risk for alcoholism. Children who later become alcoholics or who abuse drugs are more likely to have less fear of new situations than others, even if there is a risk for harm. In a test of mental functioning, alcoholics (mostly women) did not show any deficits in thinking but they were less able to inhibit their responses than nonalcoholics. It was once thought that a family history of passivity and abnormal dependency needs increased the risk for alcoholism, but studies have not borne out this theory.

*Socioeconomic Factors.* It has been long thought that alcoholism is more prevalent in people with lower educational levels and in those who were unemployed. A thorough 1996 study, however, reported that the prevalence of alcoholism among adult welfare recipients was 4.3% to 8.2%, which was comparable to the 7.4% found in the general population. There was also no difference in prevalence between poor African Americans and poor whites. People in low-income groups did display some tendencies that differed from the general population. For instance, as many women as men were heavy drinkers. Excessive drinking may be more dangerous in lower income groups; one study found that it was a major factor in the higher death rate of people, particularly men, in lower socioeconomic groups compared with those in higher groups. . . .

## Violence and Death

*How Serious Is Alcoholism?*

About 100,000 deaths a year can be wholly or partially attributed to drinking, and alcoholism reduces life expectancy by 10 to 12 years. Next to smoking, it is the most common preventable cause of death in America. Although studies indicate that adults who drink moderately (about one drink a day) have a lower mortality rate than their non-drinking peers, their risk for untimely death increases with heavier drinking. Any protection that occurs with moderate alcohol intake appears to be confined to adults over 60 who have risks for heart disease. The earlier a person begins drinking heavily, the greater their chance of developing serious illnesses later on. Alcoholism can kill in many different ways, and, in general, people who drink regularly have a higher rate of deaths from injury, violence, and some cancers.

*Overdose.* Alcohol overdose can lead to death. This is a particular danger for adolescents who may want to impress their friends with their ability to drink alcohol but cannot yet gauge its effects.

*Accidents, Suicide, and Murder.* Alcohol plays a major role in more than half of all automobile fatalities. Less than two drinks can impair the ability to drive. Alcohol also increases the risk of accidental injuries from many other causes. One study of emergency room patients found that having had more than one drink doubled the risk of injury, and more than four drinks increased the risk eleven times. Another study reported that among emergency room patients who were admitted for injuries, 47% tested positive for alcohol and 35% were intoxicated. Of those who were intoxicated, 75% showed evidence of chronic alcoholism. This disease is the primary diagnosis in one quarter of all people who commit suicide, and alcohol is implicated in 67% of all murders.

*Domestic Violence and Effects on Family.* Domestic violence is a common consequence of alcohol abuse. Research suggests that for women, the most serious risk factor for injury from domestic violence may be a history of alcohol abuse in her male partner. Alcoholism in parents also increases the risk for violent behavior and abuse toward their children. Children of alcoholics tend to do worse academically than others, have a higher incidence of depression, anxiety, and stress and lower self-esteem than their peers. One study found that children who were diagnosed with major depression between the ages of six and 12 were more likely to have alcoholic parents or relatives than were children who were not depressed. Alcoholic households are less cohesive, have more conflicts, and their members are less independent and expressive than households with nonalcoholic or recovering alcoholic parents. In addition to their own inherited risk for later alcoholism, one study found that 41% of children of alcoholics have serious coping problems that may be life long. Adult children of alcoholic parents are at higher risk for divorce and for psychiatric symptoms. One study concluded that the only events with greater psychological impact on children are sexual and physical abuse.

> *"[People with alcoholism] nearly always deny the problem, leaving it up to coworkers, friends, or relatives to recognize the symptoms and take the first steps toward treatment."*

## Medical Problems

Alcohol can affect the body in so many ways that researchers are having a hard time determining exactly what the consequences are of drinking. It is well known, however, that chronic consumption leads to many problems, some of them deadly.

*Heart Disease.* Large doses of alcohol can trigger irregular heartbeats and raise blood pressure even in people with no history of heart disease. A major study found that those who consumed more than three alcoholic drinks a day had higher blood pressure than teetotalers. The more alcohol someone drank, the greater the increase in blood pressure. People who were binge drinkers had the highest blood pressures. One study found that binge drinkers (people who have nine or more drinks once or twice a week) had a risk for a cardiac emergency that was two and a half times that of nondrinkers. Chronic alcohol abuse can also damage the heart muscle, which leads to heart failure; women are particularly vulnerable to this disorder. Contrary to many previous reports, a recent study suggested that moderate to heaving drinking (more than two bottles of beer or two glasses of wine a day) was a greater risk factor for coronary artery disease than smoking. As in other studies, light drinking (two to six drinks a week) was protective. More research is needed to confirm or refute this new study. In any case, moderate drinking does not appear to offer any heart benefits for people who are at low risk for heart disease to begin with.

*Cancer.* Alcohol may not cause cancer, but it probably does increase the carcinogenic effects of other substances, such as cigarette smoke. Daily drinking increases the risk for lung, esophageal, gastric, pancreatic, colorectal, urinary tract, liver, and brain cancers, lymphoma and leukemia. About 75% of cancers of the esophagus and 50% of cancers of the mouth, throat, and larynx are attributed to alcoholism. (Wine appears to pose less danger for these cancers than beer or hard liquor.) Smoking combined with drinking enhances risks for most of these cancers dramatically. When women consume as little as one drink a day, they may increase their chances of breast cancer by as much as 30%.

*Liver Disorders.* The liver is particularly endangered by alcoholism. About 10% to 35% of heavy drinkers develop alcoholic hepatitis, and 10% to 20% develop cirrhosis. In the liver, alcohol converts to an even more toxic substance, acetaldehyde, which can cause substantial damage. Not eating when drinking and consuming a variety of alcoholic beverages are also factors that increase the risk for liver damage. People with alcoholism are also at higher risk for hepatitis B and C, potentially chronic liver diseases than can lead to cirrhosis and liver cancer. . . .

> *"The two basic goals of long-term treatment are total abstinence and replacement of the addictive patterns with satisfying, time-filling behaviors."*

*Mental and Neurologic Disorders.* Alcohol has widespread effects on the brain. One study that scanned the brains of inebriated subjects suggested that while alcohol stimulates those parts of the brain related to reward and induces euphoria, it does not appear to impair cognitive performance (the ability to think and reason). Habitual use of alcohol, however, eventually produces depression and confusion. In chronic cases, gray matter is destroyed, possibly leading to psychosis and mental disturbances. Alcohol can also cause milder neurologic problems, including insomnia and headache (especially after drinking red wine). Except in severe cases, neurologic damage is not permanent and abstinence nearly always leads to recovery of normal mental function. Alcohol may increase the risk for hemorrhagic stroke (caused by bleeding in the brain), although it may protect against stroke caused by narrowed arteries. . . .

*Malnutrition and Wernicke-Korsakoff Syndrome.* A pint of whiskey provides about half the daily calories needed by an adult, but it has no nutritional value. In addition to replacing food, alcohol may also interfere with absorption of proteins, vitamins, and other nutrients. Of particular concern in alcoholism is a severe deficiency in the B-vitamin thiamin, which can cause a serious condition called Wernicke-Korsakoff syndrome. Symptoms of this syndrome include severe loss of balance, confusion, and memory loss. Eventually, it can result in permanent brain damage and death. Another serious nutritional problem among alcoholics is deficiency of the B vitamin folic acid, which can cause severe anemia. . . .

> *"Between 80% and 90% of people treated for alcoholism relapse—even after years of abstinence."*

*Drug Interactions.* The effects of many medications are strengthened by alcohol, while others are inhibited. Of particular importance is its reinforcing effect on antianxiety drugs, sedatives, antidepressants, and antipsychotic medications. Alcohol also interacts with many drugs used by diabetics. It interferes with drugs that prevent seizures or blood clotting. It increases the risk for gastrointestinal bleeding in people taking aspirin or other nonsteroidal inflammatory drugs including ibuprofen and naproxen. In other words, taking almost any medication should preclude drinking alcohol.

*Pregnancy and Infant Development.* Even moderate amounts of alcohol may have damaging effects on the developing fetus, including low birth weight and an increased risk for miscarriage. High amounts can cause fetal alcohol syndrome, which can result in mental and growth retardation. One study indicates a significantly higher risk for leukemia in infants of women who drink any type of alcohol during pregnancy.

*Complications in Older People.* As people age, it takes fewer drinks to become intoxicated, and organs can be damaged by smaller amounts of alcohol than in younger people. Also, up to one-half of the 100 most prescribed drugs for older people react adversely with alcohol. . . .

## Getting Treatment

Even when people with alcoholism experience withdrawal symptoms, they nearly always deny the problem, leaving it up to coworkers, friends, or relatives to recognize the symptoms and take the first steps toward treatment. . . .

One study reported that the main reasons alcoholics do not seek treatment are lack of confidence in successful therapies, denial of their own alcoholism, and the social stigma attached to the condition and its treatment. Studies have found that even a brief intervention (e.g., several fifteen-minute counseling sessions with a physician and a follow-up by a nurse) can be very effective in reducing drinking in heavy drinkers who are not yet dependent. However, the best approaches are group meetings between people with alcoholism and their friends and family members who have been affected by the alcoholic behavior. Using this interventional approach, each person affected offers a compassionate but direct and honest report describing specifically how he or she has been specifically hurt by their loved one's or friend's alcoholism. Children may even be involved in this process, depending on their level of maturity and ability to handle the situation. The family and friends should express their affection for the patient and their intentions for supporting the patient through recovery, but they must strongly and consistently demand that the patient seek treatment. Employers can be particularly effective. Their approach should also be compassionate but strong, threatening the employee with loss of employment if he or she does not seek help. Some large companies provide access to inexpensive or free treatment programs for their workers.

The alcoholic patient and everyone involved should fully understand that alcoholism is a disease and that the responses to this disease—need, craving, fear of withdrawal—are not character flaws but symptoms, just as pain or discomfort are symptoms of other illnesses. They should also realize that treatment is difficult and sometimes painful, just as treatments for other life-threatening diseases, such as cancer, are, but that it is the only hope for a cure.

*Symptoms of Withdrawal.* When a person with alcoholism stops drinking, withdrawal symptoms begin within six to 48 hours and peak about 24 to 35 hours after the last drink. During this period the inhibition of brain activity caused by alcohol is abruptly reversed. Stress hormones are over-produced and the central nervous system becomes over-excited. About 5% of alcoholic patients experience delirium tremens, which usually develops two to four days after the last drink. Symptoms include fever, rapid heart beat, either high or low blood pressure, extremely aggressive behavior, hallucinations, and other mental disturbances. . . .

*Treatment for Delirium Tremens, Seizures, and Other Severe Symptoms.* People with symptoms of delirium tremens must be treated immediately. Untreated delirium tremens has a fatality rate that can be as high as 20%. They are usually first given intravenous anti-anxiety medications and their physical condition is stabilized. It is extremely important that fluids be administered. Restraints may be necessary to prevent injury to themselves or others. . . .

## Long-Term Treatment and Relapse

The two basic goals of long-term treatment are total abstinence and replacement of the addictive patterns with satisfying, time-filling behaviors that can fill the void in daily activity that occurs when drinking has ceased. Some studies have reported that some people who are alcohol dependent can eventually learn to control their drinking and do as well as those who remain abstinent. There is no way to determine, however, which people can stop after one drink and which cannot. Alcoholics Anonymous and other alcoholic treatment groups whose goal is strict abstinence are greatly worried by the publicity surrounding these studies, since many people with alcoholism are eager for an excuse to start drinking again. At this time, abstinence is the only safe route. . . .

*Why Do People with Alcoholism Relapse?*

Between 80% and 90% of people treated for alcoholism relapse—even after years of abstinence. Patients and their caregivers should understand that relapses of alcoholism are analogous to recurrent flare-ups of chronic physical diseases. One study found that three factors placed a person at high risk for relapse: frustration and anger, social pressure, and internal temptation. Treatment of relapses, however, does not always require starting from scratch with detoxification or hospitalization; often, abstinence can begin the next day. Self-forgiveness and persistence are behaviors essential for permanent recovery.

*Mental and Emotional Stress.* Alcohol blocks out emotional pain and is often perceived as a loyal friend when human relationships fail. It is also associated with freedom and a loss of inhibition that offsets the tedium of daily routines. When the alcoholic tries to quit drinking, the brain seeks to restore what it perceives to be its equilibrium. The brain's best weapons against abstinence are depression and anxiety (the emotional equivalents of physical pain) that continue to tempt alcoholics to return to drinking long after physical withdrawal symptoms have abated. Even intelligence is no ally in this process, for the brain will use all its powers of rationalization to persuade the patient

> *"One of the most difficult problems facing a person with alcoholism is being around people who are able to drink socially without danger."*

to return to drinking. It is important to realize that any life change may cause temporary grief and anxiety, even changes for the better. With time and the substitution of healthier pleasures, this emotional turmoil weakens and can be overcome.

*Codependency.* One of the most difficult problems facing a person with alcoholism is being around people who are able to drink socially without danger of addiction. A sense of isolation, a loss of enjoyment, and the ex-drinker's belief that pity—not respect—is guiding a friend's attitude can lead to loneliness, low self-esteem, and a strong desire to drink. Close friends and even intimate partners may have difficulty in changing their responses to this newly sober person and, even worse, may encourage a return to drinking. To preserve marriages to alcoholics, spouses often build their own self-images on surviving or handling their mates' difficult behavior and then discover that they are threatened by abstinence. Friends may not easily accept the sober, perhaps more subdued, comrade. In such cases, separation from these "enablers" may be necessary for survival. It is no wonder that, when faced with such losses, even if they are temporary, a person returns to drinking. The best course in these cases is to encourage close friends and family members to seek help as well. Fortunately, groups such as Al-Anon exist for this purpose.

*Social and Cultural Pressures.* The media portrays the pleasures of drinking in advertising and programming. The medical benefits of light to moderate drinking are frequently publicized, giving ex-drinkers the spurious excuse of returning to alcohol for their health. These messages must be categorically ignored and acknowledged for what they are—an industry's attempt to profit from potential great harm to individuals.

# Children of Alcoholics Face Many Problems

**by the American Academy of Child and Adolescent Psychiatry**

**About the author:** *The American Academy of Child and Adolescent Psychiatry is a nonprofit organization composed of over 6,500 child and adolescent psychiatrists and other physicians interested in preventing, treating, and promoting an understanding of mental illness among young people.*

One in five adult Americans lived with an alcoholic while growing up. Child and adolescent psychiatrists know these children are at greater risk for having emotional problems than children whose parents are not alcoholics. Alcoholism runs in families, and children of alcoholics are four times more likely than other children to become alcoholics. Most children of alcoholics have experienced some form of neglect or abuse.

A child in such a family may have a variety of problems:

• *Guilt.* The child may see himself or herself as the main cause of the mother's or father's drinking.

• *Anxiety.* The child may worry constantly about the situation at home. He or she may fear the alcoholic parent will become sick or injured, and may also fear fights and violence between the parents.

• *Embarrassment.* Parents may give the child the message that there is a terrible secret at home. The ashamed child does not invite friends home and is afraid to ask anyone for help.

• *Inability to have close relationships.* Because the child has been disappointed by the drinking parent many times, he or she often does not trust others.

• *Confusion.* The alcoholic parent will change suddenly from being loving to angry, regardless of the child's behavior. A regular daily schedule, which is very important for a child, does not exist because bedtimes and mealtimes are constantly changing.

• *Anger.* The child feels anger at the alcoholic parent for drinking, and may

Reprinted, with permission, from the American Academy of Child and Adolescent Psychiatry, Facts for Families, #17, "Children of Alcoholics," published at www.aacap.org/factsfam/alcoholc.htm.

be angry at the non-alcoholic parent for lack of support and protection.

• *Depression.* The child feels lonely and helpless to change the situation.

## Warning Signs

Although the child tries to keep the alcoholism a secret, teachers, relatives, other adults, or friends may sense that something is wrong. Child and adolescent psychiatrists advise that the following behaviors may signal a drinking or other problem at home:

• Failure in school; truancy
• Lack of friends; withdrawal from classmates
• Delinquent behavior, such as stealing or violence
• Frequent physical complaints, such as headaches or stomachaches
• Abuse of drugs or alcohol
• Aggression towards other children
• Risk-taking behaviors
• Depression or suicidal thoughts or behavior

Some children of alcoholics may act like responsible "parents" within the family and among friends. They may cope with the alcoholism by becoming controlled, successful "overachievers" throughout school, and at the same time be emotionally isolated from other children and teachers. Their emotional problems may show only when they become adults.

Whether or not their parents are receiving treatment for alcoholism, these children and adolescents can benefit from educational programs and mutual-help groups such as programs for children of alcoholics, Al-Anon, and Alateen.

> *"Most children of alcoholics have experienced some form of neglect or abuse."*

Early professional help is also important in preventing more serious problems for the child, including alcoholism. Child and adolescent psychiatrists help these children with the child's own problems, and also help the child to understand they are not responsible for the drinking problems of their parents.

The treatment program may include group therapy with other youngsters, which reduces the isolation of being a child of an alcoholic. The child and adolescent psychiatrist will often work with the entire family, particularly when the alcoholic parent has stopped drinking, to help them develop healthier ways of relating to one another.

# Alcohol Abuse Is a Serious Problem for Teenagers

## by Center for Science in the Public Interest

**About the author:** *The Center for Science in the Public Interest is a nonprofit education and advocacy organization that seeks to reduce the damage caused by alcoholic beverages.*

For kids, alcohol is "still the one." Alcohol is the most widely used and abused drug among youth. It kills more teenagers than all other drugs combined, and is a factor in the three leading causes of death among 15–24 year olds: accidents, homicides and suicides. Nearly four million young people suffer from alcohol dependence, accounting for over one-fifth of all alcohol dependent people. Alcohol can cause serious and potentially life threatening problems for children and adolescents and can be a precursor to other drug use.

The average age at which children begin to drink today is about 13 years old. After having reached a low point in the early 1990s, the percentage of 8th, 10th and 12th graders who report having had a drink in the past 30 days, or who have been drunk in the past two weeks, has been rising steadily.

## Alcohol Is a Gateway Drug

*Alcohol is the most commonly used "gateway" drug by children and adolescents.* The term "gateway drug" refers to drugs that are the first to be used in a progression of use whose consumption is statistically associated with the use of other drugs. According to the concept of "gateway drugs" if the use of those first drugs can be prevented or delayed until the end of adolescence the likelihood that people will go on to use other drugs will be substantially diminished.

For decades public health professionals have debated whether a relationship exists between the consumption of beer, wine coolers and other alcohol by children, smoking cigarettes, and the subsequent use of other drugs such as marijuana, cocaine and heroin. In 1994 former Secretary of Health, Education and Welfare Joseph A. Califano, Jr. and his organization the Center on Addiction and Substance Abuse at Columbia University (CASA) undertook a comprehensive national analysis of the relationship of those gateway drugs to subsequent drug use. That study demonstrated a powerful statistical connection that, in Califano's words is "far more powerful than [the statistical connections] which first revealed the nexus between smoking and lung cancer and emphysema, between cholesterol levels and heart disease, and between exposure to asbestos and lung cancer."

Although everyone who drinks will not progress to other drugs, everyone who uses "harder" drugs, with rare exception, began with a "gateway drug." In a background paper on "Gateway Drugs," the White House Office of National Drug Control Policy asserts: "The science tells us that preventing or delaying tobacco and alcohol use prevents or delays the use of other drugs as well." According to ONDCP, alcohol is the precursor to marijuana and other illegal drugs for boys, and the combined use of tobacco and alcohol is the precursor for girls.

CASA found even more alarming evidence in its study: more than 67% of individuals who start drinking before the age of fifteen end up using an illicit drug, while fewer than 25% of those who delay drinking until seventeen or older progress to other drugs. Only 4% of those who never drink end up using other drugs.

Children aged 12 to 17 who drink are 22.3 times more likely to smoke marijuana than those who don't drink, and they are 50 times more likely to use cocaine.

For parents, for mayors and city councils, and for federal drug prevention efforts the message is very clear: if children delay drinking until it is legal to do so, they are almost certain to make it through life without using illicit drugs.

## Trends in Underage Drinking

It may come as no surprise that children and teenagers drink alcoholic beverages, but how much they drink and how often may be a revelation. Three out of five teenagers across the nation (61%) have had a drink in the last month. Boys under 17 drink more heavily than any other population group: nearly three in ten (29%) consume six or more alcoholic beverages each time they drink, compared to 24% of 18 and 19 year olds.

The 1998 "Monitoring the Future Study," a national survey commissioned by the National Institute of Drug Abuse and implemented by the Institute of Social Research shows that 8th, 10th and 12th graders are all much more likely to have used alcohol in the past 30 days, or the past year, than they are to have smoked marijuana or used any other illicit drug. In 1998, 44%

*"The average age at which children begin to drink today is about 13 years old."*

of 8th graders, 63% of 10th graders, and 74% of 12th graders experimented with alcohol. This compares to the 17% of 8th graders, 31% of 10th graders and 38% of 12th graders who experimented with marijuana.

Most teenagers drink: a recent survey of 4,390 high school seniors and dropouts reported that approximately 80% of them reported getting drunk, binge drinking, or drinking and driving within the preceding year.

*Alcohol Is Readily Available.* Alcohol is the easiest drug for children to obtain. In a recent study of students in Washington State, 25–30% of 6th graders said that it would be easy for them to obtain beer, wine or hard liquor. This compares with about 6–7% who say it would be easy to obtain marijuana and 0% who report it would be easy to obtain cocaine, LSD or amphetamines. As children get older, they find it easier to find drugs but alcohol remains the most accessible: 55% of 8th graders say alcohol is easy to obtain compared with 25–39% who could find marijuana easily and 10–15% who could find other drugs easily. More than one in five high school seniors (22%) report recent heavy use of alcohol compared with one in seven (15%) who report recent heavy use of marijuana.

Beer is the alcoholic-beverage of choice for kids, preferred by 61% of all children. The next favorite alcoholic-beverage, wine and wine coolers, is preferred by 27% of all children. In 1991 the Inspector General of the U.S. Department of Health and Human Services estimated that 1.1 billion cans of beer and 300 million bottles of wine coolers were consumed by junior and senior high school students every year.

*Binge Drinking.* Many adults picture drinking as a leisurely cocktail or beer after work, or an elegant glass of wine with dinner. Unfortunately, that's not the way kids drink. When they drink, they are much more likely to "drink to get drunk." According to a 1995 College Alcohol Study by the Harvard School of Public Health 52% of college students "binge drink" up from 33% in 1993. The frequency of drinking and the quantities consumed are awesome: the average teen drinks on more than five days a month, according to a study by the American Academy of Pediatrics. Kids who drink frequently consume an average of 5.6 drinks at a time. Binge drinking starts early: 39% of high school seniors report having five or more drinks at a time at least once in the previous month.

> *"More than 67% of individuals who start drinking before the age of fifteen end up using an illicit drug."*

Binge drinking is a major health problem—and has led to a number of widely publicized deaths by college students in the past year. It is also significant in alcohol's role as a gateway to other drugs: the more alcohol a child drinks, the more likely they are to progress to other drugs.

## Consequences of Early Drinking

Although there are health risks associated with drinking at any age, some risks are unique for minors. A 1997 study by researchers at the National Institute on Alcohol Abuse and Alcoholism (NIAAA) found that the age at which one begins to drink has a dramatic impact on the chances that one will develop alcohol dependence. Those who take their first drink at age 13 have a 47.3% chance of becoming alcohol dependent during their lives. For those who delay drinking until age 16, the odds drop to 30.6%; those who wait until the legal age of 21 have only a 10.0% chance of developing alcohol dependence.

The earlier one drinks, the more likely one is to end up using other drugs. Research suggests that the majority of those who begin drinking between 13 and 16 will progress to other drugs.

> *"The age at which one begins to drink has a dramatic impact on the chances that one will develop alcohol dependence."*

Young brains are more susceptible to alcohol damage than fully matured brains. Alcohol shrinks memory signals much more quickly (at a lower dosage) in adolescent brains than in the adult brain, and reduces memory acquisition. Those exposed to alcohol in adolescence show a reduced ability to learn when compared with those exposed to alcohol in adulthood.

In animal studies, alcohol consumption has been shown to delay the onset of puberty, and to result in slow bone growth and in weaker bones.

*Traffic Fatalities.* Motor vehicle crashes are the leading cause of death for 15 to 20 year olds. In 1997, 3,336 drivers 15 to 20 years old died, an additional 365,000 were injured, in motor vehicle crashes. Almost 30% of those drivers had been drinking. The estimated economic cost of those crashes totaled $31.9 billion.

Younger drivers are more likely to have been binge drinking than older drivers (39% vs. 13%) and are more likely to have consumed both their first and last drink in less than an hour (30% vs. 15%).

All states and the District of Columbia now have 21-year-old minimum drinking age laws. The National Highway Traffic Safety Administration estimates that these laws have reduced traffic fatalities involving drivers 18 to 20 years old by 13% and have saved an estimated 17,359 lives since 1975.

*Alcohol and Suicide.* Suicide is now the second leading cause of death for children aged 15 to 19 in the United States.

Alcohol use among adolescents has been associated with considering, planning, attempting and completing suicide. The more frequently an adolescent uses alcohol, the greater the likelihood they will consider or attempt suicide; alcohol is more closely correlated with suicidal thoughts than any other drug, and more closely associated with actual adolescent suicide attempts than any drug other than crack cocaine. In one study, 37% of eighth-grade females who drank heavily reported attempting suicide, compared with 11% who did not drink.

## Alcohol Consumption Contributes to Many Social Problems

*Alcohol and Educational Problems.* Drinking leads to problems in school. High school youth who are regular substance users are three to five times more likely than non-users to have given up on school, to have dropped out of school at some time, to have been suspended in the last year, and to consider it unimportant to get good grades. Regular users are also less involved in sports or other extracurricular activities.

Alcohol use by college students is a factor in 40% of academic problems, 28% of dropouts, and 80% of acts of vandalism. 95% of violent crime on college campuses is alcohol related. 90% of all reported campus rapes involved use of alcohol by the victim or the perpetrator.

*Alcohol and Youth Crime.* Alcohol and crime also go hand in hand. The majority of youths sentenced to prison have a past history of substance abuse; the most commonly abused drug is alcohol. Of 1,030 youths, aged 12 to 17, entering Texas Youth Commission facilities, the most commonly used drug was alcohol. The following table provides a breakdown of drug usage in the year prior to the month before entering the facility:

| | |
|---|---|
| Alcohol | 26.9% |
| Marijuana | 22.5% |
| Cocaine (powder) | 15.6% |
| Inhalants | 12.5% |
| Downers | 10.4% |
| Uppers | 9.3% |
| Crack | 6.4% |
| Heroin | 4.2% |

Many believe that the drug most used by youth offenders is crack cocaine. The 1997 Annual Report on Adult and Juvenile Arrestees by the National Institute of Justice tells a different story. The average age at which offenders first reported using alcohol ranged from 14.1 (Houston) to 15.8 years (Miami—results are reported city by city), while the average age at which offenders began using crack ranged from 23.3 years (Houston) to 28.2 years (Atlanta). Clearly, for youthful offenders as for the youth population generally, alcohol is the drug of choice.

*Alcohol and Sex.* Alcohol consumption is also more likely to lead to risky sexual behavior: high school students

> *"The majority of youths sentenced to prison have a past history of substance abuse; the most commonly abused drug is alcohol."*

who drink are four times more likely to have had sexual intercourse and twice as likely to have had four or more partners than non-drinkers, behaviors which increase the risk for sexually transmitted diseases, including HIV.

*Health Problems Caused by Drinking.* Young people face the same long-term health consequences as do older drinkers: alcohol is the third leading cause of death in the United States. Men and women who drink alcoholic beverages regularly have, in comparison with abstainers, higher death rates from cirrhosis, cancers of the mouth, larynx, pharynx, esophagus, and liver; from colorectal cancer, breast cancer, hemorrhagic stroke; and from injuries, violence, poisoning and suicide. Alcohol causes birth defects and can cause inflammation of the pancreas and damage to the brain. For people who may be at risk for coronary artery disease the consumption of small amounts of alcohol may offer some off-setting health benefits—but young people generally are not at risk for coronary artery disease.

## Alcohol Use by Parents

This viewpoint focuses on the use of alcohol by children, but the use of alcohol by their parents is an equally large problem for children and for society at large. CASA reports that at least seven out of ten cases of child abuse and neglect are caused or exacerbated by alcohol or other drug abuse and addiction. Any comprehensive national program to reduce or prevent the problems associated with alcohol and drug abuse needs to deal with alcohol consumption by parents as well as consumption by children.

# Binge Drinking on College Campuses Is a Serious Problem

## by J.J. Thompson

**About the author:** *At the time this viewpoint was written, J.J. Thompson was an associate editor of* U.S. News & World Report.

Jason McCray remembers drinking shots at JB's in Tallahassee, Florida, but after that the details of his 21st birthday fade. The college senior knows from photos his buddies took that, several pubs later, he forced down double shots of whiskey and later vomited under the bar. (They got photos of that, too.) "They had to carry me out," he says.

Thus ended McCray's Tennessee Waltz, a coming-of-legal-age ritual in which Florida State University students celebrate turning 21 with a free drink, in addition to those bought by friends, at each of the half-dozen or so bars along Tennessee Street.

### A Widespread Problem

McCray denies that his birthday binge is the way he typically drinks. But it does represent the manner of drinking that too many expect and experience at college. Surveys show that up to 85 percent of all college students imbibe and that nearly half drink heavily. In 1949, when the first thorough study of college drinking was made, undergraduates drank no more than others their age, and college life did not encourage excessive tippling. The same can't be said today. College students drink more because college officials are less strict and many young people drink in high school or before. The result is that students now encounter college cultures in which drinking is not only common but is done mainly to get drunk.

Schools tend to respond with handwringing, saying there is little they can do. Recent research, including a study by *U.S. News & World Report*, indicates that's not so. *U.S. News* got responses from 69 percent of the 1,320 presidents of four-year colleges and universities it surveyed to learn what makes a difference. The survey found that while college presidents try to highlight the evils of student alcohol abuse, many don't see how common binge drinking really is. Only 3 percent of the presidents responding to the questionnaire estimated a rate as high as that found by a Harvard University study and, remarkably, 21 percent couldn't say how common it was on their campuses. Some researchers argue that it is a good idea to teach students when to say when; others say it may be even better for schools to prohibit them from drinking. The *U.S. News* survey and follow-up reporting suggest that schools that allow drinking on campus are up to three times more likely to experience high numbers of binge drinkers.

College students don't just down more alcohol, experts say; many often swill stronger forms, such as "PGA" (pure grain alcohol) and potent concoctions of several alcoholic beverages—sometimes through funnels or directly from the keg taps, while hanging upside down. "When I was in school, if you got drunk once a week, you were thought to be somebody no one wanted to hang out with, never mind [getting drunk] three to four times a week," says Fran Cohen, 52, director of the Office of Student Life at the University of Rhode Island. Now she deals with students who don't seem to mind the drunken behavior, wooziness, vomiting, and passing out that accompany too much alcohol.

## Binge Drinking

A late-fall fraternity bash at DePauw University in Greencastle, Indiana, proves her point. Guests—many of whom had already achieved a buzz at smaller parties and at the football game against rival Wabash College—tossed empty beer bottles from the balcony of the Delta Tau Delta house, watching them smash in the courtyard. Their target was the fraternity crest, and guests knew to walk far clear of the area when a big bash was going on. Inside, several hundred people, many of them riding on another's shoulders, screamed over the stereo's throbbing bass. Men and women waited their turns to lie on their backs and have beer or schnapps poured out of a bell, the trophy of that day's football victory, into their mouths. After each student gulped—be it one or 12—he or she rose to the cheers of the crowd and the clanking of the bell. Meanwhile, a nauseated woman leaned over a plastic trash can for several minutes, a man holding her so she wouldn't topple in headfirst.

> *"While college presidents try to highlight the evils of student alcohol abuse, many don't see how common binge drinking really is."*

Social scientists call this "binge drinking," defined as five or more drinks for a man at any one time within a two-week period, four or more drinks for a woman. This definition doesn't mean getting falling-down drunk, says Dr. Henry Wechsler, principal investigator in the Harvard study of college drinking. Instead, having five drinks in a row indicates problems associated with drinking. What's more, he found that few students who consume five fail to drink six or more. "It's right there, it's free, it's in front of you, and the next thing you know you've had 12 drinks in an hour and you can't move," one college senior explains.

The Harvard study showed that 44 percent of all undergraduates in the United States binge drink—a rate that has been fairly constant for almost 20 years. It also found that 23 percent of the men and 17 percent of the women were frequent binge drinkers—downing a bunch of drinks three or more times in two weeks.

## A Destructive Behavior

This much drinking takes its toll. Tim Anderl, an Ohio University senior, says that typically, "By the end of the fall, you're broke and your grades are in the gutter." Indeed, many students spend more money in a semester on alcohol—over $300—than they do on books. There's also a correlation between drinking and grades. One study found that A students have, on average, three drinks a week, while those making D's and F's average 11 drinks a week.

Problems with grades aren't the only ones plaguing binge drinkers. They are two to five times as likely as other drinkers to engage in unplanned or unprotected sex, get injured, damage property, argue, fight, or face trouble with the police.

*"Having five drinks in a row indicates problems associated with drinking."*

And some die. Scott Krueger, 18, a high-achieving freshman at Massachusetts Institute of Technology, overdosed on alcohol at a fraternity party in September 1997, slipped into a coma, and died three days later. Leslie Anne Baltz was a 21-year-old honor student at the University of Virginia until November, when she drank too much at a pregame party, was left alone by friends to sleep it off, somehow tumbled down a flight of stairs, hit her head, and died. Alcohol poisoning or alcohol-related accidents killed at least five other undergraduates nationwide during the 1997 fall term. While no one counts the number of college students who die from alcohol use, Dr. David Anderson of George Mason University in Fairfax, Virginia, estimates that at least 50 die each year.

Binge drinkers also make life difficult for students who don't drink so heavily. At schools where more than 50 percent of the students binge drink, Wechsler found that a majority of the nonbingeing students complain of the second-hand effects of binge drinking, ranging "from assault to sexual assault to vandalism to just being a pain all the way around."

## Preventing Alcohol Abuse on Campus

College administrators often identify student alcohol abuse as one of the biggest challenges they face. Yet, funding for prevention programs, on the increase until 1994, has never averaged more than a few dollars per student, not counting staff salaries. Experts complain that many alcohol education programs seldom involve more than a few posters, some brochures, and an Alcohol Awareness Week, all of which students say are largely ignored.

Bill DeJong, director of the Higher Education Center for Alcohol and Other Drug Prevention in Boston, thinks colleges have to change the way they recruit students. "If their view books show scenes of small groups socializing rather than football games, tailgate parties, and so on, they will attract a different kind of student," he argues. The *U.S. News* survey of college presidents suggests that when schools included their alcohol policies and the associated penalties in recruiting materials, they were about half as likely to have high numbers of binge drinkers.

> *"[Binge drinkers] are two to five times as likely as other drinkers to engage in unplanned or unprotected sex, get injured, damage property, argue, fight, or face trouble with the police."*

That's the strategy being adopted by the University of Rhode Island, once rated a top party school. On a sunny fall afternoon, URI junior Denis Guay guides a tour of the campus for prospective students and their parents to a freshman dormitory room. After pointing out the route to the bathrooms, he states the school's alcohol policy: no drinking anywhere on campus by anyone under 21 and only one six-pack at a time per legal-age student in the dorm rooms. The first offense earns a fine of $50; the second, $100; the third, suspension.

Lee and Judi Kroll, on the tour with their son Jon, were glad to hear of the low-tolerance alcohol policy. Jon doubted the measures were actually enforced. While a number of URI students said it was possible to discreetly drink on campus, more agreed with sophomore Kira Edler, who said, "If you get caught, there are prices to pay." As a result, URI is less of a party school. Since 1990, kegs have been banned from campus, alcohol prohibited from social events, and fines instituted and raised. While the number of violations for possessing alcohol is up, other violations involving alcohol, such as violence or vandalism, have fallen sharply.

## "There's Nothing Else to Do but Drink"

The argument against such policies has always been that it pushes drinking underground. Harvard's Wechsler argues that administrators who say that are shunning responsibility. "If you let them drink on campus, it doesn't mean they'll only drink on campus," he says. He maintains that there is less binge drinking on campuses where students are encouraged to focus on other activities. One reason could be that schools with such tough antidrinking policies attract fewer students who want to party.

A number of students at Earlham College in Richmond, Indiana, said that the school's dry policy influenced their decision to attend the liberal arts college. "One thing I like about it is that if you don't want to see drinking, you can avoid it," says student Roscoe Klausing.

Writing more-restrictive policies—which 30 percent of the campuses reporting to *U.S. News* did within the past two years—is no panacea. Consistent enforcement is key, as is filling students' days and nights with meaningful activities. Friday classes are a joke on too many campuses, and grade inflation has allowed students to spend even less time on coursework. "There's nothing else to do but drink" is a common lament among college students.

In general, presidents of colleges in urban areas, where there are more recreational and cultural events to lure students, report lower binge drinking rates on campus than those running schools in less urban settings. In addition, schools with lots of older or part-time students report low binge-drinking rates, probably because those students have families, jobs, or responsibilities that keep them away from the party circuit.

## The Fraternity System

Many experts agree that alcohol abuse is perhaps most rampant and causes the most trouble in places where colleges have little or no authority, such as the fraternity system. Studies show that residents of fraternity and sorority row are up to four times as likely to be binge drinkers as other students, and their leaders are the most likely of all.

But an organization doesn't have to be Greek to encourage drinking. At St. John's University, an all-male Catholic college in central Minnesota, the school's unofficial rugby club initiated its new members one cold Saturday night at an off-campus party house known by the locals as the Far Side. The behavior is as bizarre as a Gary Larson cartoon. A chant of "Drink, [expletive]! Drink, [expletive]! Drink, [expletive]! Drink!" rings out. Two kegs of beer chill outside while inside a fifth of Jack Daniels waits on a table for the team's rookies—boys clad only in bras and panties. St. John's officials insist that the incident is not typical there, and they have met with the rugby team to plan alternatives for initiating new members.

*"There is less binge drinking on campuses where students are encouraged to focus on other activities."*

Often, though, such behavior at most colleges has received little more than a "boys will be boys" response until student injuries or deaths, as well as lawsuits and rising insurance premiums, prompt some action. Nationally, two fraternities have committed to having dry houses by 2000. In December, all 66 member fraternities of the National Interfraternity Conference passed a resolution recommending alcohol-free chapter houses. URI's Carothers has moved all but two fraternities onto campus, where they must comply with school rules. The

University of Iowa's interfraternity council has mandated that official Greek parties be alcohol free starting next fall.

While some colleges and Greek organizations are making headway, the pubs and liquor stores near colleges tend to be much less cooperative. One Cornell University senior says, "I was 17 when I got to school and I could get a drink anywhere," including several bars and convenience stores near campus, where students often present false proof of age. Ads in college newspapers tempt students with "Nickel Beer," "Beat the Clock," and "Penny 'til You Pee" nights, where drinks are discounted or served free with a small cover charge. In the crowded parking lot outside Caesar's, an oceanside bar running a busy "Slug Fest" special about 5 miles from URI, senior Anthony Antorino was insisting that students there know their drinking limits when he had to interrupt himself. "Oh my God!" he exclaimed. "Well, there's an exception." He pointed to a young woman who had just squatted by the front wheel of a car to relieve herself.

## Changing the Norm

Some college administrators have joined community leaders on "town and gown" councils to tackle this and other problems. Experts say that schools can wield their economic clout to compel local governments and alcohol control boards to action. The Presidents Leadership Group of the Higher Education Center for Alcohol and Other Drug Prevention goes a step further, urging their colleagues to work at the state level for more stringent laws. A peeved Bill Sheen knows such efforts work. After the Tallahassee police started their weekend "Party Patrol," the sophomore business major was fined $195 for holding a cup of Coke and Jim Beam whiskey outside a rowdy apartment gathering. "It sucks. We can't have a party," he says.

Colleges and universities will never rid themselves of alcohol abuse completely, Wechsler says; instead, the goal is to change the norm. Look at what happened with smoking. "No Smoking" signs are obeyed with few complaints. The designated driver, an idea unheard of 15 years ago, is now a common practice, even for partying college kids. Alcohol education did reach some of the more moderate drinkers, experts say. Now it's time to target heavy drinkers.

# The Dangers of Alcohol Are Exaggerated

## by Stanton Peele

**About the author:** *Stanton Peele is a psychologist and researcher specializing in drug and alcohol addiction, and the author of* The Diseasing of America: How We Allowed Recovery Zealots and the Treatment Industry to Convince Us We Are Out of Control.

A traditional anecdote tells of a congressman who answered a constituent's inquiry about his position on whiskey: "If you mean the demon drink that poisons the mind, pollutes the body, desecrates family life and inflames sinners, then I'm against it. But if you mean the elixir of Christmas cheer, the shield against winter chill, . . . then I'm for it. This is my position and I will not compromise!"

Unlike this apocryphal congressman, Americans and their government have staked out strong positions on alcohol. But these positions have fluctuated wildly from era to era.

### A More Positive Attitude Toward Alcohol?

There are signs that, after several decades of anti-alcohol crusading, the United States is swinging back toward a more positive attitude. The most conspicuous indicator of this shift was the federal government's acknowledgment in its 1995 dietary guidelines that alcohol has beneficial effects. Long overdue, this recognition marks a significant change from previous government decrees on the subject. Other signs of a thawing in attitudes toward alcohol are still preliminary: Several small pilot programs in the United States are challenging the dominant approach to alcohol problems, which offers abstinence as the only cure for the "disease" of alcoholism. And leading researchers, noting that the risks of fetal alcohol syndrome have been greatly exaggerated, are questioning conventional advice about drinking during pregnancy.

These positive signs should be regarded with caution. America's ambivalence about "demon rum" is deeply imbedded in our culture. For two centuries, we have fought about the role alcohol should play in our lives. Just as we turn in one direction, forces are set in motion that pull us back the opposite way.

The colonial era was the golden age of American drinking. Americans consumed three to four times as much alcohol (mostly beer and cider) as they do today, with few social problems. Legislators drank while in session; communion wine was part of Protestant services; the tavern was a family-oriented gathering place; and tavern keepers were highly respected members of the community. There was no

> *"America's ambivalence about 'demon rum' is deeply imbedded in our culture. For two centuries, we have fought about the role alcohol should play in our lives."*

anti-alcohol movement in pre-revolutionary America. There *were* drunkards, but responsibility for excessive drinking was laid at their feet and not blamed on alcohol. The distinguished Puritan cleric Increase Mather warned against drinking too much but in the same breath referred to alcohol as "God's Good Creature."

Drinking became less benign following expansion of the United States after the War of Independence. Industrialization and the institution of regular work hours made heavy drinking less compatible with daily obligations. At the same time, the social forces that kept drinking under control in colonial America began to wane. In the fabled saloons and dance halls of the West, unlike in the family tavern, the only women present were prostitutes; drunken unruliness, fist fights, and gunplay were commonplace.

## Temperance Movements

The temperance movement arose in the 19th century in response to growing problems related to drinking. Despite its name, the movement rejected the idea of moderation, maintaining that *any* drinking inevitably progressed to excess and ruin. Several states enacted—and repealed—alcohol prohibition. At the national level, the war between the "drys" and the "wets" translated into regional and group conflict—the South and Midwest versus the West and urban East, Protestants versus Catholics, native-born Americans versus new European immigrants.

When the nation embarked on "the Noble Experiment" of Prohibition in 1920, reactions were mixed, but there was little organized opposition to the 18th Amendment. Thirteen years later, wets and drys alike had become so disenchanted with Prohibition that few opposed repeal. The temperance promise that sin and poverty would be eliminated along with booze was simply not borne out, and the attempt to suppress alcohol consumption had brought a host of unintended costs. In the aftermath of Prohibition, drinking became acceptable once again.

But the feelings that gave rise to Prohibition remained just beneath the surface of the American psyche, and in the 1970s a new temperance movement emerged, manifested in the rapid growth of the recovery movement and Alcoholics Anonymous, of private alcoholism treatment à la the Betty Ford Center, and of government efforts to limit alcohol consumption. The United States quadrupled its hospital beds for alcoholics between 1978 and 1984, placed warning labels for pregnant women on alcoholic beverages, and made anti-alcohol education programs a staple not only for high school students but for children as young as six. Banners proclaiming that "alcohol is a liquid drug" appeared in schools nationwide, while "Just Say No" became a national slogan.

## The Health Benefits of Moderate Drinking

But the seeds of an opposing trend were being sown just as the new anti-alcohol movement flowered. Medical epidemiologists tracking health outcomes in large groups of people repeatedly found that abstainers suffered more heart disease than moderate and light drinkers. Since heart disease is by far America's leading cause of death, moderate drinkers had lower overall mortality rates (although mortality rates among excessive drinkers were higher than average). Such findings, which began appearing in medical journals by the 1980s, presented public health officials with a dilemma: How was it possible to tell children drinking was bad but that people who drank lived longer?

Despite much evidence to the contrary, in 1990 the dietary guidelines compiled by the U.S. Department of Health and Human Services in conjunction with the Department of Agriculture asserted that "drinking has no net health benefit." But the government faced increasing difficulty sustaining its blanket condemnation of alcohol, and the latest di-

*"There was no anti-alcohol movement in pre-revolutionary America. There were drunkards, but responsibility for excessive drinking was laid at their feet and not blamed on alcohol."*

etary guidelines, issued in January 1996, announced that drinking could be beneficial. The report even went so far as to note that "alcoholic beverages have been used to enhance the enjoyment of meals by many societies throughout human history." The change occurred in part because additional scientific evidence appeared after the 1990 report. But the real obstacle had been cultural resistance. According to Assistant Secretary of Health Philip Lee, "There was a significant bias in the past against drinking." Marion Nestle, a guidelines committee member and chair of New York University's nutrition and food science department, said the change represented "a triumph of science and reason over politics."

## Teaching Children About Alcohol

Still, the revision does not represent a flip to Mediterranean-style attitudes. For one thing, the recommended daily consumption limits—one drink for women and two for men—are quite low. In Britain (hardly a Mediterranean culture), the government's "sensible drinking" limits are about twice the American levels: two to three drinks daily for women and three to four for men. Furthermore, the U.S. guidelines emphasize that children should not consume alcohol. This is far from a universal belief. In Spain, children of any age may drink beer or wine with a parent at a cafe. This is also true in New Zealand, provided a meal is being eaten. In Switzerland, children may drink on their own at 16, and in some cantons at 14. No industrial nation other than the United States restricts drinking to people 21 and older.

Forbidding drinking by children does not seem to reduce alcohol abuse. Psychiatrist George Vaillant, who tracked a group of Boston adolescents for four decades, found that Irish-Americans were seven times as likely to become alcoholic as were Italians, Greeks, and Jews. Yet the latter groups typically introduce children to alcohol, while in Irish culture children traditionally do not drink in the home.

Despite a legal drinking age of 21, youthful overdrinking is a common feature of American life. In national surveys, about half of male high school seniors and college students say they have consumed at least five drinks at a sitting in the previous two weeks. More than a third of female students say they've had four or more drinks at a time. The figure for sorority and fraternity members is 80 percent or higher. It stands to reason that teenagers who learn to drink with friends are less likely to acquire responsible habits than teenagers who learn to drink at home in a family setting.

## Abstinence May Not Be the Best
## Way to Deal with a Drinking Problem

Among other anomalous features of Irish drinking, Vaillant's Boston study found that there were more abstainers in this group as well as more alcoholics. One reason for this dichotomy was that many excessive drinkers had sworn off drinking altogether. The Italians, on the other hand, were more likely to react to a drinking problem by cutting down.

This cultural difference reflects a larger battle in American alcoholism treatment. For many years, behavioral psychologists have claimed considerable success in teaching problem drinkers to reduce their intake. A.A. members and others who subscribe to the medical model of alcoholism, including the staffs of innumerable private treatment centers, insisted that this was impossible. But in 1992, the World Health Organization announced the results of an international study of "brief interventions" in both developed and Third World countries. Brief interventions are carried out in a general health care setting, rather than at

> *"The government faced increasing difficulty sustaining its blanket condemnation of alcohol, and the latest dietary guidelines . . . announced that drinking could be beneficial."*

alcohol treatment centers. A physician or other health care worker inquires about a patient's level of drinking, then informs heavy drinkers about healthy levels of drinking. In subsequent visits, the doctor asks about the patient's progress in reducing his or her drinking. The WHO study found that brief interventions are substantially more effective than standard alcoholism treatment of the kind practiced in the United States. They reach more drinkers with less folderol, and they avoid the conflicts associated with reformers-cum-therapists accusing heavy drinkers of being alcoholics in denial.

> *"American attitudes toward alcohol are aberrant even when compared to those of cultures . . . that share elements of the temperance tradition."*

Despite these promising results and some success at offering controlled drinking as an alternative in pilot programs at several American universities, the U.S. alcoholism treatment industry is not likely to wither away any time soon. For the foreseeable future, recovering alcoholics and expensive private hospitals will continue to hold sway over how Americans deal with problem drinkers.

## Little Evidence for the Surgeon General's Warning

Another manifestation of temperance-movement thinking is the advice given to women about drinking during pregnancy. Predictably, the 1995 U.S. dietary guidelines confirm the instruction that appears on every bottle of beer, wine, and liquor: "According to the Surgeon General, women should not drink alcoholic beverages during pregnancy because of the risk of birth defects."

Americans started hearing about the dangers of fetal alcohol syndrome (FAS) beginning in the 1980s. But subsequent investigations have revealed that FAS is exceedingly rare, even among alcoholic women. In 1995, Ernest Abel, a pioneering FAS researcher at Wright State University, performed a meta-analysis of 59 studies in various countries that looked at the relationship between maternal drinking and birth weight. Not only was there no evidence that light drinking harmed the fetus, but mothers who consumed up to one drink per day actually had heavier babies than mothers who abstained. (However, pregnant women who average two drinks a day tend to have lighter babies.) Those findings led Abel to question the wisdom of public health efforts to discourage all women from drinking during pregnancy. Once again, the evidence does not support an official U.S. health proclamation about alcohol.

## Other Nations Trust Their
## Citizens to Use Alcohol Responsibly

American attitudes toward alcohol are aberrant even when compared to those of cultures, such as Britain and Scandinavia, that share elements of the temperance tradition. Consider: Among the NATO soldiers in Bosnia, only the Americans are forbidden to drink. According to the *New York Times*, "the Norwegian soldiers here can drink in moderation, as can the French, the Danes, and the British." Apparently, other nations accept the logic that adults who are allowed to fly large aircraft and fire heavy artillery can also be trusted to consume alcohol moderately. We do not. But then, the Danes, French, British, and Norwegians have never enacted national prohibition.

# Alcohol Consumption Is Unfairly Condemned

## by Colman Andrews

**About the author:** *Colman Andrews is a food and travel writer, a restaurant critic for the* Los Angeles Times, *and the author of* Everything on the Table: Plain Talk About Food and Wine.

I'm drunk. My cheeks are flushed. My heart is beating fast. I'm not sure what time it is. As I look around the room, I find myself transfixed by insignificancies—a beam of light etching a tiny rainbow onto one side of an Evian bottle protruding from an ice bucket; a thin, translucent rim of molten wax ringing the flame of the milk-white taper on my table; a scribble of blue thread on the back of a waiter's short black jacket. I also find myself, improbably, enjoying the syrupy pianist in the corner as he oozes through his maudlin repertoire. I feel wonderful.

I'm sitting alone in the dining room of the Hôtel Beau Rivage Palace in Lausanne, Switzerland, and have just finished a simple but delicious dinner. I began my evening with a flute of champagne in the hotel bar. With my meal, I consumed a bottle of good Swiss pinot blanc. Now, with a demitasse of strong, creamy coffee, I'm starting on my second tiny glass of the aged dry white cherry brandy called *vieux kirsch*.

Do I disgust you? Do you disapprove? And if so, why? I'm not behaving oddly or inappropriately to my surroundings. I'm not singing loudly to myself or knocking things over. I may well lurch a little when I get up to leave; I'll probably snore like a foghorn tonight. But I'm not going to drive anywhere. I'm not going to abuse anyone on the way to my room. So what if I'm drunk? Maybe I'll die before you do. Maybe I won't. Maybe you're a better person than I am. I hope you are, in fact. Good night.

I wrote those words, or at least scrawled the notes on which they are closely based, in 1992, on the third evening of a 17-day business trip to Europe—a trip that was to include many more good meals and many more ascents, as I like to think of them, to a state of pleasant inebriation. I was scrawling in the first place, instead of just sitting there sipping cherry hooch and listening to "La Vie en Rose," because I had lately started thinking seriously about alcohol and (for a start) my own relation to it. Since that time, I've scrawled and thought a good deal more, drunk and sober both, not just about why I drink, but about why other people do or don't, and about why alcohol is increasingly condemned these days, by the earnest and the honest as well as by the fatuous and the self-deluding, as evil straight up.

## In Defense of Drinking

I've come to several conclusions: I think, first of all, that a lot of people who drink, and genuinely enjoy drinking, sometimes drink too much (*because* they genuinely enjoy drinking), but that when they do, it's usually no big thing. They usually don't cause anybody any problems, and they probably do no more than minor damage to themselves. (A hangover is not a pretty beast, but it is a short-lived one; and, up to a point at least, the liver has astonishing self-regenerative abilities.)

I think that if alcohol is indeed, as we are often told, "America's number-one drug problem," it is also probably America's number-one scapegoat for societal ills—ills whose real causes don't come conveniently packaged in bottle form.

And I think that, insofar as it is possible to measure such things, alcohol probably brings as much pleasure to the world as it brings pain. Plenty of people speak out against the pain. I think somebody ought to speak up for the pleasure.

## A Pleasurable Activity

I like to drink. This is no secret to anyone who knows me. Let's define some terms here, though: I don't live in a constant state of intoxication. I don't—I can't—work drunk. I don't get drunk every night. I don't get drunk on purpose. I mean, I know that alcohol will inebriate me if I consume a certain quantity of it and, in fact, appreciate that quality in it—but I don't sit down at the table, open a bottle of vodka and say, "Boy, am I gonna get blotto tonight!"

And when I talk about getting drunk, incidentally, I don't mean falling-down/throwing-up/screaming-and-flailing-or-sniffling-and-sobbing/out-of-control drunk. I mean drinking to the point that the chemical equilibrium of my body begins to be altered in various noticeable ways—my capillaries dilated, my muscles relaxed, my neurons disordered—with pleasurable effect.

Drinking is not an obsession with me. It is far from the defining activity of my life. I don't wake up in the morning imagining what alcoholic beverages I will consume that day. Drinking is simply a thing I do, a part of the mix. I drink wine—a bottle, more or less—with dinner three or four times a week. (I should mention that I'm 6-foot-1 and weigh something over 250 pounds, so I might be said to have a somewhat larger capacity than usual.) The nights I don't drink wine, I might have a small scotch when I come home or a brandy before I go to bed, or I might have nothing at all. I almost never drink at lunchtime, unless

I'm off somewhere where lunchtime drinking is the norm. Occasionally, day or night, if I'm in the mood and the circumstances permit, I exceed these limits.

I don't drive drunk, but I'd be a liar if I said that I've never driven drunk—and so would many of you. Sometimes when we drink more than we've intended to, judgment and coordination take advantage of the situation and sneak off hand-in-hand in the middle of the party, so discreetly that we don't even notice that they're gone. One of the drinker's most important responsibilities is to keep an eye on them, even through the haze, and to shut the bash down (and give up the car keys) if they disappear. (And one of the drinker's most important assets is a friend to help mount the vigil.)

> *"[Alcohol is] probably America's number-one scapegoat for societal ills—ills whose real causes don't come conveniently packaged in bottle form."*

I'm well aware of the physical dangers of alcohol—the way it can wrack the body, scramble the brain. I'm also aware of its beneficial effects (wine's apparent value to the cardiovascular system, for instance). But I neither drink nor moderate my drinking for medical reasons. I do moderate it—I drink less now than I did 20 or even 10 years ago, and will probably drink less in 1995 than I do in 1994—but only out of common sense. My body is less resilient than it used to be, and since I drink for pleasure, I try to avoid drinking to the point of displeasure.

Why *do* I drink, then? I drink because I like the way alcohol smells and tastes, especially in the forms in which I most often encounter it, which are wine, scotch, various brandies, an occasional beer, an occasional silly cocktail. I drink because I like the trappings of imbibing, the company it keeps—the restaurants and cafes and bars and (usually) the people who gather in them. And, I drink, frankly, because I like the way alcohol makes me feel. I like the glow, the softening of hard edges, the faint anesthesia. I like the way my mind races, one zigzag step ahead of logic. I like the flash flood of unexpected utter joy that sometimes courses quickly through me between this glass and that one. I like the feeling of being almost, but not quite, in control.

## A Naturally Occurring Substance

Alcohol is ancient—as old as fruit and grain. Fermentation, the process by which alcohol is produced, occurs spontaneously in nature. It is ignited by air-borne yeasts, settling by chance onto grapes or other sugar-laden fruits, vegetables, grains and such (the catalogue of willing agents is immense). The yeast secretes an enzyme called zymase, which acts upon certain of the sugars—principally dextrose and levulose—to form carbon dioxide and a carbohydrate called ethanol or ethyl alcohol ($C_2H_5OH$), which is the kind of alcohol we drink.

If alcohol is ancient, it is also ubiquitous. I don't mean just that most cultures, in most parts of the world, have discovered and enjoyed alcohol for themselves, but also that it is present in every one of us, whether we drink or not. In 1973, the Nobel Prize-winning British biochemist Sir Hans A. Krebs discovered that dietary sugars are fermented daily in the human intestine, producing alcohol in an amount said to approximate that contained in a quart of 3.2% beer. This alcohol doesn't have the effects of a quart of beer, at least in normally functioning human bodies, because it is broken down almost immediately, before it reaches the bloodstream. Still, this would seem to be further proof that alcohol is a natural substance, and that the body has the means for dealing with it, at least in modest quantity. This is accomplished initially through an enzyme known as alcohol dehydrogenase, whose function is to catalyze the first step in ridding the body of alcohol—and which, as Mark Keller of the Rutgers University Center of Alcohol Studies writes in his book "Alcohol and Alcohol Problems," "doesn't seem to have very much else to do."

It was Louis Pasteur who discovered the nature of fermentation, in 1857. Many thousands of years before that, though, human beings began to take note of both the process and its effects. According to one story, Noah drank fermented grape juice after watching goats grow tipsy from the grapes, and liked the stuff so much that he subsequently became the world's first drunkard (and planted the world's first vineyard). Another tale credits a concubine in the court of the (probably mythical) King Jamshid of Persia, who sought oblivion by quaffing a noxious, foaming liquid she found at the bottom of a bowl of rotting grapes in the palace cellar—and became the life of the party instead.

## Alcohol's Role in Human History

Distillation, the process by which whiskey, vodka, rum and other such liquors are made, is another story. Unlike fermentation, it is not a naturally occurring process, but rather a technique apparently developed by Arab alchemists in the 10th Century, originally to make perfumes and medicines. It is based on the fact that alcohol evaporates faster than water; by boiling wine, then, its alcohol can be drawn off and collected. The spirit, as it were, is extracted from the *vinum corpus*.

However fermentation was discovered, there is archeological evidence to suggest that, as long ago as 6,000 BC, the process had come under some measure of human control. The anthropologists Solomon H. Katz and Mary M. Voigt push the date back even earlier, to about 8,000 BC. They

> *"I drink, frankly, because I like the way alcohol makes me feel."*

also posit that the earliest fermented beverage, apparently a kind of beer, might have been considered so desirable by its consumers that they were willing to change their very mode of living to ensure its regular supply—actually planting grains that had hitherto been gathered in the wild. Out of cyclical, nonmigratory agriculture grew the first permanent human settlements—and the next thing anybody knew, you had rush-hour gridlock at Wilshire and Westwood.

The desire to get drunk, in other words, might lie at the very roots of human civilization.

## Alcoholism Is Too Broadly Defined

My name is Colman, and I'm an alcoholic. It says so right here, at the bottom of this questionnaire from Johns Hopkins Hospital in Baltimore. The form poses 20 yes-or-no questions. "If you have answered YES to three or more," it reads in conclusion, "you are definitely an alcoholic." They got me on four of them: (3.) *Do you drink because you are shy with other people?* Yes, sometimes, when I'm feeling out of my element. It works great; after a glass or two of something, I loosen up, start a conversation and join the party. (10.) *Do you crave a drink at a definite time daily?* Yep. Dinnertime. (16.) *Do you drink alone?* All the time, especially when I travel. I like drinking in company, but good wine tastes just as good at the solitary table. (17.) *Have you ever had a complete loss of memory as a result of drinking?* Yes, once.

> *"Is the Frenchman who consumes maybe a bottle or a bottle and a half of wine a day, every day of his life . . . an alcoholic?"*

I was young (in my early twenties), tired (I was near the end of an arduous second-class train journey from Bucharest to Paris) and unwise. Stopping between trains in Dijon, I stashed my luggage in a locker and went off to the Foire Gastronomique, an immense food and wine exhibition, at which I attempted to taste about two dozen varieties of calvados [an apple brandy]—strictly for academic purposes, of course—after already having had a bit too much wine to drink. I vaguely remember leaving the exhibition hall. The next thing I knew, my train was pulling into the Gare de Lyon some four or five hours later. Miraculously, I had all my luggage with me.

This is not the place to question the validity of facile questionnaires, to discuss the philosophies and methods of Alcoholics Anonymous and other such groups (which frequently use such questionnaires as screening devices) or to lampoon the you're-either-in-denial-or-in-recovery school of pop psychology.

But I think it might be worth noting, since it is not commonly understood by the general public, that there is no single, universally accepted medical or legal definition of "alcoholism"—and that by no means every expert on the subject accepts the fact that alcoholism is a disease at all. In his controversial but extensively documented 1988 book "Heavy Drinking: The Myth of Alcoholism as a Disease," Herbert Fingarette, a former World Health Organization alcoholism and addiction consultant, goes so far as to say that "*No* leading research authorities accept the classic disease concept [of alcoholism]."

Alcoholism is perhaps like obscenity in this respect: Almost everybody admits that it exists and most folks claim to know it when they see it. But when you try to get specific and say, This Is, This Isn't, it becomes a powerful elusive thing. Is an alcoholic, for instance, simply someone who ingests a certain pre-determined quantity of alcohol? (The Greek Stoic philosopher Epictetus thought so 2,000 years ago. "He is a drunkard," he proposed, "who takes more than three glasses, though he be not drunk.") Or should we define alcoholism in terms of physical symptoms (blackouts or the DTs, say) or of tragic social consequences (auto accidents, domestic violence, whatever)?

## A Responsible Alcoholic

My father was an alcoholic by nearly anybody's definition. For most of his life, he drank like a son-of-a-bitch. As a young dandy of a newspaper editor in Chicago, just before Prohibition, he was famous for going to bed at 4 a.m. "drunk as a skunk," then getting to the office in the morning before anybody else and knocking out stories while his colleagues were still squinting at the coffee. Later, as a Hollywood writer, he hung out at Lucey's and other movie-business watering holes, where water was rarely consumed, and downed martinis or (his trademark drink) Old Rarity and Perrier. My personal recollections of his drinking are somewhat less romantic. I recall, for example, that he used to hide bottles of whiskey in his suitcase when he went on business trips—and that when we went out to dinner as a family, he would sometimes excuse himself for a trip to the men's room, then stop on the way back to bribe a waiter to surreptitiously bring him a water glass filled with vodka.

If he was an alcoholic, though, he was also a scrupulously moral man, a stranger to violence whether drunk or sober and an almost unbelievably hard worker—a writer who sat at his typewriter for unbroken four- and five-hour stints, not even getting up to go to the bathroom or the coffee-maker, or to stretch his legs. At the age of about 60, on doctor's orders, he quit drinking. He did it cold turkey, subsequently refusing even a celebratory glass of champagne when I graduated from high school. After my mother died, I encouraged him to drink a bit again. This he did with great pleasure. "I'd forgotten how good that tasted," he said when he tried his first martini in a dozen years.

When he died himself a year later—from the effects not of his drinking but of his lifelong three-pack-a-day cigarette habit—I found nothing to suggest that he had started drinking seriously again. There was not a single bottle stashed in his apartment, not even beer in the refrigerator. If my father was an alcoholic, then, I'm tempted to say that he was not a typical one. But does a "typical" one exist?

## A Question of Context

Isn't it sometimes a question of social norms, or of context? Is the Frenchman who consumes maybe a bottle or a bottle and a half of wine a day, every day of his life (except when he's taking his annual government-subsidized, two-week "water cure" at some sulfurous-smelling spa in the mountains) an alcoholic?

What about the Greek or Italian who cannot imagine sitting down to lunch or dinner without at least a glass of wine or beer? On the other hand, what about the kid who guzzles too much Coors at a high school beer bust and pukes all the way home (and who will probably re-peat the process for a while until he grows out of it)? What about your aunt, who hadn't had a drink since George Bush was elected but who sipped a bit too much spiked eggnog a couple of nights ago and knocked

> *"Alcohol does not 'cause' automobile accidents or child neglect or rape or murder. We do, by misusing it."*

over a stop sign driving back to Mission Viejo? And if she's not an alcoholic, which I would argue she certainly isn't, then how dare our courts require, as they might well do, that she attend AA meetings as a portion of her sentence?

And, er, what about me?

Context, in fact, is the whole point. You know all about context if you've ever gone sober to a party where the drinking is heavy. Everyone seems so, well, glassy-eyed and red-faced, so loud and unfunny. It is not a pretty picture. But that's just you. You're out of place—just as you'd be out of place if you walked, glassy-eyed and red-faced, into a room full of the stone-cold sober. Wine-tasting party, wedding reception, Friday night at the tavern, table at Patina, bearskin rug by a ski lodge fire—those are drinking places, or can be if you want them to be. Freeway, office, library, schoolhouse—those are not, not *even* if you want them to be.

## Getting Drunk Is an Acceptable Activity

But the notion that there is a proper context for drinking, and for getting drunk, is rapidly disappearing in America. Institutionalized carousing is a facet of many cultures: Just as certain days are often set aside for abstinence, so certain days are set aside for popping corks and tapping kegs. We've just had such a day ourselves [New Year's Eve], and have another one coming up, on March 17. But, we are now told, it's *not OK* to get drunk on those days, or on any others. Drinking is bad, period. The consumption of alcohol is increasingly unacceptable anywhere, anytime, under any circumstances.

The three-martini lunch is an artifact today, as rare as the eight-track tape. In certain industries once famous for being practically fueled by ethanol—the movie business, journalism, advertising—drinking has become so suspect that a beer after work practically ruins reputations. In trendy restaurants, pregnant women are refused drinks by self-righteous waiters (never mind that some obstetricians permit their expectant patients an occasional glass or two of wine—or that waiters probably ought to wield no particular moral authority in this regard). Schoolchildren come home with their "Just Say No" brochures and beg their parents not to drink wine with dinner because alcohol is a drug. The line between use and abuse is blurred. If you look up "Intoxication" in the on-line catalogue at the Santa Monica Public Library, you will be asked to "See Alcoholism"—as if they are one and the same.

It's about time alcohol fell into disrepute, say anti-alcohol activists. According to some estimates, in this country it is involved in more than half of all fatal traffic accidents, more than half of all homicides, more than half of all arrests of any kind—and has a "negative economic impact" of more than $100 billion a year. It leads to suicide, broken homes, addiction to other drugs, woes of almost every kind.

## A Morally Neutral Substance

It is possible, to some extent, to defend alcohol from these charges. Who says, for instance, that the tragic character flaws blamed on drinking are always caused by drinking, rather than the other way around? How many people on Skid Row drank themselves there, and how many drink because they are there? And why, for that matter, do we lavish opprobrium on those people irresponsible enough to drive drunk and not on those who drive while under the influence of prescription tranquilizers or antihistamines (which can cause dangerous drowsiness), or the ones who nod off behind the wheel from sheer fatigue or sleep disorder, or the ones temporarily short-circuited by anger or deep sorrow?

There's a more basic response to the litany of accusations leveled against alcohol today, though: Alcohol is innocent. It has no soul. It has no intentions. It is a morally neutral substance, a mere arrangement of molecules, no more inherently good or bad than water (which both nourishes and drowns) or sunlight (progenitor of both chlorophyll and melanoma). Alcohol does not "cause" automobile accidents or child neglect or rape or murder. We do, by misusing it. Alcohol doesn't even cause alcoholism. (If it did, observed the National Institute on Alcohol Abuse and Alcoholism in 1977, "everyone who drinks would become an alcohol abuser.")

If drinking, and getting drunk, should be done in context, they should also be done with a sense of (and I hope this doesn't seem too weak a word) manners. There are, and have always been, codes of drinking. These vary according to geography and era, but they are always in place. "Make not thyself helpless in drinking in the beer shop," reads an Egyptian papyrus from about 1500 BC, "for . . . falling down thy limbs will be broken, and no one will give thee a hand."

> *"Drinking, like life, is a matter of balance."*

It is the responsibility of the drinker to know how, as well as when, to drink. There are people who Can't Drink. Something—personality, hereditary chemistry, whatever—robs them of control and of good sense when they ingest alcohol. Their etiquette is simply phrased, if not easily observed: Don't drink. There are others who can drink, and who choose to do so. Their etiquette is, or ought to be: Know yourself, and know alcohol in yourself.

## A Matter of Balance

I have two daughters, one 9 months and the other almost 4 years old, and though I've never actually sat down and thought deeply about the consequences of the messages I'm sending them by drinking so frequently in front of them—by incorporating alcohol into my life, into our family life—I am certainly very much aware that I am sending them messages.

"What are you going to do," my wife asked me recently, "if Maddy comes to you one day when she's a teen-ager and says, 'Dad, I'd like a glass of wine before I do my homework?'" I replied that I'd say no, and that I'd explain to her that there are some good things in life that you have to wait awhile for—like coffee in the morning, a driver's license and that glass of wine.

I realize, though, that that's far from enough. I realize that I have to imbue in my daughters a sense of respect for alcohol's heady powers and a sense of responsibility in its use. I hope, too, that I can inspire in them a deep affection for the concept of conviviality, and for the almost sacramental implications of breaking bread and sharing wine with someone.

> *"The consumption of alcohol is increasingly unacceptable anywhere, anytime, under any circumstances."*

But I also hope—and this is the really tricky part—that I can teach them this about getting drunk: That drinking, like life, is a matter of balance; that balance isn't always the same as moderation, though it keeps moderation at its core—and that you can't keep your balance if you can't see the edge.

# The Extent of Binge Drinking Among Young People Is Exaggerated

**by David J. Hanson**

**About the author:** *David J. Hanson is a professor of sociology at the State University of New York at Potsdam and the author of* Alcohol Education *and* Preventing Alcohol Abuse.

To most people, binge drinking brings to mind a self-destructive and unre-strained drinking bout lasting for at least a couple of days during which time the heavily intoxicated drinker "drops out" by not working, ignoring responsi-bilities, squandering money, and engaging in other harmful behaviors such as fighting. This view is consistent with that portrayed in dictionary definitions, in literature, in art, and in plays or films such as the classic *Come Back Little Sheba* and *The Lost Weekend* or the recent *Leaving Las Vegas.*

It is also consistent with the usage of physicians and other clinicians. As the editor of the *Journal of Studies on Alcohol* emphasizes, binge describes an ex-tended period of time (typically at least two days) during which time a person repeatedly becomes intoxicated and gives up his or her usual activities and obli-gations in order to become intoxicated. It is the combination of prolonged use and the giving up of usual activities that forms the core of the clinical definition of binge.

## The Expanding Definition of "Binge Drinking"

Other researchers have explained that it is counter-productive to brand as pathological the consumption of only five drinks over the course of an evening of eating and socializing. It is clearly inappropriate to equate it with a binge.

A 1995 Swedish study, for example, defines a binge as the consumption of half a bottle of spirits or two bottles of wine on the same occasion. Similarly, a study in Italy found that consuming an average of eight drinks a day was con-

Reprinted from David J. Hanson, "Binge Drinking," published at www2.potsdam.edu/alcohol-info, by permission of the author.

sidered normal drinking — clearly not bingeing. In the United Kingdom, binge-ing is commonly defined as consuming 11 or more drinks on an occasion. But in the United States, some researchers have defined bingeing as consuming five or more drinks on an occasion (an "occasion" can refer to an entire day). And now some have even expanded the definition to include consuming four or more drinks on an occasion by a woman.

> *"The unrealistic definitions [of binge drinking] being promoted by some researchers are misleading and deceptive at best."*

Consider a woman who has two glasses of wine with her leisurely dinner and then sips two beers over the course of a four or five hour evening. In the view of most people, such a woman would be acting responsibly. Indeed her blood alcohol content would remain low. It's difficult to imagine that she would even be able to feel the effects of the alcohol. However, some researchers would now define her as a binger!

How useful is such an unrealistic definition? It is very useful if the intent is to inflate the extent of a social problem. And it would please members of the Prohibition Party and the Women's Christian Temperance Union. But it is not very useful if the intent is to accurately describe reality to the average person.

It is highly unrealistic and inappropriate to apply a prohibitionist definition to describe drinking in the United States today. Perhaps we should define binge drinking as any intoxicated drinking that leads to certain harmful or destructive behaviors. Perhaps we should at least require that a person have a certain minimum level of alcohol in the bloodstream as a prerequisite to be considered a binger. Perhaps we could even require that a person be intoxicated before being labeled a "binger." But one thing is certain: the unrealistic definitions being promoted by some researchers are misleading and deceptive at best.

The conclusion is clear: Be very skeptical the next time you hear or read a report about "binge" drinking. Were the people in question really bingeing? By any reasonable definition, most almost certainly were not.

## The Extent of "Binge" Drinking

While a continuing barrage of newspaper articles, TV shows, and special interest group reports claim that binge drinking among young people is a growing epidemic, the actual fact is quite to the contrary. Binge drinking among young people is clearly declining and it has been doing so for many years.

"Binge" drinking among high school seniors has declined from 41.2% to 31.3% between 1980 and 1997. That's a drop of almost one-fourth (24%).

Similarly, the proportion of high school seniors who have consumed alcohol daily, have consumed any alcohol within the previous 30 days, have consumed within the previous year, or who have ever consumed alcohol have all dropped very dramatically since 1980.

*"Binge" drinking is also down among American college students, and it has clearly been declining for a number of years. This is indisputable.*

For example, according to a 1997 study of college drinking by Dr. Henry Wechsler of Harvard University, binge drinking has decreased significantly across the country over the four years since his earlier study. His research also found that the proportion of abstainers jumped nearly 22% in that short period of time.

These findings are consistent with data collected for the National Institute on Drug Abuse by the Institute for Social Research (ISR) at the University of Michigan. The ISR research found that college binge drinking in the United States recently reached the lowest level of the entire 17-year period that its surveys have been conducted. Similarly, it found that the proportion of drinkers has reached an all-time low among college students.

The federally-funded Core Institute at Southern Illinois University recently reported that collegiate binge drinking has dropped over 13% since 1980, when the Institute first began collecting data.

Research conducted at colleges across the United States repeatedly since the early 1980s by Drs. David Hanson (State University of New York) and Ruth Engs (Indiana University) has found declines over that time both in the proportion of collegians who drink at a high level and in the proportion who drink any alcohol.

So the facts are clear and indisputable: *"Binge" drinking is down and abstinence is up among American college students. Yet in spite of this and other overwhelming evidence, the false impression persists that drinking is increasing and that "bingeing continues unabated."*

## So What's the Harm?

This misperception is dangerous because when young people go off to college falsely thinking that "everybody" is drinking and bingeing, they are more likely to drink and to binge in order to conform. Correcting this misperception is important because it can empower young people and break the vicious self-fulfilling prophesy that helps perpetuate collegiate alcohol abuse.

Individual students almost always believe that most others on campus drink more heavily than they do and the disparity between the perceived and the actual behaviors tends to be quite large. By conducting surveys of actual student behavior and publicizing the results, the extent of heavy drinking can be quickly and significantly reduced. The most carefully assessed such abuse prevention project on campus has demonstrated a 35% reduction in heavy drinking, a 31% reduction in

> *"When young people go off to college falsely thinking that 'everybody' is drinking and bingeing, they are more likely to drink and binge in order to conform."*

alcohol-related injuries to self, and a 54% reduction in alcohol-related injuries to others. And similar results have been demonstrated at colleges across the country with this quick and inexpensive approach.

Too many college students still abuse alcohol. But people who exaggerate the problem and distort its magnitude are actually making the problem worse. If we are to further reduce alcohol abuse and the problems it causes, we have to publicize the actual facts and correct damaging misperceptions. Doing so will empower students to do what they as individuals generally want to do: drink less or not drink at all.

The challenge of correcting dangerous misperceptions about college student drinking is enormous. Many researchers and others have a vested interest in inflating the extent of "binge" drinking, and stories of drinking epidemics make dramatic headlines that sell more publications. But scare tactics are actually counterproductive and it turns out that *the most effective way to reduce alcohol abuse is simply to tell the truth and make sure that young people understand the facts.*

# Chapter 2

# Is Alcoholism a Disease?

# Chapter Preface

Many experts disagree about whether alcoholism is a disease or merely a bad habit. Supporters of the disease model, including the American Medical Association, contend that alcoholics are victims of a medical condition that develops in individuals who have certain innate risk factors for the disease, such as a genetic predisposition or unusual brain chemistry. Those who reject this view believe that alcoholism is not a biological disease, but rather a self-destructive behavior which an individual can overcome through willpower and psychological counseling.

The disease model first gained wide acceptance after the 1960 publication of E.M. Jellinek's book *The Disease Concept of Alcoholism*. Jellinek maintained that some, but not all, alcoholics have a disease. Many alcoholics become physically dependent on alcohol and suffer serious health problems as a result of their drinking; Jellinek reasoned that this type of alcoholism is an involuntary disorder that is damaging to one's health, and thus a disease. He was careful, however, to recognize that some heavy drinkers do not become dependent on alcohol, and others may be psychologically, but not physically, dependent on drinking. Jellinek postulated that an unknown biological factor caused the disease state to develop in some drinkers but not in others. Many researchers now believe that a person's genetic makeup may be this unknown risk factor: "Twin and adoption studies have, with rare exception, suggested that genetic factors play an important role in the etiology of alcoholism," says physician Kenneth Kendler.

Critics of the disease model reject the idea that alcoholism develops in certain individuals merely because they have a particular biological makeup. Instead, they believe that alcoholics drink as a way of dealing with other problems in their lives. According to this view, alcoholism is a behavioral pattern, one that is often shaped by social and cultural forces. For example, researcher George E. Valliant found that in one group of Irish and Italian neighbors, the Irish were seven times more likely to develop alcoholism. Valliant postulated that this was not because of genetic differences, but rather because "It is consistent with Irish culture to see the use of alcohol in terms of black or white, good or evil, drunkenness or complete abstinence, while in Italian culture it is the distinction between moderate drinking and drunkenness that is most important."

Although experts disagree over whether or not alcoholism is a disease, most now agree that both sociocultural and biological factors contribute to its development. The authors in the following chapter debate the relative importance of these factors, and the advantages and disadvantages of the disease model of alcoholism.

# Physicians Should Treat Alcoholism as a Disease

## by Thomas R. Hobbs

**About the author:** *Thomas R. Hobbs is medical director of the Physicians' Health Programs, an advocacy service for physicians suffering from impairing conditions.*

The debate on whether alcoholism is a disease or a personal conduct problem has continued for over 200 years. In the United States, Benjamin Rush, M.D., has been credited with first identifying alcoholism as a "disease" in 1784. He asserted that alcohol was the causal agent, loss of control over drinking behavior being the characteristic symptom, and total abstinence the only effective cure. His belief in this concept was so strong that he spearheaded a public education campaign in the United States to reduce public drunkenness.

### The Temperance Movement

The 1800s gave rise to the temperance movement in the United States. Alcohol was perceived as evil, the root cause of America's problems. Accepting the disease concept of alcoholism, people believed that liquor could enslave a person against his or her will. Temperance proponents propagated the view that drinking was so dangerous that people should not even sample liquor or else they would likely embark on the path toward alcoholism. This ideology maintained that alcohol is inevitably dangerous and inexorably addictive for everyone. Today, we know that strong genetic influences exist, but not everyone becomes addicted to alcohol.

The temperance movement picked up steam in the late 1800s and evolved into a movement advocating the prohibition of alcohol nationally. Banning alcohol would preserve the family and eliminate sloth and moral dissolution in the United States, according to supporters. Backed by strong political forces, legislation was passed and prohibition went into effect in 1920. Paradoxically, the era of prohibition also marked the death of Victorian standards. According to A. Sinclair in his book, *Prohibition: The Era of Excess*, a code of liberated

Reprinted, with permission, from Thomas R. Hobbs, "Managing Alcoholism as a Disease," *Physician's News Digest*, February 1998, published at www.physiciansnews.com.

personal behavior grew and with it the idea that drinking should accompany a full life. Drunkenness represented personal freedom. Due to public outcry, prohibition was repealed in 1933.

## The Disease Model of Alcoholism

Soon after prohibition ended, Alcoholics Anonymous (AA) was born. Formed in 1935 by stockbroker Bill Wilson and a physician, Robert Smith, AA supported the proposition that an alcoholic is unable to control his or her drinking and recovery is possible only with total abstinence and peer support. The chief innovation in the AA philosophy was that it proposed a biological explanation for alcoholism. Alcoholics constituted a special group who are unable to control their drinking from birth. Initially, AA described this as "an allergy to alcohol."

Although AA was instrumental in again emphasizing the "disease concept" of alcoholism, the defining work was done by Elvin Jellinek, M.D., of the Yale Center of Alcohol Studies. In his book, *The Disease Concept of Alcoholism*, published in 1960, Jellinek described alcoholics as individuals with tolerance, withdrawal symptoms, and either "loss of control" or "inability to abstain" from alcohol. He asserted that these individuals could not drink in moderation, and, with continued drinking, the disease was progressive and life-threatening. Jellinek also recognized that some features of the disease (e.g., inability to abstain and loss of control) were shaped by cultural factors.

During the past 35 years, numerous studies by behavioral and social scientists have supported Jellinek's contentions about alcoholism as a disease. The American Medical Association endorsed the concept in 1957. The American Psychiatric Association, the American Hospital Association, the American Public Health Association, the National Association of Social Workers, the World Health Organization and the American College of Physicians have also classified alcoholism as a disease. In addition, the findings of investigators in the late 1970s led to explicit criteria for an "alcohol dependence syndrome" which are now listed in the [American Psychiatric Association's *Diagnostic and Statistical Manual* and the World Health Organization's *International Classification of Diseases*]. In a 1992 *Journal of the American Medical Association* article, the Joint

> *"Alcoholism is a primary chronic disease with genetic, psychosocial, and environmental factors influencing its development and manifestations."*

Committee of the National Council on Alcoholism and Drug Dependence and the American Society of Addiction Medicine published this definition for alcoholism: "Alcoholism is a primary chronic disease with genetic, psychosocial, and environmental factors influencing its development and manifestations. The disease is often progressive and fatal. It is characterized by impaired control over drinking, preoccupation with the drug alcohol, use of alcohol despite adverse consequences, and distortions in thinking, mostly denial. Each of these symptoms may be continuous or periodic."

## Many Physicians Still View Alcoholism as Merely Bad Behavior

Despite the numerous studies validating the disease model of alcoholism, controversy still exists. In his 1989 book, *Diseasing of America*, social psychologist Stanton Peele, Ph.D., argues that AA and for-profit alcohol treatment centers promote the "myth" of alcoholism as a lifelong disease. He contends that the disease concept "excuses alcoholics for their past, present, and future irresponsibility" and points out that most people can overcome addiction on their own. He concludes that the only effective response to alcoholism and other addictions is "to recreate living communities that nurture the human capacity to lead constructive lives."

Surprisingly, Dr. Peele's view that alcoholism is a personal conduct problem, rather than a disease, seems to be more prevalent among medical practitioners than among the public. A recent Gallop poll found that almost 90 percent of Americans believe that alcoholism is a disease. In contrast, physicians' views of alcoholism were reviewed at an August 1997 conference held by the International Doctors of Alcoholics Anonymous (IDAA). A survey of physicians reported at that conference found that 80 percent of responding doctors perceived alcoholism as simply bad behavior.

> *"Alcoholism should not be judged as a problem of willpower, misconduct, or any other unscientific diagnosis."*

Dr. Raoul Walsh in an article published in the November 1995 issue of *Lancet* supports the contention that physicians have negative views about alcoholics. He cites empirical data showing physicians continue to have stereotypical attitudes about alcoholics and that non-psychiatrists tend to view alcohol problems as principally the concern of psychiatrists. He also contends that many doctors have negative attitudes towards patients with alcohol problems because the bulk of their clinical exposure is with late-stage alcohol dependence.

Based on my experiences working in the addiction field for the past 10 years, I believe many, if not most, health professionals still view alcohol addiction as a willpower or conduct problem and are resistant to look at it as a disease. Part of the problem is that medical schools provide little time to study alcoholism or addiction and post-graduate training usually deals only with the end result of addiction or alcohol/drug-related diseases. Several studies conducted in the late 1980s give evidence that medical students and practitioners have inadequate knowledge about alcohol and alcohol problems. Also, recent studies published in the *Journal of Studies on Alcoholism* indicate that physicians perform poorly in the detection, prevention and treatment of alcohol abuse.

The single most important step to overcoming these obstacles is education.

Education must begin at the undergraduate level and continue throughout the training of most if not all specialties. This is especially true for those in primary care where most problems of alcoholism will first be seen. In recent years, promotion of alcohol education programs in medical schools and at the post graduate level has improved. In Pennsylvania, for example, several medical schools now offer at least one curriculum block on substance abuse. Medical specialty organizations, such as the American Society of Addiction Medicine, are focusing on increasing addiction training programs for residents, practicing physicians and students.

Also, an increasing number of hospitals have an addiction medicine specialist on staff who is available for student and resident teaching, as well as being available for in-house consultations.

The American Medical Association estimates that 25–40 percent of patients occupying general hospital beds are there for treatment of ailments that result from alcoholism. In the United States, the economic costs of alcohol abuse exceed $115 billion a year. Physicians in general practice, hospitals and specialty medicine have considerable potential to reduce the large burden of illness associated with alcohol abuse. For example, several randomized, controlled trials conducted in recent years demonstrate that brief interventions by physicians can significantly reduce the proportion of patients drinking at hazardous levels. But first, we as physicians must adjust our attitudes.

## A Biopsychosocial Disease

Alcoholism should not be judged as a problem of willpower, misconduct, or any other unscientific diagnosis. The problem must be accepted for what it is—a biopsychosocial disease with a strong genetic influence, obvious signs and symptoms, a natural progression and a fatal outcome if not treated. Since 1988, the medical profession's and the public's acceptance of smoking as an addictive disease has resulted in reducing nicotine use in the United States. I feel that similar strides can be made with alcohol abuse. We must begin, as we did with nicotine, by educating and convincing our own colleagues that alcoholism is a disease. We must also emphasize that physicians have played a significant role in reducing the mortality and morbidity from nicotine use through patient education. Through strong physician intervention, I believe that we can achieve similar results with alcohol abuse.

# Addiction Is a Disease

## by Greg Skipper

**About the author:** *Greg Skipper is the medical director of Springbrook Northwest, a residential treatment program for alcoholism and other drug dependencies in Newberg, Oregon.*

The debate continues regarding whether or not addiction to alcohol or drugs is a disease. At the real heart of this debate are questions regarding the individual's responsibility for the disorder and understanding of the pathophysiology of the brain.

## Most People Misunderstand the Concept of Disease

Dorland's Medical Dictionary defines disease as "a definite morbid process having a characteristic train of symptoms; it may affect the whole body or any of its parts, and its etiology, pathology, and prognosis may be known or unknown." At first blush addiction certainly seems to satisfy this definition. The Jellinek curve graphically portrays the inexorable morbid progression of symptoms from surreptitious use, to compulsive use, to use despite adverse consequences and eventual isolation and loss of family, health, occupation and eventual incarceration or death.

In 1956 the American Medical Association (AMA) announced their opinion resolving that alcoholism is a disease. Likewise, in 1987 the AMA included drug addiction as a disease. The World Health Organization lists chemical dependence among other disorders in its International Classification of Diseases, Volume Ten (ICD-X). Most medical professional organizations consider addiction a disease, including the American Psychiatric Association who lists substance dependence criteria along with other mental disorders in the Diagnostic and Statistical Manual, Volume Four (DSM-IV).

So, if all these official organizations have agreed that addiction is a disease, where's the debate? Oddly enough, it comes from the general public, social critics, and law enforcement agencies. Most people have an erroneous view of disease as something that invades or attacks your good health; an innocent victim attacked by a "perpetrator" over whom he or she has no control. This idea

Reprinted from Greg Skipper, "Addiction . . . a Disease?" published at www.easystreet.com/sbnw, with permission from Springbrook Northwest, Inc.

of disease does not work for addiction. And here is where the controversy begins. In addiction, the person participates in or causes many of their own problems by their behavior.

## Many Diseases Are Caused by Unhealthy Behavior

In fact, most diseases are self-imposed by behavior, at least in part. If someone smokes cigarettes and eats fatty foods and then gets coronary artery disease, they have largely caused their own problem. Likewise, someone with a family history of diabetes who eats enough to become overweight and then develops diabetes has tempted fate and caused much of their own problem. They are a victim of their own unhealthy behavior. It's not that they wanted to have heart disease or diabetes but rather in the pursuit of their chosen lifestyle they inadvertently chose behaviors that have undesirable consequences. Likewise, when someone drinks it is never their goal to become addicted; however, they have caused their own problem, in part, and largely in ignorance, by their behavior. The fact that addiction is a disease should not in any way remove the burden of responsibility for causation (at least in part) or for treatment. In this way, addiction is like many other diseases.

The exact pathophysiology of addiction is not known. Theories regarding possible causes include abnormal or different receptors for neurotransmitters such as dopamine or serotonin, different neuroanatomical connections, or different chemical responses to addictive drugs. If the exact defect

> *"Most diseases are self-imposed by behavior, at least in part."*

were known the acceptance of addiction as a disease would be much easier. For example, if addiction was caused by a mutant dopamine gene structure called the A1 allele, we could then call addiction the "dopamine A1 allele disease." The fact that we don't know the pathophysiology with certainty makes it harder to understand and classify.

## Other Models for Understanding Addiction

Hester and Miller have described numerous conceptual models for understanding addiction. Including the dispositional disease model, they also list moral, temperance, spiritual, educational, social, characterologic, biologic, conditioning, sociocultural, general systems, and public health models. All of these models have merit and point out differing aspects of the complex problem of addiction.

Again addiction in this regard is like other illnesses. For example, there are differing models for understanding coronary artery disease. With coronary disease much has been said regarding personality type A and B as contributing or preventing the disease. There are also educational socioeconomic factors with heart disease. Heredity and diet are important factors as are issues of lifestyle, exercise, and self care. There is a genetic and also a biological perspective. There is even a moral model of heart disease that focuses on gluttony and/or "bad habits" as the primary cause of the problem. The exact cause of coronary disease is also not known. (See Table 1.)

## Table 1: Conceptual Models of Addiction and Coronary Artery Disease (CAD)

| Model | Causal Factors in Addiction | Causal Factors in CAD |
|---|---|---|
| Moral | Personal responsibility, self-control | Gluttony, cigarette smoking |
| Temperance | Alcohol | Cholesterol |
| Spiritual | Spiritual deficit | Stress, lack of serenity |
| Dispositional Disease | Genetic abnormality | Genetic predisposition |
| Educational | Lack of knowledge | Lack of knowledge |
| Characterological | Personality traits, defenses | Personality traits, type A/B |
| Conditioning | Classical or operant conditioning | NA |
| Social Learning | Modeling, skill deficit | NA |
| Cognitive | Beliefs, expectancies | NA |
| Sociocultural | Environmental, cultural norms | Cultural norms |
| General Systems | Boundaries and rules, family dysfunction | Stress in family systems |
| Biological | Heredity, brain physiology | Vascular physiology, biochemistry |
| Public Health | Agent, host, environment | Agent, host, environment |

None of these other models detract from the fact that addiction is a disease. It occurs in approximately 15% of Americans during their life. There appears to be a hereditary genetic component. What is inherited is the potential for addiction and not the disease. There are various degrees of severity and complexity. Treatment can be very effective, especially if long term follow-up is performed.

### Addicts Do Bad Things

One way addiction is unlike most other diseases is . . . that addicts in the course of their illness do bad things. They lie, steal, cheat, and are unreliable. The compulsion to use eventually supersedes moral restraints. The compulsion to use supersedes values. The compulsion to use is so strong it exceeds most other drives. Addicts do bad things and they should be responsible and deserve consequences. However, this still does not mean addiction is not a disease. The fact that AIDS patients have been known to steal to buy medicine does not mean AIDS is not a disease. The fact that promiscuity leads to sexually transmitted diseases does not mean syphilis is not a disease.

Addiction is a disease. Patients and family benefit from understanding this fact. This understanding helps the patient to have less shame and guilt and to begin a process of accepting help. The family benefits by decreasing their anger and frustration and they begin to support healthy rehabilitative activities and support for the patient and themselves.

# Alcoholism Has a Genetic Basis

by Marc Alan Schuckit

**About the author:** *Marc Alan Schuckit is a psychiatrist and addiction specialist who teaches at the University of California, San Diego School of Medicine, and he is the author of* Educating Yourself About Alcohol and Drugs: A People's Primer, *from which the following viewpoint was excerpted.*

It seems obvious that not everyone carries the same level of vulnerability to developing severe, repetitive problems once substance use has begun. This statement is really no different from what one would expect for most medical disorders, because different people appear to carry higher or lower levels of vulnerability toward heart attacks, cancer, obesity, and so on. Some people believe that different levels of vulnerability to developing alcohol or drug dependence are caused, at least in part, by biological differences that exist between people.

## Some Genetic Factors Appear to Be Important

Most of my research over the last twenty years has focused on one important type of biological factor that might contribute to different levels of vulnerability toward developing severe substance-related problems. This is the possible role that *genetics* might play in the development of alcohol dependence or alcoholism. By this I mean the way in which the biological material or genes passed on from parents to children might predispose someone toward a higher or lower vulnerability to developing severe and repeated alcohol-related problems.

Unfortunately, there is less known about genetic influences relating to dependence on other substances such as the stimulants, marijuana-type drugs, or opiates, but even here new and interesting data are now being developed. However, since I want to keep my major emphasis on what is known (rather than what is guessed), I have to limit the comments offered here mostly to alcohol.

The fact that alcoholism runs strongly in families has been known for hundreds of years. Until relatively recently, however, most assumed that the twofold-to-fourfold increased risk for severe alcohol problems among close relatives of alcoholics was a result of the family environment in which people were raised. For example, it was assumed that a child raised in a home in which heavy drinking was the norm might learn that alcohol is a way to deal with problems. According to this theory, later in life such a person might be expected to develop more alcohol-related difficulties than someone raised in a home in which drunkenness was frowned upon and where alcohol was consumed in only moderate amounts or not at all. However, studies conducted in the 1960s began to question this presumption about the all-important role of environmental factors in producing alcoholism.

## Studies of Twins and Adopted Children of Alcoholics

The first type of study to begin to test the relative importance of genetics versus childhood environment focused on twins. Here, researchers took advantage of the fact that nature produces two types of twins. *Fraternal twins* are born at the same time but share only 50% of their genes, the same as any full brothers and sisters. They come from different eggs and sperm, with two separate fertilized eggs being implanted in the womb at the same time. *Identical twins,* on the other hand, are also born at the same time but actually share 100% of their genes. They come from the same fertilized egg, which splits into two separate individuals after several divisions.

Both types of sets of twins are raised in the same environment and experience major childhood events at the same age and under the same general life conditions. Therefore, if severe alcohol-related life problems were the result of major events that occurred in childhood (i.e., environmental influences), then the twin of an alcoholic should have a very high risk for the disorder himself or herself, no matter whether fraternal or identical twinship is involved. On the other hand, if genetic factors are important, the identical twin of an alcoholic, sharing 100% of the genes, should be at a much higher risk for developing this problem than a fraternal twin. Almost all of the studies in this area carried out over the last twenty years show that the risk for alcoholism is much higher in the identical twin of an alcoholic (perhaps as high as 60%) than in the fraternal twins (with an estimated 30%). These findings support the view that genetic factors play an important role in determining the risk for alcoholism.

> *"Until relatively recently . . . most assumed that the twofold-to-fourfold increased risk for severe alcohol problems among close relatives of alcoholics was a result of the family environment in which people were raised."*

To me, however, the most convincing evidence concerning the importance of genetic factors in alcoholism comes from studies of children of alcoholics who were adopted away close to birth. Here one can evaluate the risk for alcoholism among biological children of alcoholics who were raised by nonalcoholics. It is remarkable that these sons and daughters still demonstrate their fourfold increased risk for severe alcohol problems, even when they had no knowledge that their biological parent had had alcoholism. In fact, even if one of the children's adoptive parents develops alcoholism, this does not raise the alcoholism risk for the adopted child any further than what is predicted by the biological parent's problem. In other words, *a high risk for severe alcohol problems is predicted by the disorder in the biological parent, not by problems in the environment in which the child is raised.*

> *"A high risk for severe alcohol problems is predicted by the disorder in the biological parent, not by problems in the environment in which the child is raised."*

## Genetic Factors Do Not Explain the Whole Picture

The discovery that alcoholism is influenced by genetic factors doesn't mean that genes alone cause severe alcohol problems. Some environmental factors must also play a role because the risk for the disorder in even the identical twin of an alcoholic is never as high as 100%. In other words, no one is predestined to become an alcoholic, anymore than anyone has a 100% chance for developing cancer or heart disease.

Thus, even if we have a higher risk for developing severe and persistent alcohol-related difficulties, we still have *choices* regarding what we do about it. We are the ones who decide whether we will drink at all, and we each determine the care we take to avoid drunkenness, the way we limit drinking at times of stress, and whether the development of more minor problems convinces us to avoid any use of alcohol in order to stop placing ourselves at risk.

# Alcoholics Should Not Be Blamed for Their Disease

**by W. Waldo**

**About the author:** *W. Waldo is the publisher of Hope and Healing Webchronicles (www.hopeandhealing.com), a website created to inform families affected by alcoholism about spiritual principles, positive perspectives, and the twelve-step philosophy of Alcoholics Anonymous.*

If a loved one was diagnosed with cancer, or diabetes, or mental disease such as schizophrenia or manic-depression, how would you respond?

Alcoholism is a disease no different than cancer, or diabetes, or mental disorders with various forms of treatments available and various levels of success with treatment attainable.

## A Disease with Biological and Genetic Causes

Alcoholism is a biological brain disease. When alcohol or other addictive drugs are introduced into a body predisposed by inherited genetics to addiction, permanent biological changes occur in the brain. These changes do not occur in someone without the genetic predisposition to addiction.

We are all born with genetic "predispositions". A heightened probability of developing certain physical or mental diseases during our lifetime based on our heritage. If mother's side of the family has members who have been diagnosed with cancer or father's side of the family has members who have been diagnosed with heart disease or diabetes, there is an increased risk for the child to manifest one of these diseases at some point in life.

Genetics play one part in the development of disease. There are emotional and environmental factors that all must come together to create disease. Possession of one part of the whole does not make a whole. Knowledge of predisposing factors are only markers, not an inescapable fate.

When all the parts do come together to make the whole and disease manifests, there is a common fate for people suffering from the disease of addiction that does not generally apply when any other disease manifests. It is to be

Reprinted from W. Waldo, "Alcoholism Is a Disease Like Any Other Disease," published at www.hopeandhealing.com/eguide21.htm, April 1998, by permission of the author.

blamed for their disease as if the disease is an indication of a weak character, moral deficiency or being without sufficient willpower and internal discipline to manage the addiction.

## Cruelty vs. Compassion

It is unimaginably cruel to blame someone for their disease, and yet, alcoholics are blamed for causing their disease whenever alcoholism is considered a lifestyle choice.

When almost any other disease is diagnosed, appropriate forms of treatment options are discussed. Odds of remission are given. One out of ten . . . five out of ten. . . . The focus is to be that 'one out of ten' or that 'one of the five'. It doesn't matter how long the treatment procedures take or how long and windy the road to recovery becomes. Setbacks are seen as a challenge to move forward with greater commitment to recovery. Loved ones never let go, friends rally around with positive affirmation and some employers will adjust work schedules to secure your position with the company.

It should be no different when the disease is alcoholism.

Initial treatment for alcoholism and drug addictions usually involves admission to an inpatient/outpatient treatment center specializing in alcoholism and drug addictions. There is a detoxification period, followed by counseling, education, support groups and 12 Step meetings. Many treatment centers have a family program involving family members in recovery.

The treatment center is a beginning point in the life of recovery.

> *"It is unimaginably cruel to blame someone for their disease."*

Continued abstinence from alcohol treats the physical; counseling and involvement in support groups treats the emotional, mental and spiritual.

As with any disease, recovery is not always a straight road of success. There can be periods of remission and possible relapse. If a relapse does occur, measured as a temporary setback and not as failure, with a challenge to modify or enhance course of treatment in an effort to find a workable mix, then recovery will likely continue forward. This would be the perspective if the treatment for cancer, diabetes or a mental disorder did not bring hoped for results.

It should be no different when the disease is alcoholism.

## A Double Standard

In the event of relapse during or after treatment for the disease of cancer, diabetes or mental illness, no one would act as if they were dealing with a willfull child who is refusing to co-operate, declare hopelessness and blame the patient for a lack of perfect first-time remission.

Unfortunately, the disease of alcoholism and success of treatment is often held to a different standard.

# The Genetic Basis of Alcoholism Has Been Exaggerated

## by Stanton Peele

**About the author:** *Stanton Peele is a psychologist and researcher specializing in drug and alcohol addiction, and he is the author of* The Diseasing of America: How We Allowed Recovery Zealots and the Treatment Industry to Convince Us We Are Out of Control, *from which the following viewpoint was excerpted.*

Alcoholics Anonymous originally claimed that alcoholics inherit an "allergy" to alcohol that underlies their loss of control when they drink. Today this particular idea has been discarded. Nonetheless, a tremendous investment has been made in the search for biological inheritances that may cause alcoholism, while many grandiose claims have been made about the fruits of this search. In 1987, almost two-thirds of Americans (63 percent) agreed that "alcoholism can be hereditary"; only five years earlier, in 1982, more people had disagreed (50 percent) than agreed (40 percent) with this statement. Furthermore, it is the better educated who agree most with this statement. Yet widely promulgated and broadly accepted claims about the inheritance of alcoholism are inaccurate, and important data from genetic research call into doubt the significance of genetic influences on alcoholism and problem drinking. Moreover, prominent genetic researchers themselves indicate that cultural and environmental influences are the major determinants of most drinking problems, even for the minority of alcoholics who they believe have a genetic component to their drinking.

## Theory Presented as Fact

Popular works now regularly put forward the theory—presented as fact—that the inherited cause of alcoholism has been discovered. In the words of Durk Pearson and Sandra Shaw, the authors of *Life Extension*, "Alcohol addiction is not due to weak will or moral depravity; it is a genetic metabolic defect . . . [just

Excerpted from Stanton Peele, *The Diseasing of America: How We Allowed Recovery Zealots and the Treatment Industry to Convince Us We Are Out of Control*, (New York: Lexington Books, 1995). Reprinted with permission.

like the] genetic metabolic defect resulting in gout." One version of this argument appeared in the newsletter of the Alcoholism Council of Greater New York:

> Someone like the derelict . . . , intent only on getting sufficient booze from the bottle poised upside-down on his lips . . . [is] the victim of metabolism, a metabolism the derelict is born with, a metabolic disorder that causes excessive drinking.

Is it really possible that street inebriates are destined from the womb to become alcoholics? Don't they really have a choice in the matter, or any alternatives? Don't their upbringings, or their personal and social values, have any impact on this behavior?

## Ambiguous Findings

Several well-publicized studies have found that close biological relatives of alcoholics are more likely to be alcoholics themselves. The best-known research of this kind, examining Danish adoptees, was published in the early 1970s by psychiatrist Donald Goodwin and his colleagues. The researchers found that male adoptees with alcoholic biological parents became alcoholics three to four times more often than adoptees without alcoholic relatives. This research has several surprising elements to it, however. In the first place, only 18 percent of the males with alcoholic biological parents became alcoholics themselves (compared with 5 percent of those without alcoholic parentage). Note that, accepting this study at face value, the vast majority of men whose fathers are alcoholics do not become alcoholic solely because of biological inheritance.

Some might argue that Goodwin's definition of alcoholism is too narrow and that the figures in his research severely understate the incidence of alcoholism. Indeed, there was an additional group of problem drinkers whom Goodwin and his colleagues identified, and many people might find it hard to distinguish when a drinker fell in this rather than in the alcoholic group. However, more of the people in the problem drinking group did not have alcoholic parents than did! If alcoholic and heavy problem drinkers are combined, as a group they are not more likely to be offspring of alcoholic than of nonalcoholic parents, and the finding of inherited differences in alcoholism rates disappears from this seminal study. One last noteworthy result of the Goodwin team's research: in a separate study using the same methodology as the male offspring study, the investigators did not find that daughters of alcoholic parents more often became alcoholic themselves (in fact, there were more alcoholic women in the group without alcoholic parents).

> *"Widely promulgated and broadly accepted claims about the inheritance of alcoholism are inaccurate."*

Other studies also discourage global conclusions about inheritance of alcoholism. One is by a highly respected research group in Britain under Robin

Murray, dean of the Institute of Psychiatry at Maudsley Hospital. Murray and his colleagues compared the correlation between alcoholism in identical twins with that between fraternal twins. Since the identical pair are more similar genetically, they should more often be alcoholic or nonalcoholic together than twins whose relationships are genetically equivalent to ordinary siblings. No such difference appeared. Murray and his colleagues and others have surveyed the research on inheritance of alcoholism. According to a longtime biological researcher in alcoholism, David Lester, these reviews "suggest that genetic involvement in the etiology of alcoholism . . . is weak at best." His own review of the literature, Lester wrote, "extends and . . . strengthens these previous judgments." Why, then, are genetic viewpoints so popular? For Lester, the credibility given genetic views is "disproportionate with their theoretical and empirical warrant," and the "attraction and persistence of such views lies in their conformity with ideological norms."

Several studies of male children of alcoholics (including two ongoing Danish investigations) have not found that these children drink differently as young adults or adolescents from their cohorts without alcoholic relatives. These children of alcoholics are not generally separated from their parents, and we know that for whatever reason, male children brought up by their alcoholic parents more often will be alcoholic themselves. What this tells us is

> *"Children aren't born as alcoholics but develop their alcoholism over the years."*

that these children aren't born as alcoholics but develop their alcoholism over the years. In the words of George Vaillant, who followed the drinking careers of a large group of men over forty years:

> The present prospective study offers no credence to the common belief that some individuals become alcoholics after the first drink. The progression from alcohol use to abuse takes years.

## Why Do Some People Drink More than Others?

What, then, do people inherit that keeps them drinking until they become alcoholics? Milam asserts in *Under the Influence* that the source of alcoholism is acetaldehyde, a chemical produced when the body breaks down alcohol. Some research has found higher levels of this chemical in children of alcoholics when they drink; other research (like the two Danish prospective studies) has not. Such discrepancies in research results also hold for abnormalities in brain waves that various teams of researchers have identified in children of alcoholics—some find one electroencephalogram (EEG) pattern, while other researchers discover a distinct but different pattern. Psychiatrist Marc Schuckit, of the University of California at San Diego Medical School, found no such differences between young men from alcoholic families and a matched comparison group, leading him to "call into question . . . the replicability and generalizability" of cognitive impairments and neuropsychologic deficits "as part of a predisposition toward alcoholism."

Washington University psychiatrist Robert Cloninger (along with several other researchers) claims that an inherited antisocial or crime-prone personality often leads to both criminality and alcoholism in men. On the other hand, antisocial acting out when drinking, as well as criminality, are endemic to certain social and racial groups—particularly young working-class and ghetto males. The Cloninger view gets into the slippery realm of explaining that the underprivileged and ghettoized are born the way they are. In addition, Schuckit has failed to find any differences in antisocial

> *"Not even genetically oriented researchers . . . deny that cultural and social factors are crucial in the development of alcoholism and that, in this sense, alcoholism is driven by values and life choices."*

temperament or impulsiveness to differentiate those who come from alcoholic families and those without alcoholic siblings or parents. Instead, Schuckit believes, one—perhaps the—major mechanism that characterizes children of alcoholics is that these children are born with a diminished sensitivity to the effects of alcohol (although—once again—other researchers do not find this to be the case).

In Schuckit's view, children of alcoholics have a built-in tolerance for alcohol—they experience *less* intoxication than other people when drinking the same amounts. (Note that this is the opposite of the original AA view that alcoholics inherit an allergy to alcohol.) In the Schuckit model, alcoholics might unwittingly drink more over long periods and thus build up a dependence on alcohol. But as a theory of alcoholism, where does this leave us? *Why* do these young men continue drinking for the years and decades Vaillant tells us it takes them to become alcoholics? And even if they *can* drink more without experiencing physical effects, why do they tolerate the various drinking problems, health difficulties, family complaints, and so on that occur on the road to alcoholism? Why don't they simply recognize the negative impact alcohol is having on their lives and resolve to drink less? Certainly, some people do exactly this, saying things like "I limit myself to one or two drinks because I don't like the way I act after I drink more."

## Cultural and Social Factors Play an Important Role

One insight into how those with similar physiological responses to alcohol may have wholly different predispositions to alcoholism is provided by those who manifest "Oriental flush"—a heightened response to alcohol marked by a visible reddening after drinking that frequently characterizes Asians and Native Americans. Oriental flush has a biochemical basis in that Asian groups display higher acetaldehyde levels when they drink: here, many believe, is a key to alcoholism. But individuals from Asian backgrounds who flush do not necessarily drink more than—or differ in their susceptibility to drinking problems from—those who don't flush. Moreover, groups that show flushing have both the highest alcoholism rates (Native Americans and Eskimos) and the lowest rates (Chinese and Japanese) among ethnic groups in the United States. What distinguishes between how people in these two groups react to the same biological phenomenon? It would certainly seem that Eskimos' and Indians' abnegated state in America and their isolation from the American economic and achievement-oriented system inflate their alcoholism rates, while the low alcoholism rates of the Chinese and Japanese must be related to their achievement orientation and economic success in our society.

Not even genetically oriented researchers (as opposed to popularizers) deny that cultural and social factors are crucial in the development of alcoholism and that, in this sense, alcoholism is driven by values and life choices. Consider three quotes from prominent medical researchers. Marc Schuckit: "It is unlikely that there is a single cause for alcoholism. . . . At best, biologic factors explain only a part of" the alcoholism problem; George Vaillant, quoted in an article in *Time*: "'I think it [finding a biological marker for alcoholism] would be as unlikely as finding one for basketball playing.' . . . The high number of children of alcoholics who become addicted, Vaillant believes, is due less to biological factors than to poor role models"; Robert Cloninger: "The demonstration of the critical importance of sociocultural influences in most alcoholics suggests that major changes in social attitudes about drinking styles can change dramatically the prevalence of alcohol abuse regardless of genetic predisposition." In short, the idea that alcoholism is an inherited biological disease has been badly overstated, and according to some well-informed observers, is completely unfounded.

# Treating Alcoholism as a Disease Harms Alcoholics

**by Edward A. Dreyfus**

**About the author:** *Edward A. Dreyfus is a clinical psychologist in private practice in the Los Angeles-Santa Monica area of California.*

Many mental health practitioners are promoting the notion that alcohol abuse, drug abuse, overeating, gambling, anorexia, bulimia and smoking are diseases. By using the disease model, its proponents believe that people are more apt to seek help because having an "illness" is more acceptable than having psychological or behavior disorder. I am reminded of the effects of saying that people with emotional difficulties were "sick," and suffering from a "disease." Psychology and psychiatry moved a long way forward when we listened to Thomas Szasz declare that mental illness was a myth, to Karl Menninger discussing degrees of personality organization, and to Benjamin Rush when he spoke of problems in living. Now it appears we are moving backwards. What will be the next "disease" to appear in the news media?

The disease model states that alcoholism and compulsive over-eating, for example, are diseases and can be compared to diabetes in that diabetics react to sugar in a similar way that over-eaters have a reaction to food and alcoholics to liquor. Therefore, in both instances the individuals must carefully monitor their intake. If they do not rigidly adhere to their respective diets there will be dire consequences. The compulsive over-eater, for example, maintains that if he/she does not monitor food intake, there is a chemical imbalance which takes over and control over one's eating is no longer possible. So, the theory maintains, the compulsive over-eater is not "normal" insofar as eating is concerned, but rather he or she has a "disease" and is "sick."

The question that this thesis does not address, however, is: Why do compulsive over-eaters and alcoholics, knowing that they are not able to control their substance abuse once it is started, persist in breaking their diet? The diabetic's disease is the failure of the body to produce sufficient insulin; the disease is not

Reprinted from Edward A. Dreyfus, "Compulsive Behavior: Disease or Symptom?" published at http://hometown.aol.com/edreyfus/dreyfus.htm, by permission of the author.

the individual's failure to stay on a diabetic diet. It is not the *behavior* that is the disease, it is the manner in which the body metabolizes alcohol that may be the disease, leading to the necessity for dietary control, or in the case of the substance abuser and alcoholic, abstinence. While there may be a biological or chemical basis for some compulsions, the disease model does not account for the compulsive *behavior* itself; it only accounts for the specific substance.

## Historical Perspective

Many years ago mentally disturbed persons were considered to be inhabited by the devil; they were ostracized from their communities and families and were treated with disdain. They were locked up, deprived of their human rights, and often killed. Pinel, in the 18th century, cut the chains of the inmates of the insane asylum at Bicitre and freed them, declaring that they were not possessed of evil spirits, but rather that they were medically ill. This was the beginning of a movement which sought to achieve humane treatment for the mentally disturbed. It was an extremely important step forward. By declaring these people ill, the indignities they suffered were reduced. It was *necessary* to call them "sick" in order to obtain humane treatment.

As the theories of Sigmund Freud were made available and became acceptable, it was discovered that many of these individuals were not ill in the medical sense, but rather they were psychologically disturbed. The "talking cure," as psychoanalysis was then called, demonstrated that mental "illness" could be cured through words. This was another very important step, for now, people with psychological disorders could be viewed with some dignity and could potentially be treated by nonmedical practitioners. Unfortunately neither the patients nor the practitioners were accorded the same respect as those with physical ailments who were being treated by physicians. In fact, many people still believe it is much more acceptable to be physically ill than it is to be psychologically disturbed.

So, instead of being chained in dungeons and forgotten, the mentally ill were locked in hospitals and treated. However, it gradually became obvious that they were still ostracized from the community, and were being treated as second class citizens. Though they were treated better physically, they still carried the stigma of being "sick," which was almost as dehumanizing as being thought of as "in-

*"It is pitiful that a society has to resort to seeing people as sick in order to be compassionate towards them."*

habited by the devil." Now they were pitied, but they still lost their freedom, their dignity, and their human rights.

The movement away from the disease model toward a psychological model helped pave the way toward integrating the "mentally ill" into the community rather than segregating them. It had the effect of gaining more respect, understanding, and dignity for all people with emotional difficulties. Instead of seeing these people as "sick", we began seeing them as having "problems in living," which could be understood and resolved. Such a psychological model permitted greater numbers of non-medical practitioners to "treat" these individuals and has made such treatment more available and more affordable to more people. People began to feel more comfortable treating troubled people humanly without having to see them as "sick." (In fact, they found that the disease model interfered with effective treatment.) People trying to cope with internal or external stress may do so in maladaptive ways. This does not make them "sick."

## Consequences of a Disease Model

When it came to compulsive behaviors, however, even the most compassionate individuals had difficulty accepting that people did not seem able to control their own behavior. Hence, they treated alcoholics as "bums," over-eaters as "fatsos," gamblers as "stupid," etc. And these people viewed themselves similarly. So, the concept of illness was invoked once again. And once again people were treated for their "illness" and others viewed them more compassionately as, "Don't laugh at your overweight Aunt Mary, she has an illness," or "Your drunk Uncle Charley is sick." I think it is pitiful that a society has to resort to seeing people as sick in order to be compassionate towards them. And I believe it adversely affects people's self esteem to have to consider themselves sick in order to be related to humanly. I find it sad that people, so hungry for acceptance, both self-acceptance or acceptance from others, will accept the appellation "sick."

> *"[Advocates for various self-help groups] promote the concept of disease in order to entice substance abusers into treatment."*

The advocates for various self-help and other groups that deal with compulsive substance abuse view these compulsions as diseases. They promote the concept of disease in order to entice substance abusers into treatment. If they can convince these people that they are "sick" and they are suffering from a "disease" then it is believed that more people will accept treatment.

We live in a society that loves labels whether on clothes or on people. We tend to relate to the clothes people, with the labels on the outside, just as we treat the labels we pin on people: schizophrenic, alcoholic, ACA [adult child of an alcoholic], incest survivor, borderline personality, etc. And people seem to need to view themselves as "sick" in order to be treated humanly (and in order to treat themselves with care.)

Psychology strove for years to move away from the medical/disease model so that healers would relate to people as people, not as labels, not as "sick." This was called the humanistic movement and eschewed the medical model and sought a psychological model. I see a reversal of this effort and find it regressive. And I think, in this context, that 12-step programs with their emphasis on disease and "sickness," fosters this regressive type of thinking.

While I do not object to the results or even some of the methods employed, I do object to the use of the terms "disease" and "sick" as a means for effecting these results. There are consequences to using a disease model which extend beyond merely controlling substance abuse. In our quest for expediency, we are often short-sighted.

## Social Consequences

I object to the idea that compulsive *behavior* is a disease. It does not matter whether there is a chemical imbalance that leaves these people vulnerable to gaining weight and drinking, the disease concept is not appropriate for the compulsive behaviors. Society decides on what is compulsive, and using the disease concept, any one of us could be viewed as "sick" for any behavior that people deem compulsive. Thus someone who is a "workaholic," a smoker, or a nail-biter could be considered "sick." Don't people have the right to engage in activities, even unhealthy activities, without being considered "sick"?

Compulsive behavior is rewarded in our society. Indeed, people are taught to be compulsive; that is, we are taught to be punctual, orderly, committed, organized, etc. We are taught to hide our feelings through activity. We are taught to keep busy when we are feeling badly. We are taught to whistle when afraid, think about something else when we are sad, and even to eat when we are "blue." All compulsive individuals are taught at an early age to deny feelings through some form of activity. And if you learn your lessons well, you could be considered "sick."

## Psychological Consequences

Some psychological consequences of the disease model are:
1. Individuals tend to give up responsibility for their life; they can see themselves as victims because the "disease" is not their fault.
2. Individuals seek someone to "fix" them without examining the causes or issues which may produce the compulsion; only the symptom is examined.
3. There is a loss of dignity and self-esteem in believing that one is "bad" or "sick" for having gone off a diet, or drinking, etc.
4. Individuals often use "illness" or "disease" to avoid taking responsibility for their behavior just as they might have gotten "sick" to avoid going to school.
5. This kind of infantilization has long-term consequences to one's self-esteem and self-confidence, though it may have immediate results. Patronizing others does not enhance one's self-concept.
6. By seeing oneself as "sick," one invites compassion and pity; and one then begins to see oneself as pitiful, hoping for a magical cure that someday will be discovered if one is "good."

Because we live in a society that also looks askew at individuals with psychological problems, especially compulsive disorders (they tend to be viewed as lacking in will-power or lacking in moral fiber), it is much more palatable to talk in terms of the "disease" which needs to be treated than it is to deal with maladaptive coping behaviors. It is more acceptable to go to the medical doctor's office than it is to go to the psychotherapist's office. So the disease model has much more appeal for the majority of our society.

Thus, what started out as a humane approach to a problem has become in itself a problem. Originally, calling compulsive behaviors a disease was for the purpose of increasing compassion toward the obese, the alcoholic, or the gambler. Gradually the solution has produced the very effect it sought to eliminate—namely, reducing human dignity and reinforcing the notion that one is not a responsible adult. Rather, the compulsive substance abuser is viewed as a helpless child who is "sick" and needs to be told what to do. (In fact, in some of these self-help programs, members are referred to as "babies.")

> *"Individuals often use 'illness' or 'disease' to avoid taking responsibility for their behavior just as they might have gotten 'sick' to avoid going to school."*

There is no doubt that were we to promote a psychological model of abuse rather than a disease model, many individuals would not seek treatment; that would be their choice. However, in my opinion, there is greater harm to many more people from the potential loss of responsibility, choice, and dignity by invoking a disease model. What will be the next "sickness" for which treatment will be given? When do we have the right to behave differently than society dictates without being labeled "sick"?

## Political Consequences

If we accept a "disease" model for compulsive behavior, then what will stop people from thinking about other psychological disorders as disease? And if this happens, we will be back where we were 50 years ago, believing that all people with emotional problems are "sick." Who will treat these "sick" people? Clearly the medical profession has a vested interest in promoting a disease model, for it is physicians who treat the "sick." It does not matter to the public that the "disease model" was only a *metaphor* used to encourage people to seek help. Over time the metaphor is lost and we are left with a model that is inappropriate. While the idea of using a disease model as a metaphor, to make it more palatable for some people to accept treatment, has some short range appeal, the long range consequences may be less attractive.

Many people do not comprehend the use of the disease model as a metaphor or as a theoretical model for generating hypotheses. Metaphors and models often become functionally autonomous; they take on a reality of their own. Yesterday's metaphors become today's reality. As the use of the term "disease" increases, and with more public acceptance of the notion that compulsive behaviors are diseases, we must become concerned with the long term consequences on our thinking about the relationship between emotional disorders and disease.

Are we heading toward a time when, once again, people with problems in living and emotionally disturbed human beings will be viewed as "sick" and in need of medical, not psychological, treatment?

## An Alternative Model

I think that a model based on integrating psychological, biological, and social factors for understanding and treating chemical dependency, addictions, and compulsive behaviors is more appropriate than a disease model. Such a model takes into account biological (including genetics, physiological predisposition, and chemical components), social, and psychological factors in understanding compulsive behaviors without invoking "sickness" or disease as causative. The individual, in this model, remains responsible for how s/he deals with their life without the loss in dignity.

This model accepts that there may be genetic, chemical, biological, etc. factors involved in some addictions (for not being able to metabolize alcohol, for example), but this does not account for why an individual continues to rely upon their addiction for dealing with problems in living. It recognizes that there are social issues involved in compulsive behavior which have nothing to do with biology or chemistry. It further states that psychological, not medical, factors are the most powerful in understanding and controlling human behavior. It accepts the basic principle that human beings are fundamentally responsible for their own behavior and have the power to choose how they will conduct their lives. It accepts that people are free to choose how they will live their life; even if that choice is self-destructive, it is still their choice. People can choose to play the game of life differently than most without being labeled "sick." They must, however, accept full responsibility for the consequences of that behavior.

> *"The 'disease model' was only* **a metaphor** *used to encourage people to seek help."*

# Chapter 3

# How Effective Is Alcoholics Anonymous?

# Chapter Preface

Alcoholics Anonymous is the most well-known and popular treatment for alcoholism. Roughly one million people in the United States alone participate in the program, in which recovering alcoholics provide each other with mutual support and guidance. AA is considered so effective that many courts require individuals convicted of alcohol-related crimes to attend AA meetings, and the twelve-step philosophy created by AA founder Bill Wilson has been adopted by other organizations such as Narcotics Anonymous and Gamblers Anonymous.

The twelve steps require alcoholics to overcome denial by admitting that they are powerless over alcohol and acknowledging the harm that drinking has caused themselves and others. Other important steps require alcoholics to turn to a higher power to help them control their addiction, and to help other alcoholics to achieve sobriety.

Countless recovering addicts praise the twelve steps, but many others have had only negative experiences with AA. James Christopher in his book *How to Stay Sober: Recovery Without Religion* and Charles Bufe in *Alcoholics Anonymous: Cult or Cure?*, charge that AA, with its emphasis on a "higher power," is actually a religious organization, and that it is unconstitutional for the courts to require participation in the program. The authors recommend nonspiritual programs such as Rational Recovery and Secular Organizations for Sobriety. Others disagree with the idea that alcoholics are "powerless" over their addiction: Groups such as Moderation Management feel that learning to control one's drinking may often be a more attainable goal than AA's insistence on complete abstinence.

Officially, AA does not concern itself with these criticisms. To help assure alcoholics that their identities will remain anonymous should they come to an AA meeting, the organization avoids becoming involved in public controversies, not wanting to involve itself in "outside issues." "Our primary purpose is to stay sober and help other alcoholics to achieve sobriety," states AA literature.

Nonetheless, AA has its defenders. Harvard University addiction researcher Steven Hyman credits AA with a breakthrough: "What AA understands is that the essence of dealing with alcoholism is not to blame people for having the disease, yet nevertheless demand that they take responsibility for themselves." One AA member insists that the program is simply "one alcoholic talking to another and saying, 'I've been where you are, and this is what I've done to not be there anymore.'" "If we stick to that," she says, "I think we will survive."

The debate over AA's effectiveness is an emotional one. Those whose lives have been rescued by the organization defend it vigorously; others are equally eager to offer alternative solutions. The authors in the following chapter debate whether AA's widespread popularity is justified.

# Alcoholics Anonymous Is Effective

## by Robert Zimmerman

**About the author:** *Robert Zimmerman is a writer who specializes in alcohol and drug topics and is editor of the quarterly* Prevention File.

*Editor's note: This viewpoint was published on June 25, 1995, just prior to the 60th anniversary convention of Alcoholics Anonymous in San Diego, California.*

Members of Alcoholics Anonymous coming to San Diego this week are calling their international convention a celebration. Most of all they'll be celebrating their own sobriety. Recovery from alcoholism—a day at a time, as they say in AA—deserves a celebration. But this year is also the 60th anniversary of the founding of AA, and that's something the whole world can celebrate.

AA is a unique made-in-USA creation that has been able to take root and thrive in other countries and cultures. The San Diego convention comes at a time when the AA fellowship is seeing a burst of international growth with widening recognition of its power to change the course of human lives.

### Treating Alcoholism with the 12 Steps

Besides helping countless alcoholics pull back from the brink of self-destruction, AA has changed the way most people think about personal problems and the efficacy of mutual-help support groups. AA's founding in 1935 has become a bit of American folklore—the story of how Bill W. and Dr. Bob, two alcoholics deemed hopeless by their family and friends, discovered they could sustain their own recovery through faith in a higher power and helping other alcoholics get sober.

They and their followers worked out 12 suggested steps for personal recovery in a book called "Alcoholics Anonymous" first published in 1939. The AA "Big Book" has sold a phenomenal 15 million copies in 31 languages and spawned a variety of spinoffs that deal with drug addiction, gambling, overeating and what

Reprinted from Robert Zimmerman, "AA Success Is Cause for Celebration," *San Diego Union-Tribune*, June 25, 1996, by permission of the author.

have you. A survey published in 1991 identified 260 12-step programs aimed at problems other than drinking.

Alcoholics entering treatment facilities in the United States today generally are introduced to the 12 steps of Alcoholics Anonymous and urged to become active members of AA when they leave treatment. A physician wrote recently in the *Journal of the American Medical Association* that medical practitioners are unable to do better than AA in helping alcoholics maintain long-term sobriety. The reliance of therapists on AA principles as part of a treatment regimen, he said, is a recognition that chronic alcohol abuse is "an error of the soul as well as the body."

The most exhaustive academic study of AA ever undertaken has just been completed by a consortium of 18 researchers from eight countries with support of the World Health Organization. Klaus Makela of the Finnish Foundation of Alcohol Studies, the project director, will report on it at the 37th International Congress on Alcohol and Drug Dependence at the University of California at San Diego on August 20–25. To be published later this year by the University of Wisconsin Press, the study finds AA to be "the prototype of a new kind of social movement" having an impact far beyond our borders.

## A Positive Social Movement

The researchers chose to look at Alcoholics Anonymous as a social movement even though it has no goal of changing society. It does not crusade for temperance or prohibition and pointedly stays out of public policy debates. Though its program has a spiritual dimension it steers clear of identification with any religion.

Still, according to the international scholars, AA has "invented new forms of communication and fosters new types of social relationships. . . . Its international diffusion is evidence that the globalization of ways of thinking and being has reached a new level—that a system of thought and a program of action developed in middle-class North America in the 1930s can be adapted and made relevant, while still maintaining its core features, in cultural environments as diverse as the slums of Mexico City, the factory towns of Poland, and the agricultural villages of Switzerland."

AA has held together and flourished for 60 years with an organizational scheme that looks from the outside like a recipe for anarchy. As a reporter in 1959 I interviewed Bill W. over lunch at a New York restaurant

> *"Medical practitioners are unable to do better than AA in helping alcoholics maintain long-term sobriety."*

when the AA co-founder was coming up on the 25th anniversary of his sobriety—his "birthday" in AA parlance. When I began by asking about his organization he quickly pointed out that AA wasn't an organization and it wasn't his.

Most of our hour together went to an explanation of how AA manages to exist without a hierarchy of leadership, a governing body or an organizational bureaucracy. It's all done on the strength of 12 "traditions" that grew out of the experience of the first AA groups just as the 12 steps grew out of the personal experience of the first alcoholics who stayed sober together. Bill W. died in 1971 but the loose-knit system he helped foster is still in place.

There are no dues for AA membership. There are no membership rolls. People are members of AA when they say they are; the only requirement is a desire to stop drinking. AA groups are regarded as autonomous as long as anything they do does not affect the fellowship as a whole. A General Service Conference of delegates elected from around the United States and Canada meets once a year and tries to resolve policy issues through consensus. One researcher concluded that the lack of a conventional power structure in AA gives it the tone of the "classic anarchy" that social philosophers only dream about.

> *"There are no dues for AA membership. There are no membership rolls. People are members of AA when they say they are; the only requirement is a desire to stop drinking."*

These loose reins, according to the international study, have saved AA from the kind of factional disputes that often break up social movements as they grow. Members don't get into quarrels over property because AA doesn't own any. It doesn't run any institutions for members to try to control. Its money comes mainly from sale of literature and passing the hat at meetings, with a board of trustees—which includes some non-alcoholics—overseeing its New York office and publishing enterprise. There are relatively few paid employees and assignments are rotated to avoid empire-building.

## Crossing Political and Cultural Boundaries

The international study examined how AA leaps over political and cultural boundaries. The fellowship sends out no missionaries but members in one country often contribute time and money to help start groups in another. In the early years AA groups abroad generally were started by American expatriates living in foreign capitals. Groups proliferate in the native population as AA literature is translated into more and more languages.

A generation ago many observers believed membership would be unlikely to grow beyond the cultural sphere of North America and the largely Protestant countries of Northern Europe. That indeed was the pattern of AA growth in its first decades, but a second wave of growth occurred in the 1980s in Catholic countries of Europe and Latin America, especially Mexico. By 1988, Latin America accounted for one-third of AA's world membership. A third wave of growth is now under way in the old communist bloc.

John G., international coordinator in the AA General Service Office in New York, has just returned from a swing through Eastern Europe and says he was amazed at the rapid growth of the fellowship he encountered. "Six years ago we knew of only two AA members in Budapest. Today there are at least 60 groups in Hungary." After an era in which possession of AA literature could have landed one in jail, the program is taking off in former Iron Curtain countries. The growth in Poland has been phenomenal—from six groups in 1980 to 960 today. "There are always more groups than we know about," says John. "We know of about 60 groups in Russia but I have a hunch there are many, many more."

Larry N., a San Diegan who is one of AA's trustees, visited Russia last year at the invitation of members of fledgling AA groups in that country. They are setting up an "All Russia Service Council" patterned on the AA structure in the United States. A conference held at Petrozavodsk, north of St. Petersburg, attracted delegates from as far away as Magadan on the Pacific coast of Siberia.

"They're having lots of problems with things we take for granted here, like paying for postage to send out literature," Larry says. "Everything has to be done by volunteers because there isn't enough money to staff an office." He says the Russians are getting help from AA members in Finland who now can cross into Russia without the border hassles of the past. "It's going to take a while for the Russians in AA to get on their feet but I'm sure they'll do fine in the long run."

## AA's Phenomenal Worldwide Growth

AA considers its worldwide membership to be about 2 million, with 91,000 groups in 141 countries. There was an attendance of 5,000 at its first convention, in Cleveland in 1950. This week in San Diego it will take nearly that many volunteers from AA groups in Southern California just to be greeters, guides and interpreters for an attendance expected to exceed 60,000.

If there is going to be a fourth wave of AA growth it is likely to occur in Asia. Those registering for the convention in San Diego include sober alcoholics from the Fiji Islands, Singapore, Guam, Hong Kong, India, Japan, the Philippines, South Korea, and Thailand.

John G. reports that two more translations of the AA "Big Book" are in the works. The languages? Hindi and Nepali.

# AA's Emphasis on Spirituality Benefits Alcoholics

by William W. May

**About the author:** *William W. May is a professor of religion at the University of Southern California in Los Angeles.*

The single most important event for an addict or alcoholic to experience in early recovery is the beginning of a distinct spiritual focus for living. In many cases the alcoholic or addict is cynical, agnostic, or atheistic—or their spiritual view of life is identical to their religious upbringing. In the last instance, the person manifests extreme guilt; the former is contemptuous of spirituality. A new or different spiritual focus for life emerges gradually during abstinence, beginning during the initial days of recovery. Upon intake into rehabilitation treatment, clinical assessments and formal treatment plans to facilitate this process should be started immediately by staff.

## Alcoholism Is a Spiritual Disorder

The need has been well documented by case histories published by Alcoholics Anonymous. Dr. William Silkworth, who aided the recovery of one of the founders of Alcoholics Anonymous (Bill W.), addressed both the reality and complexity of this phenomenon as early as 1939:

> "We doctors have realized for a long time that some form of moral psychology was of urgent importance to alcoholics, but its application presented difficulties beyond our conception. The cases we have followed through with have been most interesting; in fact, many of them are amazing. The unselfishness of these men as we have come to know them, the entire absence of the profit motive, and their community spirit, is indeed inspiring to one who has labored long and wearily in this alcoholic field. They believe in themselves, and still more in the Power which pulls chronic alcoholics back from the gates of death."

Reprinted from William W. May, "Spiritual Focus as a Therapeutic Strategy," *Behavioral Health Management*, September 1, 1994, by permission of the publisher. (A List of References in the original has been omitted in this reprint.)

Dr. Silkworth's observation has a contemporary ring for those who labor in the addictions field. We see the same results in those who return for informal visits long after leaving our rehabilitation unit. Although we psychologists eschew the term "moral" in our discipline today, the approach to treatment in our rehabilitation unit places great emphasis on this area. We focus on such constructs as "emotional unmanageability," "rigorous self-honesty," "cognitive restructuring," and the like, all of which are forms of moral rehabilitation.

> *"The single most important event for an addict or alcoholic to experience in early recovery is the beginning of a distinct spiritual focus for living."*

These are some of our treatment goals, but what of the patient's motivation to work toward them? The frequent query by our staff is "Does the patient have internal motivation to recover?" By this we are really asking, "Is the patient willing to change his behavior for internal satisfaction?" In order to have the internalized drive to change, the patient must have hope that the change will work, that it will pay off. Patients who strive for non-material payoffs (i.e. peace of mind, time in recovery, etc.) have better treatment experiences than those who are fixed on material gain. A spiritual experience is a common precursor for hope in finding a way out of the morass of active alcoholism or addiction. (Carl Jung speculated there was no coincidence that alcoholic drink is referred to as spirits.) Therefore alcoholics are thirsty for spirit, and alcoholism could be considered, by this token, a spiritual disorder or condition.

## What Is a "Spiritual Experience"?

It is any life event, however great or small, that an individual believes to be a result of an unseen force. This belief cannot be—as a rule—linked to any one sense, and it is blocked by analytical thought. A dramatic case is found in the spiritual awakening of Bill W. To this experience he attributed his life-long sobriety and dedication to helping other alcoholics recover. He later called it "the moment of clarity," and provided a brief account of it in Alcoholics Anonymous: "Simple, but not easy; a price had to be paid. It meant the destruction of self-centeredness. I must turn in all things to the Father of Light who presides over us all. These were revolutionary and drastic proposals, but the moment I fully accepted them, the effect was electric. There was a sense of victory, followed by such a sense of peace and serenity as I had ever known. There was utter confidence. I felt lifted up, as though the great clean wind off a mountain top blew through and through. God comes to most men gradually, but His impact on me was sudden and profound."

Experiences such as Bill W.'s are rare in my encounters with addicts and alcoholics in treatment; yet, many men and women have had brief "moments of clarity" that get progressively longer with time being abstinent. A distinctly new spiritual focus emerges out of this. As Dr. Silkworth aptly points out, these briefer moments of clarity gain spiritual significance through a psychic change in the individual. Those psychic changes the person can perceive as originating from a spiritual source, or God as they understand God. The immediate result of this change in perception is a sense of serenity, peace, and oneness never experienced in their immediate past. A powerful incentive is then in place to motivate the individual to experience more of this new serenity. I have seldom found exceptions to this in the men and women who have been my patients in our rehabilitation unit, or those I have interviewed who are active members of Alcoholics Anonymous.

## Case History: Roger S.

After six months of sobriety in A.A., Roger S. came to me for help in adjusting to a recent divorce. Hearing Roger's account of what caused him to stop drinking helped me gain a better insight into the vagaries of that initial shift in spiritual focus described above. Roger had drunk alcoholically for 27 years, and over the last 10 years of his drinking was experiencing increasingly volatile rages. During the three days preceding his first day of abstinence, Roger said he consumed about one gallon of rum and was full of hate for his wife and stepchildren. I was curious as to what had caused him to change from a chronic alcoholic to a sober member of Alcoholics Anonymous. Roger said:

"Recalling the events of the previous evening, I felt shame, and feared facing my wife with no alibi in mind. The house was quiet, but outside birds fluttered and white clouds floated

> *"A spiritual experience is a common precursor for hope in finding a way out of the morass of active alcoholism."*

through a bright blue sky. My wife and her son had gone, the wreckage of the previous night was all about me—upturned chair, broken glass, broken fan. Two fifths of rum were on the counter, one almost empty, the other almost full. Outdoors was cheery, peaceful, and bright, while in my house it was dreary and wrecked. That I felt so calm and steady bothered me such that I looked at my face in the mirror—no puffiness or blood-shot eyes. I couldn't at first understand it. I simply sat and drank iced tea and stared out the kitchen window, and began having clear reveries of my past with alcohol. I actually felt another presence in the room with me at times, which strengthened my hope that the way out of my present mess was to stop drinking, and stop for good. I could, that day, remember other times and places where I had the same choice as I did then—either the bottle or life—but chose to rationalize my way back to drinking.

"I gradually accepted that the stark contrasts I was viewing that day were no coincidence. They were another set of markers being given me by a superior consciousness—God?—which said, 'Well, here you are again at a crossroad in life. Which path will you choose this time?'

"I'm not very good at talking about this stuff, but I know that the longer I reviewed my past and looked at the symbolism of that moment, the calmer and more peaceful I felt. I looked at my life that day as I had never been able to do before. I know that I could not have done that on my own, and that some spiritual force was guiding me. All I know is, that I absolutely accepted two things as true by that afternoon. One, I could not safely drink ever again. My violent temper was escalating every time I drank now, and I was afraid I would eventually hurt my wife. Second, I personally did not have any ideas on how to stay stopped from drinking; moreover, I knew nothing of how to get along with people.

"From that point I made a commitment to daily ask God to relieve me of my temper, I wouldn't drink, and I would never rely on other people to resocialize me. I started getting answers before the day was over, and by the end of the week I was in my first A.A. meeting. The temper has not returned, and I am more confident than ever that I am on the right path."

Roger has now been sober several years without any reversion to his violence-prone past. His story is unusual in my experience, in that Roger's immediate sense of relief and hope stimulated a rapid growth of a distinct spiritual focus for him in recovery. The more common reaction of addicts/alcoholics is to rationalize their "moment of clarity," thereby stunting the development of a spiritual focus in their lives. When these individuals arrive on the inpatient unit, the clinician, realizing the value of this spiritual development, must use special diagnostic and intervention strategies.

## Spiritual Interventions

As an initial intervention, one needs to assess the patient's spiritual focus upon entering treatment. The use of M. Scott Peck's "world view" strategy is useful here. Does the patient see life as strictly deterministic, or more a random pattern of events where he/she is the hapless victim? Are they "hard" agnostics or do they subscribe to a fatalistic view of life? According to Peck, even the atheist has a "world view," and Bill W. points out that the atheist gains a spiritual focus for sobriety more easily than the agnostic. This is because the agnostic must abandon his/her empirical test of God before adopting a spiritual basis for recovery.

> *"The . . . common reaction of addicts/alcoholics is to rationalize their 'moment of clarity,' thereby stunting the development of a spiritual focus in their lives."*

Conversely, the devout patient must abandon his/her religious dogma before a new spiritual focus may be obtained. Patients I have had who are over 50 years old—especially Roman Catholics and Southern Baptists—are prone to attribute their shame from addictive behavior to their violation of church dogma. Moreover, they tend to believe that alcoholism and drug addiction are moral weaknesses to be punished by God. Their sense of "unworthiness" makes it all the more difficult for them at times to stop using.

A second intervention is that of helping clients recall those experiences which resulted in a decision to seek help. I call this a "search for the spiritual dilemma." To recall the experience, but not know what caused it, is a dilemma, and the skillful therapist can at this point begin to guide the patient to accept a spiritual power as the cause.

> *"Every man and woman who is enjoying long-term sobriety has had at some point . . . a change in their perception of life."*

I make an assumption with new patients that their "moment of clarity" preceded their admission to treatment, but has to varying degrees been repressed. Patients often begin to recall these moments during the intake interview.

## Case History: Jimmy C.

Jimmy C. is a 45-year-old chronic alcoholic with posttraumatic stress disorder (PTSD) who sought admission initially under duress from his probation officer. Anxious and angry during my intake interview, he began recounting an argument he had had with his girlfriend during a pass he had been given to visit home between detox and rehabilitation. The argument reached a volatile point and Jimmy then stormed into the kitchen, took a beer from the refrigerator, and went outside and opened it. Immediately he heard a voice say, "What do you think you are doing?" He stopped, looked down at the beer, repeated the statement, and poured the beer out.

I started quietly asking questions, "Where do you think the voice came from?" "Did the color of the trees, grass, or sky seem any different to you after that experience?" and "How did you feel right then?" With my probing, Jimmy slowly relaxed; his voice softened, he stared off into space, and began to talk of that moment for the first time since he had had it. Finally, he said, "You know, I never thought much about it before, but something was guiding me then. I felt different afterwards. Calm." Once he had reached this conclusion, I was able to direct him to further develop the experience he had just related through a written treatment plan.

Common tasks set for patients during our staff's spiritual interventions include: a) read "We Agnostics" in the Big Book; b) meditate on nature once a day; c) read page 449 in the Big Book; and d) construct a "daily gratitude list." Other interventions might include study of Eastern and Native American traditions and meditation methods, as well as self-studies into other spiritual dilemmas in the patients' experiences.

## Spiritual Awakening Is the Key to Sobriety

It is my belief that every man and woman who is enjoying long-term sobriety has had at some point from the calamity of their last drink to their first few months in sobriety a change in their perception of life. They talk of life having purpose and meaning, and of feeling a firm yet gentle guidance in their activities. An intuitive "knowing" that solutions to life problems are readily available is a consistent comment among these individuals. A.A. promises that "We will intuitively know how to handle situations that used to baffle us." This is comparable to the insight phenomenon first shown by Wolfgang Kohler in his "aha!" effect; similar to the "moment of clarity" described by Bill W., where the clouds of illusion are swept away, the reality of the addiction is laid bare, and serenity is felt. At that precise moment, the addict or alcoholic begins the spiritual awakening that is discussed in A.A. For the first time the person experiences hope that there is a solution.

The experience described above conflicts with the agnostic world view of most alcoholics and addicts. Though they share the experience, they question its nature: Did a higher power sweep the illusion away, or was it merely chance? This is a crucial dilemma. The dilemma between the intuitive knowing and resulting sense of serenity (often motivating the person into treatment) versus the addictive thinking that strives to rationalize the experience is quite strong. I believe that nearly all patients entering rehabilitation are already rationalizing this dilemma to fit their denial system.

The mission of the clinician then becomes one of assisting in patients' retrieval of the initial spiritual experience that brought them to treatment, giving it validity, and expanding on it throughout the treatment stay.

# Alcoholics Anonymous Is Ineffective

## by Michael J. Lemanski

**About the author:** *Michael J. Lemanski is a member of the National Association for Children of Alcoholics and coordinator for Self-Management and Recovery Training in Massachusetts.*

William Griffith Wilson, the founder of Alcoholics Anonymous, was born November 26, 1895, in East Dorset, Vermont. When he was nine, his parents divorced, apparently because of his father's drinking, and he was left in the care of his grandparents. In 1918, Wilson married Lois Burnham and began a career as a stockbroker; he also continued his father's career of drinking.

Later, after years of alcohol abuse and its associated miseries, Wilson began admitting himself to the Charles B. Towns Hospital in Manhattan. On December 11, 1934, he admitted himself for the fourth time and was treated by a neurologist named William Duncan Silkworth. Dr. Silkworth sedated Wilson and began administering treatment with belladonna. What happened next can best be described in Wilson's own words from his book *Alcoholics Anonymous Comes of Age:*

> My depression deepened unbearably and finally it seemed to me as though I were at the very bottom of the pit. I still gagged badly on the notion of a Power greater than myself, but finally, just for the moment, the last vestige of my proud obstinacy was crushed. All at once I found myself crying out, "If there is a God, let Him show Himself! I am ready to do anything, anything."

> Suddenly the room lit up with a great white light. I was caught up into an ecstasy which there are no words to describe. It seemed to me, in a mind's eye, that I was on a mountain and that a wind not of air but of spirit was blowing. And then it burst upon me that I was a free man. Slowly the ecstasy subsided. I lay on the bed, but for a time I was in another world, a new world of consciousness. All about me and through me was a wonderful feeling of Presence, and I thought to myself, "So this is the God of the preachers!"

Wilson's psychic conversion was accomplished. On the surface, at least, he was a changed man.

Reprinted from Michael J. Lemanski, "The Tenacity of Error in the Treatment of Addiction," *The Humanist*, May/June 1997, by permission of the author.

This experience kept him sober for five months. Then, while on a business trip in Akron, Ohio, he was overcome by the fear of relapse and panicked. It was here that he came into contact with a doctor named Robert Smith, who was also a drinker, and the two men had what has been regarded as the first Alcoholics Anonymous meeting.

Nan Robertson, in her book *Getting Better Inside Alcoholics Anonymous,* suggests that Wilson's deep religious experience at Towns Hospital may have been the result of hallucinations during his withdrawal, induced or precipitated by his medication. Belladonna is an atropine powder derived from the leaves and roots of *Atropa belladonna,* a poisonous Eurasian plant popularly known as "deadly nightshade." In any event, Wilson was apparently never able to recapture his original high (which he in his later years would call his "hot flash") and continued to seek some form of spiritual transformation. His pursuit of spirituality through séances and experiments with LSD, as well as megavitamin therapy, ultimately scandalized AA.

> *"[AA founder William] Wilson developed a formula that was remarkably egocentric. The basic concepts of AA embody the parochial singularities of his own recovery experience."*

## The Twelve Steps of Recovery

But AA was the result of more than just a hot flash and a chance meeting. Its basic philosophy was derived from the Oxford Group Movement, founded in 1921 by Frank N.D. Buchman, a spirited evangelist and self-proclaimed "soul surgeon." Smith introduced Wilson to the Oxford Group Movement. Buchman's religious ideas of human powerlessness, redemption from above, the value of taking a moral inventory of oneself, and the value of making amends to others inspired Wilson to develop the "Twelve Steps of Recovery," which, referring to alcoholism only twice, reads:

We:

1. Admitted we were powerless over alcohol—that our lives had become unmanageable.

2. Came to believe that a power greater than ourselves could restore us to sanity.

3. Made a decision to turn our will and our lives over to the care of God as we understood Him.

4. Made a searching and fearless moral inventory of ourselves.

5. Admitted to God, to ourselves, and to another human being the exact nature of our wrongs.

6. Were entirely ready to have God remove all these defects of character.

7. Humbly asked Him to remove our shortcomings.

8. Made a list of all persons we had harmed and became ready to make amends to them all.

9. Made direct amends to such people wherever possible, except when to do so would injure them or others.

10. Continued to take personal inventory and when we were wrong promptly admitted it.

11. Sought through prayer and meditation to improve our conscious contact with God, as we understood Him, praying only for knowledge of His will for us and the power to carry that out.

12. Having had a spiritual awakening as the result of these steps, we tried to carry this message to alcoholics, and practice these principles in all our affairs.

Wilson started his recovery program in 1935 as part of the Oxford Group but broke from the movement to form Alcoholics Anonymous in 1936. Beyond his assimilation of many of Buchman's ideas, Wilson developed a formula that was remarkably egocentric. The basic concepts of AA embody the parochial singularities of his own recovery experience and are spelled out in his book *Alcoholics Anonymous*—nicknamed "The Big Book"—which is essentially the bible of AA.

> *"Limitations on freedom of inquiry and discussion are common throughout the wider [twelve-step] movement."*

The first such concept is that of "hitting bottom": reaching a state of total emotional collapse and depression. He viewed this as an essential component to the recovery process: emotionally, you have to feel as though you are "at the bottom of the pit."

The second concept is that of "deflation of ego in depth": essentially, the admission and acceptance of defeat. Desperation is viewed as an essential component, with Wilson saying that "proud obstinacy" has to be "crushed." Desperation is necessary for a "conversion experience."

The third concept is that of a "higher power": the turning of one's life and will over to an external entity that is more powerful and capable of managing one's life. In essence, this entails psychic surrender—turning one's life and will over to "the God of the preachers" or at least to the group pressure and collective belief system of AA.

Because AA came into being at a time when modern methods of medical therapy, clinical psychology, clinical sociology, and professional counseling were all but nonexistent in the field of addictions treatment, AA filled a vacuum. The medical and psychological communities had failed to provide appropriate and adequate care for those addicted to alcohol, and so AA got the franchise. This meant that, for decades after AA's founding, expensive and lengthy addictions treatment programs adopted and offered essentially the same basic philosophy and methodologies as AA.

## A One-Size-Fits-All Approach

In 1951, the organization known as Al-Anon was founded. It follows the same basic philosophy of AA, utilizing the twelve-step approach, but provides a support network for the recovering alcoholic's family and friends. In 1953 came Narcotics Anonymous, a twelve-step program and support network for recovering drug addicts. Then, through the 1970s and into the 1980s, there was an explosion of twelve-step recovery programs. New organizations emerged until the self-help domain had expanded to include just about every compulsive or self-defeating behavior one could think of. It was like an evangelical movement: each program was a part of the larger AA religion, each one reframing reality to conform to the same monolithic culture and belief system. The growth was therefore lateral instead of vertical—a widening application of a single set of ideas rather than a progressive, research-oriented development of new ideas and improvements. With its one-size-fits-all approach, this larger AA movement was entirely formulaic; any self-defeating or compulsive behavior called for the same prescription, the formation of yet another twelve-step program.

A simple listing of existing groups is instructive: Adult Children of Alcoholics, Al-Anon, Alcoholics Anonymous, Alcoholics Victorious of the Institute for Christian Living, ARTS (Artists Recovering Through the Twelve Steps) Anonymous, Augustine Fellowship: Sex and Love Addicts Anonymous, Calix, Cocaine Anonymous, Codependents Anonymous, Codependents of Sex Addicts, Debtors Anonymous, Drug-Anon Focus, Dual Disorders Anonymous, Emotional Health Anonymous, Emotions Anonymous, Ethics Anonymous, Gamblers Anonymous, Incest Survivors Anonymous, Naranon, Narcotics Anonymous, Nicotine Anonymous, Obsessive-Compulsive Anonymous, Overcomers Outreach, Overeaters Anonymous, Pill Addicts Anonymous, Pills Anonymous, Prostitutes Anonymous, Sex Addicts Anonymous, Sexaholics Anonymous, Survivors of Incest Anonymous, and Workaholics Anonymous. Though some of these groups offer their own minor variations on the twelve steps, all have the same spiritual-religious orientation.

> *"If a majority of the world's population could be described as essentially codependent or dysfunctional, the global solution was simple and obvious: therapy for everyone in conjunction with the twelve steps."*

The general nature of all these groups is best seen in the pamphlet *Al-Anon Spoken Here*, which I found so objectionable at my first Al-Anon meeting. In it, guidelines for the operation of the meetings are provided. The reader is told that, within meetings, only Al-Anon "conference approved" literature can be read and discussed; sources of information from outside the program are not to be used because they "dilute" the spiritual nature of the meetings. Therapy, therapists, and professional terminology are also taboo topics of discussion, as are other recovery or treatment programs.

Such limitations on freedom of inquiry and discussion are common through-out the wider movement. The twelve-step philosophy is essentially static and resistant to change. New ideas aren't readily embraced and new methodologies from outside any given program are viewed as a threat. The peculiar thing about this is an ironic relationship to the "denial" that is so often discussed within meetings. When AA-style programs discourage objective and critical thinking, as well as new information, they essentially embrace a blatant and collective denial system of their own.

> *"[AA] suffers from two central problems: it scarcely works, and its cure is almost as bad as the malady."*

Worse, if an individual in AA, for one reason or another, doesn't make adequate progress, the typical view is that he or she isn't adequately "working the program." The usual prescription, then, is to attend more meetings. This is another form of denial: the program can never be the problem.

In 1983, therapist Janet Geringer Woititz published a book entitled *Adult Children of Alcoholics,* which describes the syndrome associated with individuals raised in an alcoholic family. This book became a best seller. After its success, a number of other authors began publishing on adult children of alcoholics, as well as on codependence in general. Within the framework of the twelve steps, both the ACoA and codependence movements grew rapidly, gaining considerable media attention.

Of course, true to form for any AA movement, acceptance of these new ideas was not easy or immediate. Within Al-Anon, for example, a large proportion of the membership banded together to resist incorporating ACoA groups into their program. Though this incorporation eventually occurred, it was only after the twelve steps had been safely imposed upon the membership within the newly formed meetings.

The next development occurred in 1986 when therapist Anne Wilson Schaef, in her book *Codependence Mistreated-Misunderstood,* expanded the concept of codependence from its original clinical application—involving the spouse of an alcoholic—to declare "that it includes the majority of the population of the United States." Along the same line, Herbert Gravitz and Julie Bowden prefaced their 1987 book *Recovery: A Guide for Adult Children of Alcoholics* with the statement, "Children of alcoholics are but a visible tip of a much larger social iceberg which casts an invisible shadow over as much as 96 percent of the population."

The next logical step was reported in an article entitled "Healing Ourselves and Our Planet" in the winter 1992 issue of *Contemporary Drug Problems,* in which Robin Room, vice-president for research and development at the Addiction Research Foundation in Toronto, described the way in which many individuals within the growing twelve-step movement—particularly in Northern California—moved between programs for a variety of life problems. He then warned of the potential emergence of "a generalized twelve-step consciousness" with a "sociopolitical agenda." The message was clear: if a majority of the world's population could be described as essentially codependent or dysfunctional, the global solution was simple and obvious: therapy for everyone in conjunction with the twelve steps.

The first important challenge to this growing absurdity came from psychologist Stanton Peele in 1989. His book *Diseasing of America* questioned the efficacy of the proliferating twelve-step programs and described the movement within the addictions field as "out of control." He included an important quote from Donald Goodwin, pioneering researcher in the inheritance of alcoholism, who charged:

> Therapists "invented" the concept that adult children of alcoholics have special problems that can be treated through therapy. They were able to sell this concept to the public and now they are eligible for reimbursement from insurance companies. In short, it was a way for therapists to tap into a new market and make money.

And so, in the fall of 1991, at the national conference of the American Association for Marriage and Family Therapy, psychiatrist Steven J. Wolin, a keynote speaker, publicly denounced the ACoA and codependence movements, declaring that "the recovery movement and its lopsided counsel of damage has become dangerous." After this statement, he received a standing ovation from the five thousand members in attendance. When a ranking member of the ACoA movement was later asked by a reporter from *USA Today* to respond, he answered, "They're just jealous of all the money we're making."

In 1992, Terence Gorski, a prominent spokesperson within the field of addictions, addressing a conference of the National Association of Alcoholism and Drug Abuse Counselors, stated:

> If I were hired by the enemies of the chemical dependency field . . . I couldn't give them a better strategy [to destroy the field] than the adult children of alcoholics movement and the codependency movement. When we as a field expanded addictions to include all compulsive disorders we destroyed our constituency base . . . destroyed our funding base . . . destroyed our economic stability.

## The Belief System Perpetuates Itself

. . . The addictions field is one of the few areas of professional endeavor where the counselors and the patients are drawn from the same constituency, hence the twelve-step bias. It's not just what these individuals embrace in terms of a belief system that's important; it's *how* they believe it. Their faith in the twelve-step approach is quite literally as if their lives depended on it. True believers recruit other true believers, and the belief system perpetuates itself. This creates an obvious resistance to any other treatment possibilities that might be proposed.

Not surprisingly, because so many addictions professionals are as dependent upon the twelve steps as their clients, it is not at all uncommon at professional addictions conferences, workshops, and seminars for twelve-step support groups to be made available for the benefit of the professionals in attendance. This is almost always done to the exclusion of any other type of support group with a differing philosophy.

All this calls into question the health of the addictions field. With the majority of its professionals having had a personal and intimate relationship with addiction, either through their own or through parental addiction within their families of origin, they often lack the emotional and psychological detachment necessary to maintain objectivity when providing treatment and open-mindedness when assessing new scientific data.

Is such therapeutic distance and new scientific data actually needed? After all, one could argue that just because the AA movement has a religious origin and nature, the features of which are significantly tied to the singularities of the founder's recovery experience; just because it is a one-size-fits-all dogma that is offered as a panacea for so broad a range of problems that nearly everyone in the world is thought to need it; and just because most of the people who administer its treatments are also among the treated, that doesn't logically prove that there's anything wrong with it. The AA method could be wonderfully effective nonetheless.

## AA Is Ineffective

But it is not. It suffers from two central problems: it scarcely works, and its cure is almost as bad as the malady.

George E. Vaillant, in his 1983 landmark book *The Natural History of Alcoholism,* describes the natural healing process associated with individuals addicted to alcohol. Without AA, therapy, or any other outside intervention, a certain percentage of the population addicted to alcohol will reach a point when they will, of their own volition, choose to abstain from the drug. Vaillant's question was: does the AA modality improve on this percentage? Compiling forty years of clinical studies, including an eight-year longitudinal study of his own, he was able to determine that this treatment approach produces results no better than the natural history of the malady.

> *"To the extent that AA and other twelve-step programs work, they do so for only a tiny percentage of the addicted population."*

Initially such programs do produce dramatic results, as the testimonials attest. However, over the long run, the "cured" population, through relapse, like water seeking its own level, asymptotically approaches the low water mark. With or without the AA approach, approximately 5 percent of the alcoholic population Vaillant surveyed managed to achieve *sustained* abstinence. Subsequent studies have produced similar results. Therefore, to the extent that AA and other twelve-step programs work, they do so for only a tiny percentage of the addicted population.

Overall, the best hard research evidence available indicates that the most commonly employed addiction treatment modalities in the United States and Canada have questionable efficacy and consistently produce negative treatment outcomes. Extensive research in a comparative analysis of treatment outcomes, conducted and compiled by Reid K. Hester and William R. Miller at the Center on Alcoholism, Substance Abuse, and Addictions—places Alcoholics Anonymous, educational lectures and films, general alcoholism counseling, and psy-

> *"Since twelve-step recovery programs admittedly offer no cure—only a lifetime of participation in a recovery group—the advantage to the professionals is obvious."*

chotherapy at the very bottom of the list in terms of effectiveness. On the other hand, modalities which include brief intervention, coping and social skills training, motivational enhancement, community reinforcement, relapse prevention, and cognitive therapy—when employed within the context of a client-to-program matching system typically found in Europe—consistently produce positive treatment outcomes. A statement by Miller in the September/October 1994 issue of *Psychology Today* puts it best: "The drug treatment community has been curiously resistant to using what works."

## AA Is Harmful

In fact, it has been curiously attached to that which is harmful. Twelve-step groups offer what is, in reality, the antithesis of therapy. There is no cure; the solution provided by such programs entails an endless attendance at meetings. An old slogan says it best: "You never graduate from Al-Anon." And you don't; you become addicted to it, desperately hanging on to the program like a spiritual lifeline in a sea of sin and death.

Somewhere within the quagmire of the AA movement and all of the twelve-step programs associated within it, the meaning of *recovery* was lost. By definition, recovery is a retrieval and reclamation process, not a surrender and abdication. The process of recovery or emotional balance and psychological well-being entails independence from addictive chemicals, compulsive behaviors, therapists, and recovery groups. To transfer dependence on chemically addictive substances to emotional or psychological dependence on a group or recovery program is not recovery in the true sense of the word.

Looking back to William Wilson, we might do well to describe him as an untreated adult child of an alcoholic and an untreated codependent. Given the patterns of his behavior and his life-long spiritual quest for an external solution to an internal problem, he effectively institutionalized both syndromes into his twelve-step program.

This can be readily seen by returning to the original definition of the term *codependence.* Prior to having been expanded, convoluted, and rendered empty, the term had meaning in a limited clinical setting for a specific population. In her book *Choice-making,* Sharon Wegscheider-Cruse quotes Robert Subby, director of Family Systems, Inc., of Minneapolis, who defined *codependency* as "an emotional, psychological, and behavioral condition that develops as a result of an individual's prolonged exposure to, and practice of, a set of oppressive rules—rules which prevent the open expression of feelings, as well as the direct discussion of personal and interpersonal problems." Using this as a base, Wegscheider-Cruse expands her own definition: "Codependency is a specific condition that is characterized by preoccupation and extreme dependence (emotionally, socially, and sometimes physically) on a person or object. Eventually, this dependence on another person becomes a pathological condition that affects the codependent in all other relationships." These definitions are significant in that they describe so well both the nature of twelve-step programs and the relationship of the participants in these programs to their groups.

And if the problem of AA addiction isn't bad enough on its own, there's an economic incentive to keep it going. Since twelve-step recovery programs admittedly offer no cure—only a lifetime of participation in a recovery group—the advantage to the professionals is obvious. Each new client can be viewed as offering the potential financial equivalent of an annuity. People looking to break a dependency on alcohol may find greater success as a participant in one of the many nonspirituality-based treatment programs [such as Drinkwise, Moderation Management, Rational Recovery, Secular Organizations for Sobriety, and Self-Management and Recovery Training (SMART)] which, although not as widely publicized, are available as alternatives to AA-style programs.

# AA's Methods Harm Many Alcoholics

by Ursula Kenny

**About the author:** *Ursula Kenny is a contributor to* Independent on Sunday, *a British newspaper.*

To the casual observer, Alcoholics Anonymous is an absolute good. It is tacitly accepted that it's beyond reproach and must do nothing but good, probably because we have all at least heard of someone who swears by it. But AA (and the 12 Step approach to addiction recovery it pioneered and patented) is currently very much in the dock [on trial]. A number of ex-members and addiction treatment professionals have accused it of having cult-like qualities and using brainwashing and bullying methods that weak and vulnerable people are particularly susceptible to. In the US, the anti-AA lobby has been further fuelled by the recent publication of two books: *Alcoholics Anonymous: Cult or Cure?* by Charles Bufe and *The Real AA* by Ken Ragge. There is also a support group on the Internet called Recovery From 12 Steps.

In Britain, another side to the 12 Step/AA story is also emerging. Which is good to know when you consider that there are currently 3,350 AA groups in the UK, and counting. *Addiction Counselling World* magazine also lists 23 UK 12 Step fellowship groups in its current issue (including Survivors of Incest Anonymous, Workaholics Anonymous and Sex Addicts Anonymous). The ever-expanding world of 12 Step Recovery is hugely successful for a lot of people—according to research by Dr Bryan Hore at the University Hospital of South Manchester, 12 Step has a success rate of as high as 70 per cent. But, given its omnipotence, it's worth knowing when and why it's not.

## Alcoholics Anonymous Is for Life

AA started in the Thirties in the US but, despite 60 years of expansion, its core programme has remained unchanged. Anyone who wants to stop drinking can go to one of hundreds of meetings held every night across the country and will be introduced to the 12 Steps and the Big Book (of guidance and member

Reprinted from Ursula Kenny, "Cult or Cure: The AA Backlash," *The Independent on Sunday*, May 10, 1998, by permission of Independent Newspapers Ltd., London.

stories) as well as a sponsor for one-to-one support. They will listen to other members' stories and tell their own. AA members can use this support system for life, and clinical psychologist Oliver James feels that this is a large part of AA's problem—people are encouraged to stay in AA for life. Once you are an alcoholic you are always an alcoholic. In AA you can never move on.

"After a year with AA, you're like a Moonie and you're probably in a relationship with another AA member," says James. "By the end of your second year, you are definitely cured of your physical addiction, but not the underlying causes—and AA does nothing about this. It merely replaces one dependency with another. The AA approach is authoritarian and fascistic, which is very effective when it's getting you to stop taking your drug of choice. With any addiction, that is the most urgent need initially; you have to stop killing yourself. But then, at some stage, you have to break away. Once you've been clean for, say, two years, you should move on to therapy. You have to get away from the AA paternal structure that may have been missing in your childhood. People use addiction as a substitute for intimate relations and AA cleverly provides an intimate relationship."

## AA as a Religion

Caroline (not her real name), 39, took four years to break away from AA and looks back with loathing at what she now sees as its self-serving and coercive methods. "I had doubts from the start but I carried on because, at the time, I had very low self-esteem and no confidence. AA only works if you're prepared to take it on as a religion. I should know, I was brought up a Jehovah's Witness until I was 18 and the similarities are astounding."

Indeed some of the AA steps make no bones about this. Step Two talks of believing "in a power greater than ourselves", Three of turning "our lives and wills over to the care of God" albeit "as we understand him", while 11 encourages prayer and meditation. This aspect of AA rhetoric is supposed to be negotiable nowadays, but Caroline disagrees: "As with any religion, you have to play by their rules or you're out. They have a Big Book which is their equivalent of the Bible. Your sponsor encourages you to pray and refers you to the Big Book at times of stress. I'd done all that sort of stuff before with the Jehovah's Witnesses. It's about control, and AA controls you by telling you that alcoholism is for life; they offer no hope of recovery. Members feed off each other in a very unhealthy way; it's

> *"The AA approach is authoritarian and fascistic."*

like a dating agency. Opposition is not encouraged; I once made the mistake of mentioning to another member that I was in contact with a woman who had dropped out. He was very critical that I would still speak to someone who had 'fallen away'. I went for it all at first. I wanted friends and I wanted to be liked but now I've detached. It's sold to you as if you're part of a special order.

You're not. You just can't have a drink. I've been emotionally damaged by their mind games to keep you a member, to keep you needing them. It's a bullying environment."

David Oddy, 43, went to AA for eight years on and off before leaving to cure himself through therapy. He agrees: "I did an undercover story about the Moonies for a local radio station once and the approach is the same. AA is bondage of another form. It is evangelical and rabid in outlook. It doesn't empower or encourage independence."

## A Disempowering Philosophy

Oliver James and other professionals also have problems with the AA identification of alcoholism as a disease. "It places an unhelpful emphasis on genes," James says. "Scientific evidence does not support this theory. The majority of addicts become so because of something that happened in their childhood." Dr Richard Hammersley at Sheffield University also agrees that the Disease Model approach can be a problem but feels that AA meetings nowadays would be tolerant of non-subscribers. Still, some ex-members found the thought that they could never recover disempowering.

There is also a view that AA is only of real use to people who are very far down the line. Sue Baker, who is the Assistant Director of Alcohol Concern, doesn't feel that AA's line on complete abstinence is always appro-

> *"It's about control, and AA controls you by telling you that alcoholism is for life; they offer no hope of recovery."*

priate. "For some people the disease/abstinence method works," she admits, "but it is entirely possible that others could return to drinking in a safe and moderate way."

"AA," James continues, "doesn't touch on the use of other drugs either. Obviously this is vital and clearly sensible when you're coming off one drug already and that is your most urgent need, but later on this approach blocks progress when say, antidepressants and therapy would help."

Nigel Walsh, 37, attended various AA meetings over a three-month period and found the approach wilfully inward looking. "Ridiculous though it sounds, they focus far too heavily on alcohol and its effects. For me it was obvious what it had done—buggered up my life. Eventually I gave AA up and went into rehab of a totally different type, where the emphasis was on feelings and emotions. That worked for me. The thing is that the principles were put in place years ago and society has moved on."

David Oddy's memories are similar. "Fourteen people would sit around a table and discuss alcohol. All they ever discussed was booze. What practical use is that for moving on? My advice to anyone who feels they have a problem with alcohol would be to go into detox initially and then find a trained and accredited therapist."

## Not for Everyone

AA themselves are not in the business of defending their position. A spokesperson was happy to provide facts and figures but felt unable to officially comment on the issues raised here. "Our policy is not to get into dialogue about outside issues." She was pleasant and not remotely defensive and it is worth mentioning again that AA and the 12 Step approach to curing addiction does work for huge numbers of people. But if it doesn't work for you it seems there are good reasons, and being in denial isn't necessarily one of them. Other treatments are available. Start with your [doctor].

# Chapter 4

# Does the Alcohol Industry Market Its Products Responsibly?

# Chapter Preface

In November 1998, the nation's largest tobacco companies agreed to pay $208 billion to the states over a period of 25 years. This settlement was the culmination of years of so-called "tobacco wars" in which more than 40 states sued the tobacco industry in order to recoup the health care costs of treating people with lung cancer and other smoking-related illnesses. The tobacco settlement has left many people wondering whether manufacturers of other potentially harmful products, such as alcohol, guns, and fatty foods, should also be held accountable for the health problems such products cause.

The states claimed that the tobacco companies had helped cause smoker's illnesses and therefore were responsible for the cost of treating them. In the past, tobacco companies had traditionally won such lawsuits, arguing that smokers know the potential health risks of smoking and therefore assume responsibility for their own behavior. But some critics charged that the industry used advertising tactics that targeted teenagers and children rather than adults. Then, beginning in 1994, the publication of secret industry documents and the testimony of former industry employees suggested that tobacco companies had tried to hide evidence about how dangerous and addictive their products were. These incidents led to several court victories for the states, and the tobacco industry finally agreed to the 1998 settlement in exchange for immunity from further such lawsuits.

Many public health advocates, having made a successful case against tobacco, question whether the alcohol industry should also be held accountable for the health problems that drinking can cause. They contend that both industries produce harmful, addictive products, and that, with ad campaigns featuring young people, parties, and animal icons like Joe Camel and the Budweiser frogs, both industries market to children and teenagers. At least, public health advocates argue, alcohol ads should be banned from television and radio in the same way that cigarette ads are. Defenders of the alcohol industry counter that, unlike tobacco companies, alcohol manufacturers have not tried to disguise the fact that alcohol is dangerous or addictive, but instead worked to promote responsible drinking. Some also argue that alcohol harms only the drinker, whereas second-hand smoke harms nonsmokers.

Observers will continue to debate exactly why it was that in the 1990s, after decades of smoking in America, the tobacco industry suddenly came under such heavy criticism. Undoubtedly one of the major reasons was that many Americans felt the tobacco companies' marketing practices were overly manipulative, deceptive, or otherwise unethical. The authors in this chapter debate whether alcohol companies are guilty of similarly irresponsible practices.

# The Government Should Not Regulate Alcohol Advertising

## by Thomas A. Hemphill

**About the author:** *Economist Thomas A. Hemphill is a fiscal officer for the New Jersey Department of State.*

In the fall of 1995, TBWA Chiat/Day, a New York City advertising agency, began pitching a potential ad campaign for Seagram's Absolut vodka, the number one selling distilled spirit in the United States. It aimed the pitch at a number of cable television networks, including CNN, Comedy Central, E!, and Bravo. The marketing probe by Seagram America initiated what has become a direct challenge to a voluntary broadcast ban, begun in 1936 for radio and in 1948 for television, by the Distilled Spirits Council of the U.S. (DISCUS). The Washington, D.C.–based national industry association, to which Seagram belongs, represents liquor producers and marketers. Liquor producers have resented for years the fact that beer and wine manufactures have more freedom to advertise on television and radio. . . .

## Challenging the Ban on Liquor Advertising

The liquor industry in America initiated its self-imposed ban on radio advertising as a concession to those angered by the repeal of Prohibition. The beer and wine industries, not looked upon with quite the disfavor as hard liquor, saw no need for initiating such a restriction. But falling sales in the past decades has put the liquor industry at a greater competitive disadvantage and made the move to change the self-imposed broadcast ad ban seem more imperative.

In June 1996, Seagram aired its first television commercial on NBC affiliate KRIS-TV in Corpus Christi, Texas, touting Crown Royal Canadian whiskey. In October 1996, Seagram began running radio commercials for a new product, Lime Twisted Gin. Grand Metropolitan PLC's Paddington Corp., distiller of Baileys Original Irish Cream, followed Seagram's lead. It instructed its New

Excerpted from Thomas A. Hemphill, "Harmonizing Alcohol Ads: Another Case for Industry Self-Regulation," *Regulation*, Spring 1998, by permission of the Cato Institute.

York City advertising agency, Interpublic Group, to inquire about airing liquor advertisements to local television stations. Another spirits distiller, Sidney Frank Importing Co., soon followed the lead of its two competitors. Moreover, in October 1996, the *Wall Street Journal* reported that a majority of DISCUS members supported a recision of the voluntary broadcast ban.

But increased liquor industry broadcast activity elicited vocal criticism from the political front. Both President Bill Clinton and Federal Communications Commission (FCC) Chairman Reed E. Hundt assailed Seagram's for proposing to air television commercials. In his 15 June 1996 weekly radio address to the nation, the President announced that he was "disappointed" that a major company would air television ads and expose "our children to liquor before they know how to handle it or can legally do so." He strongly urged Seagram's return to the voluntary association ban. In a subsequent letter to Hundt, President Clinton requested that the FCC, the independent federal agency that regulates the nation's radio, television, wire, and cable industries, conduct an inquiry into the issue of liquor advertising on television. . . .

At a 7 November 1996 DISCUS meeting, an eight-member policy board, representing about 90 percent of the distilled spirits sold in the United States, voted unanimously to rescind the self-imposed voluntary television and radio advertising ban. The association viewed the media advertising ban as an anachronism, embraced at a time when the liquor industry was attempting to make peace with neo-Prohibitionist groups. DISCUS announced that its decision was designed to "end discrimination against

> *"[The Distilled Spirits Council of the United States] viewed the media advertising ban as an anachronism, embraced at a time when the liquor industry was attempting to make peace with neoProhibitionist groups."*

distilled spirits products" and give liquor marketers equal opportunity to broadcast media presently used by beer and wine advertising. But the decision was not without further political repercussions.

## The Public Response

The response from the White House and Capitol Hill to the DISCUS decision was immediate. President Clinton, in his 9 November 1996 weekly radio address, compared alcohol companies to cigarette manufacturers and exhorted the industry to "get back on the ban." Senate Majority Leader Trent Lott (R-Miss.) joined the President in condemning the recision of the ban, calling the decision "a big mistake." Hundt, who described the decision as "disappointing for parents and dangerous for kids," called on television executives to reject all liquor advertising. Representative Joseph Kennedy II (D-Mass.) characterized the DISCUS decision as "outrageous" and promised to reintroduce his legislation to regulate alcoholic beverage broadcast advertising.

The Federal Trade Commission (FTC) initiated an investigation of the impact on American youth of televised advertising of alcoholic beverages. During its history, the FTC, the independent federal agency charged with preventing unfair or deceptive trade practices, has frequently ordered companies to cease advertising that exploits young people. Television commercials under investigation by the FTC include those for Stroh Brewery Co., Miller Brewing Co., and Anheuser-Busch as well as Seagram America's liquor products. All three breweries have subsequently pulled their ads from MTV. The current FTC probe will probably be based on the "unfair advertising" rationale that was previously used by the agency to investigate the cigarette industry in 1994. Using that approach, the FTC would attempt to prove that Seagram ads target underage audiences and have a corresponding harmful effect on them. But in a *Wall Street Journal* interview on 8 November 1996, Jodie Bernstein, director of the FTC's Bureau of Consumer Protection said that "it would be hard to make the case" that liquor should be treated differently than beer and wine. "As long as [the advertising] is not deceptive or unfair, it would be hard to differentiate."

At the state level, the attorney general of Alaska petitioned the FCC to adopt a rule prohibiting television and radio stations from broadcasting advertisements for distilled spirits. Following Alaska's lead, ten other states and Puerto Rico filed similar petitions with the FCC. Public interest groups were equally vocal in their criticism. The Center for Science in the Public Interest (CSPI) sent out Community Action Kits to assist 750 community groups across the nation to protest the DISCUS decision. Then president-elect, now president of MADD, Karolyn Nunnalee, announced that MADD planned to formally complain to the FCC about the DISCUS decision and would support legislation limiting alcohol advertising. According to Hundt, "a huge number" of public interest groups proclaimed that "hard liquor should not be on the airwaves."

The broadcast industry quickly responded to the criticism from Washington and the calls for advertising restraint. The National Association of Broadcasters, which represents the television and radio networks, issued a statement saying it was "disappointed" with the DISCUS decision despite its "staunch support of the First Amendment rights of broadcasters to advertise legal products." Representatives of three of the four major networks, ABC, CBS, and Fox, quickly announced that they would refuse to accept liquor commercials while NBC left the decision up to its station general managers, although the network recommended against it.

> *"Each subsector of the alcoholic beverage industry has its own code governing advertising and marketing practices addressing issues of social responsibility and underage drinking."*

Major cable channels, such as ESPN, MTV, Lifetime, and Turner Broadcasting System announced that they would not accept liquor spots. Other independent networks, such as Gannett, Cox Broadcasting, LIN Television, and Freedom Communications also announced that they did not accept liquor advertisements and have no plans to change their policy. Only the Black Entertainment Television and Continental Cablevision networks agreed to accept liquor commercials. Major radio station groups, such as CBS/Westinghouse/Infinity Broadcasting and American Radio Systems issued blanket rejections of distilled spirits advertising, even though they previously had broadcast them without consumer complaint. . . .

## The Political Aftermath

In March 1997, the Center for Media Education, a Washington, D.C. children's advocacy group, accused distilled spirits and beer companies of using over two dozen World Wide Web sites to promote their products to underage audiences. Pointing out Internet sites that include music audios and interactive games, the Center is requesting that Congress and federal regulators investigate the alcoholic beverage industry's on-line advertising.

On 1 April 1997, President Clinton again went on record strongly encouraging the distilled spirits industry to reinstate its voluntary broadcast advertising ban. He praised Hundt for considering "any and all actions that would protect the public interest in the use of the public airwaves." In a letter to Hundt, the President asked the commission to explore the effects on children of the distilled spirits industry's decision to advertise on television and to determine an appropriate response. However, the President did not request that the FCC inquiry include beer and wine broadcast advertising. . . .

In January 1998, the National Institute on Alcohol Abuse and Alcoholism released a major study (forty-three thousand interviews) on alcohol abuse among American youth. According to the study results, young people who began drinking before age fifteen were four times more likely to develop alcohol dependence (alcoholism) than those who began drinking at age twenty-one. The risk that a person would develop alcohol abuse, defined as a maladaptive drinking pattern that repeatedly causes life problems, was more than doubled for persons who began drinking before age fifteen compared with those who began drinking at age twenty-one.

Commenting on the study results, U.S. Secretary of Health and Human Services Donna E. Shalala urged, "prevention agencies, communities, businesses (especially the alcohol beverage industry), schools, and parents need to act together and to tell our young people unequivocally and with one voice that under-age drinking is dangerous and wrong." In addition, the Secretary warned that "we need to avoid glamorization of drinking, including misleading linkages between sports and alcohol.". . .

## The Need to Stay Competitive

Competitive market forces motivated Seagram America, and eventually the distilled spirits industry, to lift its voluntary ban of broadcast advertising and risk social scorn and more regulation. Distilled spirits, wine, and beer are the three subsectors of the alcoholic beverage industry. But distilled spirits has been the victim of hard economic times. Since 1979, that industry's best selling year, domestic sales of distilled spirits have declined from about 200 million nine-liter cases to 135 million cases in 1996. From 1970 to 1995, the distilled spirits market share of the alcoholic beverage industry dropped from 44 percent to 29 percent, while beer's market share increased from 45 percent to 59 percent. Since 1979, liquor sales have declined 32 percent while beer and wine sales are up 5 percent.

> *"Alcohol advertising only shifts consumers' allegiance from one brand to another."*

According to a August 1997 issue of *Beverage Industry,* a national trade publication, distilled spirits industry analysts offer a number of reasons for the decline: the evolution of active, health-conscious lifestyles; increased consumer sensitivity to DWI (Driving While Intoxicated) traffic laws; a general trend by consumers away from high-proof beverages; and increased competition from alternative beverages, both alcoholic and nonalcoholic. Moreover, most of the sales volume loss has been in whiskeys ("brown" goods), while vodka, rum, and tequila ("white" goods) have been expanding their market shares. . . .

The distilled spirits industry's stated desire is to compete against beer and wine products on "a level playing field." Some alcoholic beverage industry analysts believe that the distillers are following a win-win political strategy. If their efforts to advertise on television and radio succeed, the playing field becomes level. If regulators begin a crackdown on alcoholic beverage broadcasting, the distillers benefit from reduced advertising by the wine and, especially, the beer industry. Other alcoholic beverage analysts believe that the distillers' long-term strategy is to get on television now to guarantee a place when the next wave of technological advances occurs in home electronics, for example, the Internet.

## Industry Self-Regulation vs. Government Control

The public policy controversy over the broadcast airing of distilled spirits commercials has reached an important regulatory juncture. It is likely that liquor producers will face or be forced to accept one of a number of regulatory arrangements. . . .

In April 1997 DISCUS called on the President to convene a meeting of the alcoholic beverage industry (i.e., distilled spirits, brewers, and vintners) and broadcasting industry (television and radio) for the purpose of developing a common code of advertising. Currently each subsector of the alcoholic beverage industry has its own code governing advertising and marketing practices addressing issues of social responsibility and underage drinking. A common code will offer clear guidelines on alcoholic beverage advertising for the broadcast industry. That position has support in Congress from many in the Republican majority, including the chairman of the House Subcommittee on Telecommunications, Trade, and Consumer Protection, W.J. Tauzin. The proposal has not generated support from the White House, the Beer Institute, the Wine Institute, or public interest groups. Nevertheless, this regulatory strategy merits serious consideration as a possible solution to the dispute.

The efforts by critics of alcoholic beverage broadcast advertising to initiate a regulatory response so far have met failure. The President's efforts to involve the FCC in hearings on the distilled spirits issue have been stymied. The Republican-controlled Congress has not exhibited an appetite for hearings that will probably not result in any legislative remedy. Because of the virtually nonexistent probability of passing any regulatory bill, Democrats are not introducing any legislation for consideration. The political influence of the alcoholic beverage industry cannot be ignored either. For 1995 and 1996, the top thirty beer, wine, and distilled spirits companies contributed over $1.6 million to the political campaigns of Congressional and presidential candidates. The National Beer Wholesalers Association accounted for over $1 million of that financing, with the bulk of the contributions going to Republicans. Finally, the recent Supreme Court rulings upholding First Amendment rights of advertisers' free speech would make it difficult, if not impossible, for Congress or regulatory agencies to place broad restrictions on alcoholic beverage advertising—especially since studies have not proven a link between advertising and alcohol consumption. . . .

## The Case for Industry Self-Regulation

From a public policy perspective, industry self-regulation and the harmonization of advertising and marketing codes across the alcoholic beverage industry might be the best option to head off regulation in the future that could seriously harm the industry. Industry self-regulation is defined by the University of Maryland's Anil K. Gupta and Butler University's Lawrence J. Lad, as "a regulatory process whereby an industry-level, as opposed to a governmental body or a firm-level, organization, such as a trade association or professional society, sets and enforces rules and standards relating to the conduct of firms in the industry." While the "free rider" problem—where "renegade" firms in the industry do not abide by the self-regulating regime and therefore benefit at the expense of complying firms—and antitrust policies have restricted the widespread implementation of industry self-regulation in the United States, there are empirical examples of such regulatory schemata involving various levels of government intervention and industry self-regulation.

According to Harvard University's David A. Garvin, the regulatory spectrum includes pure self-regulation (motion picture and television rating and censorship); self-regulation plus government provision of technical information (voluntary product standards and the National Bureau of Standards); self-regulation plus government policing of deceptive practices (securities industry self-regulation and the Securities and Exchange Commission); and self-regulation plus an autonomous government agency with rule-making authority (National Advertising Review Council and the FTC). Garvin recommends that the greatest potential for industry self-regulation lies in "mixed systems that combine industry rule-making with federal oversight." Gupta and Lad concur with Garvin that "some form of government oversight and threat of direct regulation often coexist alongside industry self-regulation."

Currently, the distilled spirits, beer, and wine segments of the alcoholic beverage industry each have their own voluntary code of responsible advertising and marketing practices: the *Code of Good Practice for Distilled Spirits Advertising and Marketing* (DISCUS); the *Advertising & Marketing Code* of the Beer Institute; and the *Code of Advertising Standards* of the Wine Institute. Each subsector's code addresses, to varying degrees, issues concerning underage drinking and responsible product imagery.

## The Broader Issue

While the present controversy centers on distilled spirits broadcast advertising, the larger public policy issue for the broadcast industry is addressing criticism of alcoholic beverage advertising and marketing practices. The broadcast industry, which is regulated by an FCC charged with "public interest" stewardship, needs the voluntary self-regulating mechanism as well as political protection that a common code of responsible advertising and marketing offers a significant revenue source. But there are two important issues supporting the development of a common industry code which require further explanation: the measured effects of alcoholic beverage advertising and the concept of beverage equivalency.

The hypothesis that alcoholic beverage advertising is closely linked with an increase in alcohol use or abuse has been intensely researched. The FTC has reviewed the scientific literature on "cause-and-effect" between advertising and alcoholic beverage consumption and "found no reliable basis to conclude that alcohol advertising significantly affects consumption, let alone abuse." The evidence suggests that alcohol advertising only shifts consumers' allegiance from one brand to another. Dr. Morris E. Chafetz, founding director of the National Institute of Alcohol Abuse and Alcoholism, U.S. Department of Health and Human Services recently editorialized that "there is not one single study—not one study in the United States or internationally—that credibly connects advertising with an increase in alcohol use or abuse. Any assertion or assumption that alcohol ads increase use and abuse is fantasy, not fact."

*"There is not one single study—not one study in the United States or internationally—that credibly connects advertising with an increase in alcohol use or abuse."*

The second point to consider is the concept of beverage alcohol equivalence.

A standard serving of beer, wine, and spirits, i.e., a twelve-ounce can of beer, a five-ounce glass of wine, and a 1.5 ounce cocktail of eighty proof spirits, all contain the same absolute amount of alcohol. The National Institute on Alcohol Abuse and Alcoholism, the Departments of Agriculture, Transportation, and Education, MADD, the National Council on Alcoholism and Drug Dependence, Blue Cross/Blue Shield, and the National Alcohol Beverage Control Association all measure beverage alcohol equivalence using the standard serving criteria. Moreover, alcohol warning labels, minimum drinking age laws, and drunk driving laws do not distinguish among distilled spirits, beer, and wine. In spite of that beverage alcohol equivalence consensus, the Beer Institute emphasizes the so-called "obvious, significant differences between beer and hard liquor." The Wine Institute "strongly reject(s) the erroneous premise that equates wine, beer, and distilled spirits as simply quantitative variations of 'alcohol.'" Nevertheless, from a public policy perspective, "alcohol is alcohol is alcohol."

> *"While policy makers are correct to act aggressively to prevent highway deaths caused by drunk driving, worries that liquor advertising could lead to increased accidents [are] premature."*

The alcoholic beverage industry is feeling the fallout from the Food and Drug Administration's 1995 regulations restricting the advertising, promotion, distribution, and marketing of cigarettes to teenagers. Moreover, the proposed $368.5 billion agreement reached by state attorneys general, public health officials, and the tobacco companies to settle lawsuits by states and individuals also includes industry provisions to restrict cigarette advertising and monetary penalties if the percentage of youth smoking fails to decline.

## Drunk Driving Among Youth Is Down

As another so-called "sin" product, alcoholic beverages are always vulnerable to public criticism—especially when it concerns youth. In 1996, according to statistics compiled by the National Highway Traffic Safety Administration, 21 percent of the fifteen- to twenty-year-old drivers who were killed in crashes were legally intoxicated, with a blood alcohol level of 0.10 g/dl or higher. Further, almost 30 percent of those drivers who were killed, while not legally drunk, had been drinking.

It is important to note that in both the categories of drivers killed and drivers involved in fatal automobile crashes, the numbers of drivers fifteen to twenty years old who were intoxicated dropped by 54 percent between 1986 and 1996—the largest decline of any age group. That seems to imply that, while policy makers are correct to act aggressively to prevent highway deaths caused by drunk driving, worries that liquor advertising could lead to increased accidents [are] premature. Yet public interest groups like MADD and their Clinton administration and congressional allies are keeping a sharp focus on the alcoholic beverage industry's advertising and marketing practices.

## Self-Regulation Mechanisms

Forestalling government regulation would be a primary motivator for industry self-regulation. The need for a common code of advertising and marketing practices is justified by the FCC's threat to restrict alcoholic beverage broadcast advertising under the agency's legislative mandate for establishing and monitoring moral standards. An FCC regulatory decree could limit the hours when such advertising could be aired or influence the nature of commercial advertising.

How would the alcoholic beverage industry self-regulation process unfold? Under the auspices of the National Advertising Review Council, the Distilled Spirits Council of the United States, Inc., the Beer Institute, and the Wine Institute might meet with the National Association of Broadcasters to establish a voluntary code of advertising and marketing practices for the alcoholic beverage industry. The alcoholic beverage common code would incorporate salient aspects of the existing sector codes of responsible advertising and marketing practices. The broadcast industry would evaluate the common code and request further guideline clarification where needed.

There could be pressure for alcoholic beverage producers to supplement such an approach with an advisory committee of stakeholders, representing, for example, the FCC, FTC, Congress, the White House, and public interest groups. Such a group could review and, where needed, offer constructive criticism of the proposed industry guidelines. Creation of such a committee might help to reduce pressure for government action against the industry. On the other hand, the industry might feel that acting on its own will reduce pressure enough to avoid government controls. In any case, a committee could create a dangerous precedent, blurring further freedom of speech, free exchange, and the rule of law.

> *"Responding to public concerns has traditionally been a charge that the alcoholic beverage industry has voluntarily embraced."*

After the iterative code development process is complete, the final product will be a set of voluntary guidelines that will be consistently applied by all members of the broadcast media and will ostensibly defuse the threat of increased government regulation.

## The Industry Will Voluntarily Respond to Public Concerns

The alcoholic beverage industry is one of the most highly regulated sectors of the American economy. But based on exhaustive scientific evidence and expert opinion, there is no apparent need for further federal regulation of alcoholic beverage broadcast advertising. The First Amendment right to truthfully advertise a legal product will continue to allow the alcoholic beverage industry to market their spirits, wine, and beer over the broadcast airwaves. Yet the political climate is ripe to further broadcast restrictions. Supporting this assertion is a *Wall Street Journal*/NBC News Poll released 24 April 1998, which reveals that 44 percent of Americans polled believe the federal government is doing too little to regulate alcohol. That contrasts with 38 percent of those polled who believe the same about tobacco. And even if the alcohol industry could hold off regulators for a time, it could be bled dry by court costs and other costs of defending its interests.

Providing the broadcast industry with a common code of responsible alcoholic beverage advertising and marketing practices is an extension of the industry tradition of self-regulation. The broadcast industry needs guidelines that will be applied to all alcoholic beverage products. Because of the "public interest" nature of its business, the broadcasters are more susceptible to political pressure. The broadcast industry's fear is that widespread airing of liquor commercials will lead to a public backlash that could eliminate highly profitable beer advertising.

While not presently a threat to the status quo, distilled spirits could gradually increase their presence on the broadcast airwaves. A common code could offer the broadcasters the mechanism to stymie the political controversy, the threat of further government regulation, and the potential loss of revenue from foregone beer advertising. The common code will build on the already established subsector codes. Notwithstanding, each alcoholic beverage industry subsector can voluntarily exceed the common code's recommended advertising and marketing practices.

Responding to public concerns has traditionally been a charge that the alcoholic beverage industry has voluntarily embraced. Recognition of the true nature of that public concern should bring a consensus on extending the successful use of voluntary distilled spirits, beer, and wine industry subsector advertising and marketing self-regulation to the alcoholic beverage industry.

# Alcohol Advertising Does Not Promote Underage Drinking

by Morris E. Chafetz

**About the author:** *Morris E. Chafetz is the founding director of the National Institute on Alcohol Abuse and Alcoholism, president of the Health Education Foundation in Washington, D.C., and the author of* The Tyranny of Experts: Blowing the Whistle on the Cult of Expertise.

As a psychiatrist, scientist, and former architect of the national effort to prevent alcohol problems, it was my job to seek out the best science, both biomedical and behavioral. Today, a heated debate swirls around the issue of restricting alcohol advertising on TV. Assorted opponents who argue that advertising contributes to alcohol-related problems—especially among young people—are way off base.

## Where Is the Evidence?

When I consider the pros and cons of alcohol advertising and its alleged effect on problem drinking, I find myself asking the crucial question: Where in the name of science is there proof that alcohol advertising is bad for society? Shouldn't there be some science to say it's so?

In 1996 I was asked to write a review for the *New England Journal of Medicine* on how advertising affects alcohol use. I did not find *any* studies that credibly connect advertising to increases in alcohol use (or abuse) or to young persons taking up drinking. The prevalence of reckless misinterpretation and misapplication of science allows advocacy groups and the media to stretch research findings to suit their preconceived positions.

For example, one study showed that adolescents who drank alcohol could remember alcohol ads better than adolescents who did not drink. But what does that prove? If researchers found that green-colored automobiles had more acci-

Reprinted from Morris E. Chafetz, "Should the Government Restrict Advertising of Alcoholic Beverages?—No," *Priorities*, vol. 9, no. 3, 1997, by permission of *Priorities*, a publication of the American Council on Science and Health, 1995 Broadway, 2nd floor, New York, NY 10023-5860.

dents than cars of other colors, would that prove the color green causes accidents?

Another study, supported by the Center on Alcohol Advertising, purportedly showed that people who knew about the federal guidelines on moderate drinking drank less than people who didn't know. Poppycock! The many variables that affect behavior and define moderate drinking are scientifically uncontrollable. Anyone with any scientific knowledge knows the study is nonsense.

## The Zealotry of Protecting Youth

But the issue of whether alcohol advertising should be restricted goes beyond what I have noted. Nowhere is this emotional issue more conspicuous than in the zealotry of protecting youth. A recent newspaper editorial reflects the hypocrisy at work here. The editorial advised banning TV alcohol advertising to protect young people. Yet I know of no newspaper publisher ready to forgo alcohol-ad revenue. Members of the print media rationalize this hypocrisy by calling television the medium that reaches most minors. The adage that it's easy to give advice one needn't take applies here.

Deaf to advice and blind to facts, anti-alcohol advocacy groups continue their mission to protect young people from the dissoluteness of the adult world. And they amass statistics on all kinds of problems to increase their power. During our adolescent years we tested the world by taking risks, and we made it. So will the present generation of teenagers. But there endures a sturdy, albeit insecure, band of believers dedicated to the idyllic dream of the innocent, sheltered child.

*"In their zeal, child-protection advocates may be contributing to the problems they work so hard to prevent."*

The results of a national survey of high-school students belie this perfect-child fantasy. In the study, researchers with the Addiction Research Foundation in Ontario, Canada, found that 76 percent of twelfth graders and 69 percent of tenth graders in the United States drank alcohol in 1996. State surveys have shown even higher rates of consumption by young people: An analysis of four large surveys of eleventh graders in Ohio showed that 87 percent of the boys and 82 percent of the girls drank alcohol.

A book from England, *The Normal and the Abnormal in Adolescent Drinking*, provides a realistic picture of alcohol and adolescence. The authors contend that adolescent drinking is a normal part of the socialization process, wherein teenagers experiment with and acquire adult behavior. The high incidence of adolescent drinking buttresses this argument. But the authors further contend that adolescent *abstinence* is as deviant as excessive drinking. I agree with their position. Abstinence and excessive drinking are unhealthy extremes. Neither behavior should be encouraged, for in the real world drinking alcohol in moderation is socially acceptable.

The idea of considering teenage abstinence abnormal will shock most Americans. But evidence that most tenth, eleventh, and twelfth graders in the United States drank some alcohol last year suggests that abstinence is indeed abnormal in this age group. Thus, the goal of abstinence for adolescents is unrealistic. It is common worldwide to view both abstinence and excessive drinking as abnormal. Experts in many countries do not make abstinence the only acceptable treatment goal for people recovering from alcoholism. The Puritans held that temptation was to be avoided at all costs, since it would surely lead one down the road to perdition. Are America's all-or-nothing principles part of their legacy?

## Young People Do Not Mindlessly Obey Advertisements

The U.S. Supreme Court made a telling point when it decided to overturn the Rhode Island ban on advertising alcoholic-beverage prices: "Keeping users of a product ignorant [in order] to manipulate their choices just doesn't work." The time has come for us to reexamine our attitudes toward teenage drinking. Teaching adolescents how to drink sensibly is a good way to begin.

Advocacy groups claim, without evidence, that alcohol advertising encourages young people to drink. With such an easy target as alcoholic beverages, evidence seems unnecessary. And the lust to blame something or someone for youthful waywardness is so intense that parents can be held legally responsible for their children's wanton acts.

Trying to lend young people a helping hand is, in itself, exemplary. But in their zeal, child-protection advocates may be contributing to the problems they work so hard to prevent. The cult of expertise has made parents feel incapable of raising their children. But as a parent and a psychiatrist, I trust the instincts of parents more than I do the hubris of child-protection experts.

Advertising has long been an accepted part of our daily lives. And because marketing tools are ubiquitous, some people attribute an omnipotence of sorts to Madison Avenue. Money spent on advertising a product is well spent when the advertising is directed to people inclined to purchase that product. But advertising money is wasted when the aim is to induce people to behave contrary to their wishes.

In *Advertising, Alcohol Consumption, and Abuse*, Joseph C. Fisher states: "I have developed a profound respect for consumers. They are not vulnerable, gullible, or easily malleable, but rather know their own minds and act accordingly." Critics

> *"[Consumers] are not vulnerable, gullible, or easily malleable, but rather know their own minds and act accordingly."*

claim that advertising influences young people to use "forbidden" products. They cite young people's rote responses as proof that they have been seduced. But such arguments imply that young people are like animals that respond mindlessly to stimuli.

Advocacy groups claim that alcohol advertising seduces young people to drink before they "know better," predisposing them to physiological and psychological addiction in adulthood and making freedom of choice moot. But the claim that advertising can lead anyone down the bottle-strewn garden path not only to drink alcohol but to abuse it, is pure hokum.

And reckless warnings can increase the allure of a product to people with self-destructive tendencies. According to some studies, putting warning labels on products can have the opposite effect.

## Paternalism Tends to Backfire

Marion Winik's description of her youth in *First Comes Love* illustrates how anti-alcohol efforts can backfire: "The minute someone said I shouldn't do something or couldn't have something, this is not allowed, don't go there, stay away, every cell in my body rushed toward it, every synapse in my brain started firing. I had to turn that 'no' into a 'yes' or die trying."

This natural tendency to "go against the grain" is a reality of teenage life. Risk is part of growing up. Young people are not robotic anonyms and should not be regarded as such. They are human individuals and have an ancient, instinctive need to experiment. Paternalism dampens the spirit, fosters resentment, and perpetuates itself.

Events in the former Soviet Union cast doubt on the assertion that alcohol advertising causes undesirable behavior: In an attempt to stem serious nationwide alcohol-abuse problems, the Communist government banned all promotion of alcoholic beverages—after which intemperance increased and Russia arguably became the world leader in drinking problems.

And so, beware! If we invoke science to dress prejudice as policy, we do not merely pervert science: We demean policy and the laws we live by as well.

# The Alcohol Industry Should Be Permitted to Advertise the Health Benefits of Moderate Drinking

by Stephen Chapman

**About the author:** *Stephen Chapman is a nationally syndicated columnist.*

In olden times, kings and emperors trampled on the rights of their people simply because they had the power to do so. In modern democracies, governments often encroach on liberties, but they always do it with the comforting assurance that it's for our own good. Increasingly, the only freedoms entrusted to ordinary people are the ones that have been certified as harmless.

The public-health school of thought believes that we have a duty to take good care of our bodies and that enforcing this duty is government's noblest purpose. The result is an assortment of assaults on tobacco—banning smoking in office buildings and restaurants, raising cigarette taxes to onerous levels, bringing tobacco under the formidable regulatory authority of the Food and Drug Administration, and suing the pants off cigarette-makers for having the nerve to supply willing consumers with a legal product.

## The Next Target for the Nanny State

With tobacco virtually vanquished, the next inviting target for the nanny state is alcohol, which has not been so besieged since Carry Nation was doing the Lord's work by busting up saloons. Drinking has been on a steady decline for a decade and a half, but anti-alcohol forces aren't content to see individual adults cheerfully electing to reduce their consumption. They insist on enlisting government power to push more people into making the approved choice.

For years, the wine industry has asked the Bureau of Alcohol, Tobacco and

Reprinted from Stephen Chapman, "Peripatetic Pursuit of Hazards," syndicated column, March 5, 1999, by permission of Stephen Chapman and Creators Syndicate.

Firearms to let it discreetly publicize research on moderate drinking. On Feb. 5, 1999, the agency grudgingly agreed to permit wine labels advising consumers to consult their physicians or the government's official dietary guidelines to learn more about "the health effects of wine consumption."

Winemakers have some interest in this matter because scientific studies show that drinking can be good for your health. The federal guidelines note that "moderate drinking is associated with a lower risk for coronary heart disease in some individuals." The American Heart Association goes further: "The incidence of heart disease in those who consume moderate amounts of alcohol (an average of one to two drinks per day for men and one drink per day for women) is lower than in nondrinkers."

Note that the labels don't mention "health benefits," though bottles are already required to carry a stern warning that alcohol "may cause health problems." But even the neutral language was enough to send the industry's critics screaming from the room.

## Overzealous Anti-Drinking Forces

"Some consumers may interpret 'health effect' as 'health benefit' and end up drinking more than they should," lamented the Center for Science in the Public Interest (CSPI), which possesses the wisdom to know exactly how much each of us "should" drink. The new labels, warned journalist Michael Massing in the *New York Times,* will "simply encourage more people to drink" and "drive moderate drinkers to drink more heavily, with potentially steep medical and social costs."

This warning conjures up the bizarre image of whip-cracking vintners "driving" modest tipplers to chug those wine bottles or else. In fact, all the wine industry is permitted to do is invite consumers to acquire reliable data about alcohol, something truth-seeking journalists should not find inherently alarming.

Accurate, nondeceptive information is supposed to be good for consumers. But anti-drinking forces want to ban any communications that could possibly be good for sales of alcoholic beverages. Even more alarming than the new wine labels is the expansion of broadcast and cable advertising by makers of distilled spirits. Neo-Prohibitionists would dearly love to outlaw wine and beer commercials, and their aversion to bourbon and scotch ads is more intense still.

> *"Increasingly, the only freedoms entrusted to ordinary people are the ones that have been certified as harmless."*

The industry used to voluntarily refrain from this sort of marketing, only to see liquor consumption drop by 40 percent in the last two decades. Acting on the impeccable logic that alcohol is alcohol, whether it comes in a beer can or a highball glass, booze-makers have decided it's only fair they should be able to air radio and TV ads the same as Budweiser and Fetzer. But CSPI insists that the campaign "flies in the face of a national policy designed to decrease alcohol consumption as part of a broad national-health initiative."

## Treating People Like Adults

Bureaucratic words, those, but translated into English, they have a clear meaning: Regardless of our personal preferences, people who hate alcohol have decided we should drink less. If they have to suppress honest communications between competent adults to achieve that goal, then censor they will.

Those of us with an atavistic desire to be left alone to make our own choices really ought to get over it. When all is said and done, we'll still have the one freedom worth having: the freedom to do what others think is good for us.

# The Government Should Combat the Influence of Alcohol Advertising on Youth

## by George A. Hacker

**About the author:** *George A. Hacker is director of the Alcohol Policies Project, a program of advocacy group Center for Science in the Public Interest that works to curb alcohol-related problems.*

After more than 50 years of honoring its pledge not to advertise distilled spirits in the broadcast media, the liquor industry, in November 1996, finally lost its grip on good corporate citizenship. Following the lead of the Seagram Company, which began airing advertisements for its Crown Royal Canadian whiskey on a Corpus Christi, Texas, television station in June of that year, the Distilled Spirits Council of the United States (DISCUS) abandoned its long-standing, voluntary ban on broadcast liquor advertisements. As recently as 1993, its president had described the ban to a Senate committee as part of the liquor industry's "responsibility to combat alcohol abuse."

## Claiming Discrimination

The decision to dump the restraint resulted from desperation over two decades of plummeting liquor consumption; envy of beer marketers' ability to reach mass audiences of young, heavy-drinking consumers; and a perceived belief of cultural and economic victimization at their own and regulators' hands. In short, the industry was suffering from a big inferiority complex, which it now hopes to cure.

The liquor industry wants to open the airwaves to liquor to "end discrimination against distilled spirits products." It hopes to level the alcohol playing field it shares with brewers. So far, distillers have done little more than stir the politi-

Reprinted, with permission, from George A. Hacker, "Liquor Advertisements on Television: Just Say No," *Journal of Public Policy and Marketing*, vol. 17, no. 1 (Spring 1998), pp. 139–42, published by the American Marketing Association. (A list of references in the original has been omitted in this reprint.)

cal waters regarding all alcohol advertisements (chiefly beer) rather than flood the airwaves with new promotions for booze. Broadcasters' massive resistance to the advertisements (the big networks will not run them) and distillers' unwillingness to make serious financial investments in them (Seagram, for example, spent just $197,100, or 4.2% of its 1996 Crown Royal advertising budget, on spot television), together with widespread public opposition, have succeeded, until now, to preserve the status quo.

Despite the liquor industry's inability to break brewers' virtual monopoly on television advertising (94% of all alcoholic-beverage spending in that medium in 1996), there is plenty of room for concern about a potential new flood of alcohol advertisements in broadcast and substantial reasons to oppose the liquor industry's "nothing-to-lose" efforts.

For 20 years, the liquor industry lost ground to brewers and vintners. Liquor consumption fell 29% between 1980 and 1995. Since the advent of television, in the late 1940s, the amount of alcohol consumed as liquor per capita stayed constant. In contrast, the alcohol consumed as beer increased 20%.

During the past 40 years, brewers have used massive broadcast media exposure to promote "America's beverage," inseparable from baseball, family picnics, and barbecues and increasingly perceived as distant from the nether side of drinking—car

> *"The Budweiser frogs are more recognizable to young children than all but one other commercial television critter."*

wrecks, spousal abuse, rapes, crime, and addiction related to excessive alcohol consumption. Distilled spirits never overcame its "hard-stuff" moniker. By the 1990s, such distinctions, which translated into regulatory differences, such as substantially higher excise tax rates and fewer retail sales outlets for liquor, became too much for the liquor industry to bear. It demanded equity.

## The Price of Equity Is Too High

The price of equity for the liquor industry is simply too high, especially for America's kids, who are burdened by too many of the costs. Young people begin drinking in junior high school and binge drink (five or more drinks per occasion) at the rate of 30% by the time they are high school seniors. Four million children are alcoholics or problem drinkers. Alcohol, by far, is the most used and abused drug among young people. It is a major factor in the three leading causes of death for 16- to 24-year-olds. It is also the third leading killer overall (behind tobacco and diet/activity problems), contributing to more than 100,000 deaths each year in the United States. The economic costs associated with alcohol consumption total more than $100 billion each year.

In 1996, the airwaves carried some $675 million in beer and wine advertisements and approximately $1.3 million in advertisements for distilled spirits. Note the results of this level of exposure: Junior high school kids can name more beer brands than they can presidents, the Budweiser frogs are more recognizable to young children than all but one other commercial television critter, and beer is the alcoholic beverage of choice and a gateway drug for teenagers. Do we want young people to start drinking liquor instead?

## Children Sing the Jingles

Past experience with beer advertising demands that people "just say no" when it comes to opening the airwaves to liquor. For too long seductive broadcast promotions for beer have been tolerated. Those advertisements teach the virtues and pleasures of beer: too many of the messages rub off on consumers who legally cannot buy, possess, or consume it. Although it may be virtually impossible to prove conclusively the obvious—that advertising intends (and can be effective) to stimulate demand for beer—children see many of the advertisements, they sing the jingles, and they mimic the characters. In short, they learn when, where, why, how, and with whom to drink beer. The advertisements sell beer drinking, as much as beer brands, as the ticket to friendships, success, happiness, athletic accomplishment, and sexual conquest.

To pretend, as alcohol marketers do, that the advertisements do not have an effect on consumption is disingenuous at best. First, consider that they spend hundreds of millions of dollars advertising their products. One would think they have some faith in that investment. Try finding an advertising agency modest enough to confess that marketers have been wasting all (or even some of) that money. Second, alcohol marketers' vociferous defense of their "rights" to advertise—and their push to expand liquor advertising to the electronic media—speak volumes about the connection between media exposure and the bottom line. Advertising might work to shift consumers from one brand to another. But to suggest that it does not help bring in new consumers and encourage current users to consume more begs credulity. Trusting one's eyes and ears makes more sense.

Advertising is not the sole, nor the most potent, influence on alcohol consumption by youth or adults. However, it is a measurable, modest contributing factor. Even research cited by the industry as support for the "null effects" hypothesis concedes the connection. Other studies take the link even further, relating advertising expenditures positively to the number of young people killed in automobile crashes.

The documented effects on children of frequent exposure to televised beer advertising provide adequate reason to oppose liquor advertisements on the air. Those effects include the

- ability to recognize and recall brand names advertised,
- ability to match brand names and slogans,
- formation of beliefs about beer consumption that relate it to good times and fun more often than caution and risk, and
- association with having a moderate to high expectation to drink as an adult.

Television advertising for beer affects the manner, style, and meanings of drinking in society. It defines beer drinking as a positive and normative behavior. The ubiquity of the advertisements promotes an exaggerated view of how many people drink and how much. The advertisements provide drinking lessons for kids that ought to be left to parents and less self-interested parties.

The liquor industry's call for equity and the experience so far with the few televised liquor advertisements leave little doubt that distillers want access to the same youthful targets so assiduously courted by brewers. Look at the youthful demographic they reach in *Spin, Swing, Details,* and *Rolling Stone* magazines. Or view Seagram's Crown Royal dogs parading to high school graduation theme music during prime-time television shows and weekend football games. Note also that many of the radio stations on which Seagram advertisements for Lime Twisted Gin ran feature youth-oriented rock-and-roll music formats, especially designed for the 18+ demographic.

> *"To pretend, as alcohol marketers do, that the advertisements do not have an effect on consumption is disingenuous at best."*

An expansion of broadcast liquor advertising could reach millions of underage persons who are not exposed to those messages now. Data from Nielsen Media Research indicate that, on a national basis, as many as 18 million 2- to 17-year-olds watch television during the 9:00 to 9:30 P.M. prime-time segment, the time that broadcasters have indicated liquor advertisements would run. Those young people constitute more than 30% of the entire population for that age group and total more than 17% of the viewing audience during that time slot.

Liquor advertisements, like those for beer, influence the perceptions of millions of children regarding the uses of alcohol. Repetitive advertising images gently massage youth's understandings of the role of alcohol in our culture and in their lives. Those messages exaggerate alcohol's importance and whitewash the potentially negative effects of drinking. The introduction of broadcast liquor advertisements inevitably will unleash new competitive forces and lead to increases in advertising expenditures for all types of alcoholic beverages. That only can increase the pressure on young people to drink and motivate them to use even more concentrated forms of alcohol.

## Other Downsides of Broadcast Liquor Advertisements

The increased dependence of broadcasters on revenue from alcoholic-beverage producers also may have more subtle and undesirable effects. Those include influencing station programming decisions, compromising news and public service coverage of alcohol health and safety issues, jeopardizing broadcast licensees' implementation of their public interest responsibilities, and hardening broadcaster opposition to policy efforts to balance pro-drinking advertisements with public health information about the risks of alcohol consumption and messages that deglamorize drinking among underage persons. Paranoia?

Many studies have documented how the heavy reliance by some magazines on tobacco advertising revenues has distorted—and in some cases extinguished—their coverage of health issues related to smoking.

A substantial expansion of liquor advertising to television also likely will add to the number of new, specialty alcohol products that are introduced in the marketplace. Many of those products, such as low-alcohol "refreshers," "alcopops," and wine coolers, appeal to new consumers who do not like the taste of alcohol and often are packaged to resemble nonalcoholic fruit drinks. A proliferation of advertisements for those products will hamper efforts to deter underage drinking and to reduce the toll of alcohol on young people.

Drawing a line in the sand to block broadcast liquor advertising does not concede the legitimacy of beer and wine advertisements in broadcast, nor does it accept the myth that beer and wine are somehow less harmful. It simply rejects backsliding and reflects a determination to protect children from additional, potentially harmful influences. It reflects current political realities that impede controls on beer advertising. It is admittedly a defensive effort rather than the solution to the problem of alcohol advertising.

## Proposals for Reform

Outside of the liquor and advertising industries and a few needy broadcasters, there is virtually no support for liquor advertisements on television. President Clinton and Senator Trent Lott agree that distillers should go back to the voluntary ban. Attorney General Janet Reno, like the President and 26 members of Congress, has asked the Federal Communications Commission (FCC) to investigate what it can do to protect children from broadcast liquor advertisements. Fourteen state's attorneys general went even further, petitioning the FCC to ban such advertisements.

More than 250 public-interest organizations also have asked the FCC to determine whether airing liquor advertisements meets broadcasters' responsibilities to operate in the public interest. Although FCC Chairman Reed Hundt's effort to undertake a Notice of Inquiry (NOI) fell one vote short in July 1997, an FCC with four new commissioners might be more favorably disposed toward action. An NOI would respect the views of the American people, 52% of whom support a ban on broadcast liquor advertisements; more than 80% support other proposed advertising restrictions [according to a poll conducted by Michigan State University researcher Charles Atkin].

> *"Television advertising for beer affects the manner, style, and meanings of drinking in society. It defines beer drinking as a positive and normative behavior."*

Many proposals have been offered to combat the influence of broadcast liquor, beer, and wine advertisements. None appears to be on a political fast-track, but each presents lawmakers and regulators with potentially powerful tools to protect children and secure a better balance of societal information about America's most used and abused drug. The measures have broad popular support and the backing of the largest and most prestigious health, safety, religious, education, and antidrug groups.

> *"[The proposed measures to combat the influence of alcohol advertising] respect the industry's right to convey truthful, nonmisleading information about their products to adult consumers."*

The proposed measures do not call for a blanket ban on broadcast alcohol advertising. They respect the industry's right to convey truthful, nonmisleading information about their products to adult consumers. They recognize the political and (possibly) legal obstacles to formulating advertising standards that differentiate between beer, wine, and liquor. They are tailored narrowly to provide a balance of information helpful to consumers without impeding other avenues of commercial communications. Substantively and legally, they have ample precedent in the public health campaigns against tobacco, and they facilitate broadcasters' compliance with statutory obligations to operate in the public interest.

## Safety Messages and Counteradvertising

One measure that has been lurking in Congress since 1990 would require health and safety messages in all alcoholic-beverage advertising. The Sensible Advertising and Family Education Act of 1996 (H.R. 3474), introduced by Representative Joseph P. Kennedy, calls for a series of rotating warnings in advertisements. On television, the warnings would be displayed as banners during the advertisement, accompanied by a voice-over reading of the message. The messages would caution consumers about alcohol risks, including drinking during pregnancy, drunk driving, drinking while taking certain medications, and drinking too much too fast.

Once a pipe dream, the measure got an unexpected boost when the Seagram Company, out of frustration at broadcaster reluctance to run its advertisements, offered to lead proposed new advertisements with a modest six-second warning encouraging "responsible" drinking and discouraging underage drinking, drinking and driving, or drinking during pregnancy. The warning would not define "responsibility" and would be limited to voice-over intonation. It is hardly effective as a serious warning, but certainly is enough to prompt widespread scrutiny and criticism of beer and wine advertisements that fail to provide similar cautions. Although far from perfect, Seagram's latest voluntary gambit adds fuel to the current debate on broadcast advertising; it also, in principal, endorses the Kennedy approach.

Recent studies reported by the U.S. Department of Health and Human Services confirm the effectiveness of this approach: "[S]upplementing beverage container warnings in print and broadcast advertisements is likely to improve the dissemination of the warning information significantly. The delivery of strong, conspicuous warnings in a combined audio and video mode appears most effective."

Experience with counteradvertising in the "tobacco wars" indicates that a balance of commercials that inform consumers of the risks of excessive drinking, discourage over-consumption, and deglamorize drinking by underage persons would provide effective relief from the one-sided promotion of drinking. If they appeared in sufficient proportion to the commercials for alcoholic beverages and aired at times the target audience was viewing, counteradvertising, which ultimately drove cigarette advertisements from broadcast, could have substantial informational and political impact. Mandatory counteradvertising for all alcoholic-beverage advertisements, if produced by sources independent of the affected industries, even might be worth allowing liquor advertisements on the air.

In addition to information-oriented approaches, activists have proposed several measures to keep alcohol advertisements from reaching large audiences of young people with images, characters, and sounds designed to entertain and attract them. In the future, people may have to stay up late in the evening to catch the funny, lively, lifestyle advertisements for drink. Commercials during youth-viewing periods (say, 7:00 A.M. to 11:00 P.M.) might be limited to objective information about the products

> *"Experience with counteradvertising in the 'tobacco wars' indicates that a balance of commercials that inform consumers of the risks of excessive drinking ... would provide effective relief from the one-sided promotion of drinking."*

only: price, appearance, and availability. Some advertisements still might appear during sports programming, but athletic themes, race cars, hard bodies, and rock-and-roll music will not be in them.

The combination of warning requirements; counteradvertising; and time, place, and manner restrictions certainly would discourage most alcohol advertisers from spending tens of millions of dollars on television commercials. Wishful thinking? A walk back down "tobacco road" reveals how cigarette advertisements disappeared from television. The tobacco industry itself approached Congress for a ban, rather than tolerate the mandated counteradvertisements that were killing sales even faster than cigarettes were killing smokers.

## A Serious Threat to Public Health

Alcohol is not tobacco. However, using our most powerful communications media to promote the use of liquor (and beer and wine) to audiences that include substantial numbers of children poses similar, serious public health and safety concerns. Thank you, Seagram: thank you, DISCUS, for pressing the battle for equivalence among alcoholic beverages. Your efforts may not get many liquor advertisements on the air, but you will have helped focus needed attention on the televised beer advertisements that drown our children today. Saying no to liquor advertisements is only a warm-up for saying no to those advertisements too.

# The Alcohol Industry Should Not Be Permitted to Advertise the Health Benefits of Moderate Drinking

## by Robert Zimmerman

**About the author:** *Robert Zimmerman is a writer who specializes in alcohol and drug topics and is editor of the quarterly* Prevention File.

Let's hear it for moderation! We're all for moderation, aren't we? Well, it depends.

Senator Strom Thurmond is proposing that the warning labels on alcoholic beverages be broadened to mention that even moderate consumption of alcohol may lead to alcoholism or can cause health problems such as hypertension and breast cancer.

His bill sends a shudder through the Napa Valley and the rest of the wine country. The vintners have been trying to convince the government that it would be all right to put a label on their bottles associating "moderate wine consumption" with good health. We can't have it both ways.

### The Health Benefits of Alcohol Are Exaggerated

Research on alcohol and health appears to be moving faster than federal agencies can decide what to say about it. In 1991 a "60 Minutes" feature about the so-called French paradox fell like manna from heaven for the wine people. The French, it seems, eat the kind of fatty diet that clogs arteries. Yet the French have lower rates of heart disease than such a diet would suggest. Why? Because the French drink lots of wine. Scientists have confirmed that a glass or two of

Reprinted from Robert Zimmerman, "Moderation and Drinking Don't Mix," *San Diego Union-Tribune*, April 22, 1998, by permission of the author.

wine per day—or the equivalent amount of alcohol from any other source—can lower one's risk for heart trouble.

This evidence was compelling enough for the Public Health Service in 1995 to include a mention of it in its "Dietary Guidelines for Americans," being careful to point out that the benefit comes from a "moderate" amount of alcohol—one drink a day for women or two for men. The guidelines define a drink as 12 ounces of regular beer, 5 ounces of wine, or a 1.5-ounce shot of distilled spirits.

But the *Journal of the American Medical Association* in February [1998] published new research indicating that a woman's risk of breast cancer begins to rise with one glass of wine per day and is fully 40 percent greater if she drinks from two to five glasses in a day. And the recent Bill Moyers PBS special on addiction summarized new research on how alcohol affects the brain in ways similar to illegal drugs and can lead to addiction. To their credit Moyers and the PBS producers did not go along with the effort by alcoholic beverage companies to keep beer, wine and whiskey from being identified with other addictive drugs.

## Too Vague a Term

So what should the government say about "moderate" use of alcohol? Not only is alcohol dangerous for some people, but so is the word "moderate." Health professionals who screen patients for alcohol abuse are familiar with how slippery "moderation" can be, like the guy who describes himself as a moderate drinker because he only drinks one six-pack of beer every evening.

The federal Center for Substance Abuse Prevention ran a test on how drinkers would interpret a reference to "moderate wine consumption" as it would appear on proposed wine labels. Most of the 400 people in the survey said they had read or heard news stories about the link between wine and reduced risk of heart disease, and some said they were drinking more wine as a result. But the majority said they don't usually read wine labels, and if they read one like the sample they doubt if it would change their drinking behavior.

What was most striking about the survey is what it revealed about the meaning of the term "moderate." It means whatever anyone wants it to mean. Moderate in the minds of those interviewed ranged from one or two drinks in a month, to a whole bottle of wine in an evening.

"The word 'moderate' when associated with drinking has virtually no meaning," the researchers concluded. "The more one drinks, the more drinking one thinks is moderate."

The average number of drinks per occasion that heavy drinkers thought was moderate was almost six—which is more than the generally accepted definition of "binge" drinking.

> *"Not only is alcohol dangerous for some people, but so is the word 'moderate.'"*

In the 1970s the National Institute on Alcohol Abuse and Alcoholism launched a campaign to encourage "responsible" drinking. The program was quietly buried when it became obvious that no one could define exactly what "responsible" drinking amounted to. Is a message about "moderate" drinking any more likely to be understood? Apparently not.

## Any Amount of Alcohol Is Dangerous for Some People

Wine bottles and other alcoholic beverage containers since 1989 have carried a government-mandated warning that women should not drink during pregnancy because of the risk of birth defects, and that consumption of alcohol impairs one's ability to drive a car and operate machinery, and may cause health problems.

If Senator Thurmond wants to add a specific warning about alcoholism and breast cancer, fine. There needn't be a reference to "moderate" drinking because consuming any amount of alcohol is dangerous for some people, as the research shows.

And the Bureau of Alcohol, Tobacco and Firearms, which has jurisdiction over labels, should tell the wine people to forget about trying to capitalize on the French paradox.

# The Alcohol Industry Has Too Much Political Influence

## by Michael Massing

**About the author:** *Journalist Michael Massing is a contributing editor of the* Columbia Journalism Review *and the author of* The Fix: Solving the Nation's Drug Problem.

Shortly after 9 o'clock in the morning of Dec. 3, 1997, the 14 members of the Governor's Task Force on Driving While Intoxicated and Vehicular Homicide took their seats in a hearing room in the Louisiana State Capitol Building in Baton Rouge. The issue before them: whether the state should add a provision to Louisiana's drinking law that would prohibit 18- to 20-year-olds from entering bars. The law currently allows them into bars, even while it prohibits them from buying or drinking alcohol. The law is widely flouted, however, and most of the task-force members—highway officials, state legislators, local sheriffs, a representative from Mothers Against Drunk Driving (MADD)—were united on the need to change what they saw as a loophole. The loophole, they believed, was encouraging college students to spend their nights carousing rather than studying. They also felt it was contributing to the carnage on the state's highways. In 1995, Louisiana had 883 traffic fatalities, of which slightly more than half were alcohol-related—the third highest rate in the country.

## Trying to Enforce the Legal Drinking Age in Louisiana

In seeking to close the loophole, however, the task force faced a formidable obstacle: Charles Tapp, one of its members. A lobbyist for the state alcohol industry, the silver-haired, tart-tongued Tapp was on the attack from the moment the first witness was seated. "You're the executive director of what organization?" he snarled at Sharron Ayers, who represented the Louisiana Alliance to Prevent Under-Age Drinking, a coalition of grass-roots groups, state agencies and private organizations. Closing the loophole, she said, would make it harder for young people to drink.

"Why do you call it a loophole?" Tapp asked gruffly.

"It makes it very hard for law enforcement to enforce the law," Ayers replied, uncertainty creeping into her voice. "It's had a lot of effects on young people. They're out drinking, not studying. You know what happened recently at L.S.U."

Ayers was referring to the fateful night in August 1997 when several fraternity members at Louisiana State University dropped by Murphy's, a local bar. There they downed pitchers of a potent concoction called Three Wise Men—151-proof rum, Crown Royal whisky and Jägermeister, a sweet liqueur. By midnight the students were so drunk that they had to be wheeled out in shopping carts to waiting cars. After they returned to their frat house, the campus police were alerted, and, rushing over, they found nearly two dozen people passed out. Four of them had to be hospitalized, and one, a 20-year-old named Benjamin Wynne, died. An autopsy found that his blood-alcohol content was six times over Louisiana's legal intoxication limit. Generating headlines nationwide, the event had strengthened the task force's conviction that it was time to act.

"What would you do about an 18-year-old student who works in a bar?" Tapp snapped.

"We don't have that defined yet," Ayers admitted.

"What about a 19-year-old who owns a bar?" he pressed on.

"What we are concerned with is the average student going into bars," she replied.

"What do you mean by average student?"

"The average 18-, 19- and 20-year-old who goes into a lounge. We don't know whether their purpose in going in is to drink, but we do know they are drinking."

"Do you know that?" Tapp challenged her. "Oh, we know about what happened at L.S.U., but were they going in to play pool, maybe, and not drinking?"

By the end of her testimony, Ayers was literally shaking. And so it went for the rest of the three-hour hearing. After Dr. Deborah Cohen, a professor at the L.S.U. Medical Center, expressed her support for closing the loophole, Tapp accused her of engaging in "social" legislation. "We've seen a tremendous movement in that direction in the last three to four years," he said. At several points, Tapp asserted that because the state's legal age of majority is 18, any effort to close the loophole would constitute age discrimination.

> *"Big Alcohol is not about to go the way of Big Tobacco. Aggressive, flush with cash and fortified with lessons from the war on cigarettes, the alcohol lobby is fighting back with the many weapons at its command."*

Watching Tapp's performance, his fellow panel members struggled to keep their cool, waiting for the final vote to express their own views. It went 13 to 1 in favor of recommending that the Governor, M.J. (Mike) Foster, a Republican, introduce a bill to close the loophole and make it illegal for 18- to 20-year-olds to enter bars. For the state's alcohol-control forces, it was a sweet victory, if a small one.

## Citizens' Groups Versus the Alcohol Lobby

In recent months, citizens' groups across the nation have been organizing against the alcohol industry. Spurred by growing concerns over drunk driving, under-age drinking and alcohol-related crime, these groups—made up of parents and educators, churchgoers and community activists—have been pressing for higher taxes, restrictions on advertising and crackdowns on problem outlets. Not since Prohibition has the alcohol industry been so under siege. But Big Alcohol is not about to go the way of Big Tobacco. Aggressive, flush with cash and fortified with lessons from the war on cigarettes, the alcohol lobby is fighting back with the many weapons at its command.

In Louisiana, its chief weapon is George Brown. The executive director of Louisiana's Beer Industry League (and Tapp's boss), Brown is considered by many to be the state's most powerful lobbyist. He has known virtually every Governor in the last 30 years and is on a first-name basis with many state legislators. At the league's office, a red-brick bungalow a few blocks from the Capitol building, Brown and his staff frequently play host at fund-raisers for candidates, with the beer flowing free of charge.

> *"The practices the [alcohol] industry uses to market its products . . . in many ways seem indistinguishable from those of tobacco."*

The influence of Brown and the Beer Industry League generally is apparent in Louisiana's lax alcohol laws. *"Laissez les bon temps rouler"* is the state's informal motto, and with a total of nearly 13,000 places where you can buy alcohol, it's easy to see why the good times keep rolling. Many gas stations sell beer, wine and spirits, allowing you to stock up while filling your tank; some cities and parishes have drive-in daiquiri stands. There is no last call in New Orleans, and for those wanting to carry their drinks onto the street—it is legal to drink in public in the city—bars keep plastic "go cups" on hand.

The day after the task-force meeting, I went to see George Brown. A crusty, balding 74-year-old, he motioned me into a chair across from him. Looking around his office, I saw that its walls were covered with photos of Brown with various state luminaries. When I mentioned the 13-to-1 task-force vote in favor of closing the loophole, he seemed unconcerned. For this was only a recommendation; both the Governor and the Legislature had to act on it for it to become law. "I promise you, there's going to be a good fight on this," Brown said with a twinkle.

To reinforce the point, he handed me a list of upcoming fund-raisers for state legislators, pointing out those the Beer Industry League was supporting. He also alluded to the backing he could expect from restaurateurs, bar owners, casino operators and other members of the state's powerful "hospitality industry." On top of it all, Brown noted, he could count on the help of Anheuser-Busch, the beer giant, which had its own lobbyist in Baton Rouge. "He may know somebody I don't," he observed genially. "That might be good for a vote or two." All in all, Brown did not seem to be a man about to panic.

## Alcohol Is a Public-Health Menace

The growing outcry over tobacco as a public-health menace has raised the inevitable question, Is Booze Next? Smoking is far more lethal than drinking, claiming an estimated 400,000 lives a year to alcohol's 110,000. But most of tobacco's victims are well along in years, while alcohol cuts down many in their primes. About 28,000 die from cirrhosis of the liver; more than 17,000 perish in traffic accidents. Alcohol is a factor in about half of all robberies, homicides and rapes, as it is in many cases of child abuse and wife battering. Fetal alcohol syndrome is the leading preventable cause of birth defects in the Western world. "Binge" drinking, meanwhile, is widely regarded as the single-most-serious problem on college campuses. Overall, some 14 million Americans suffer from alcohol abuse or alcoholism. According to the National Institute on Alcohol Abuse and Alcoholism, alcohol causes "more economic and social damage than any other public-health problem."

It is not simply these glum statistics that spark concern. It is also the practices the industry uses to market its products—practices that in many ways seem indistinguishable from those of tobacco. Where R.J. Reynolds had Joe Camel to tout its products, Anheuser-Busch has had a whole menagerie of lovable animals, including dogs, alligators, frogs and lizards. Like Joe, these characters have high recognition ratings among adolescents. Unlike Joe, they are regularly paraded on prime-time television. Anheuser-Busch was the single-largest advertiser during the [1998] Super Bowl, buying four minutes to show Louie the Lizard's efforts to electrocute the popular frogs. Miller Brewing, meanwhile, ran its own Super Bowl promotion—a contest to select "cheerleaders" to send to the event. Not many cheerleaders are over 21.

## Failed Attempts to Regulate the Alcohol Industry

A few politicians have tried to make an issue of this. William Kennard, the recently appointed chairman of the Federal Communications Commission, has called for a study of liquor advertising on television. Representative Joseph Kennedy Jr. (Democrat of Massachusetts), a longtime industry adversary, has introduced a bill to discourage drinking that, among other things, would restrict the types of ads that could appear on prime-time television. In 1997, Senator Robert Byrd (Democrat of West Virginia) introduced a bill to eliminate the tax deductibility of money spent on alcohol advertising: alcohol, Byrd declared, was tobacco's "evil twin." And in March 1998, President Clinton publicly urged Congress to tighten the nation's laws against drunk driving.

> *"Alcohol has a presence in nearly every state and city."*

For the most part, though, the alcohol lobby has managed to fend off these attacks. Byrd's proposal was defeated 86 to 12, and Kennedy's bill has attracted few co-sponsors. Unlike tobacco, moreover, alcohol has not been hit with many personal-liability suits. And no state has sued the industry to recoup the medical costs incurred by alcohol abuse.

As a drug, of course, alcohol differs from tobacco in several key respects. Unlike cigarettes, which are toxic in any quantity, alcohol can be consumed responsibly—and it is by tens of millions of Americans. There is growing evidence, in fact, that moderate drinking can be beneficial, protecting against coronary disease and other killers. Then, too, alcohol executives have long acknowledged that their products can cause harm, and for years they have sponsored messages encouraging people to "know when to say when"—a far cry from the self-immolating denials of health consequences by tobacco executives.

## The Political Power of Big Alcohol

Such differences alone, however, cannot explain alcohol's invulnerability. An even more important factor is the industry's political power. Simply put, Big Alcohol is richer, savvier and more influential than Big Tobacco. For all its storied clout, tobacco has always been a regional product, cultivated in a handful of Southern states. By contrast, alcohol has a presence in nearly every state and city.

Consider wine. In 1997, the American wine industry racked up sales in the billions, with more than 90 percent of the wine produced by California's vintners; not surprisingly, the state's Congressional delegation is almost uniformly supportive of them. To further push their interests, the nation's vintners underwrite the Wine Institute, a $6.5 million operation with a staff of 26 in San Francisco, satellite offices in seven other cities and lobbyists in more than 40 states. The institute's Washington office is commanded by Robert Koch, a onetime staff director for Representative Richard Gephardt (Democrat of Missouri); Koch also happens to be George Bush's son-in-law.

John DeLuca, the Wine Institute's president, has long studied the travails of the tobacco companies, and he has built a whole strategy around differentiating his product from theirs. Every time a new study comes out showing alcohol's health benefits, he makes hundreds of copies and distributes them to journalists, congressmen and government officials, then follows up with phone calls and invitations to lunch. "We've worked very hard on the dietary, nutritional and lifestyle front," said DeLuca, a cultivated, serious man whose conversation is laced with references to vineyards, Italy and the Mediterranean diet. "People don't look on us as 'booze merchants.'" It was largely because of DeLuca's prodding that for the first time, the most recent U.S. Dietary Guidelines, issued in 1995, mentioned alcohol's benefits to health, a fact the institute never fails to note in its promotional literature.

The distillers, meanwhile, are represented in Washington by the Distilled Spirits Council of the United States, which employs 45 and has a budget of $7.5 million. One of its largest members, Seagram, was the top "soft money" donor to the Democratic Party in 1996, giving a total of $1.2 million; its chairman, Edgar Bronfman Sr., personally donated $160,000 to the party, and his son, Edgar junior, gave $435,000. Seagram was also one of the top 10 soft-money donors to the Republican Party.

## The Beer Lobby

For sheer political might, however, neither wine nor spirits can compare with beer. Beer accounts for nearly 90 percent of all alcohol consumed in the United States, and it runs a political machine to match. The Beer Institute, a lobbying and public relations outfit in Washington, has an annual budget of roughly $2 million; its president, Ray McGrath, is a former congressman from Long Island. Miller Brewing has its own lobbyist in the capital and, when needed, can draw on the formidable resources of its parent, Philip Morris. Coors, meanwhile, has won political influence by financing conservative groups in Washington, including the Heritage Foundation.

> *"Beer accounts for nearly 90 percent of all alcohol consumed in the United States, and it runs a political machine to match."*

Then there's Anheuser-Busch. The world's largest brewer, it controls 45 percent of the American beer market; its flagship, Budweiser, sells nearly as many cases as all Miller brands combined. The company has a payroll of nearly 25,000, annual revenues of $11 billion and brewing plants in 11 states. To defend this far-flung empire, Anheuser-Busch has a lobbyist in every state capital. In Sacramento, it has Dane Starling, a retired Army general who served as Norman Schwarzkopf's right-hand man in the gulf war. In Washington, the company has two full-time lobbyists plus 13 outside agencies ready to help with everything from antitrust matters to public relations. By a happy coincidence of geography, Anheuser-Busch is situated in the Congressional district of Dick Gephardt, the House minority leader, and over the years it has contributed generously to his campaigns.

Anheuser-Busch has also backed the Democratic Party. During the 1992 Presidential campaign, Anheuser-Busch gave $105,000 to the Democratic National Committee. And during Clinton's first term, August Busch 3d, the company's chairman, was an occasional visitor to the White House; among other things, he attended the President's first state dinner, for the Emperor of Japan. In the 1996 election cycle, Anheuser-Busch donated more than $400,000 to the Democratic Party. No wonder the company's trademark Clydesdales were invited to march in the inaugural parade. More important, the Clinton Administration has not proposed a single new tax or advertising restriction on beer or alcohol generally.

## The National Beer Wholesalers Association

No group better exemplifies Big Alcohol's aggressiveness than the National Beer Wholesalers Association (N.B.W.A.), which has recently emerged as one of the Republican Party's biggest backers. The beer wholesalers are the people who deliver beer from the brewery to the retailer. The typical wholesaler owns a warehouse and a fleet of trucks, has three dozen employees and takes in $9.3 million a year. Most are prominent citizens accustomed to speaking their minds. And they are found in every Congressional district, providing a powerful network that can be mobilized at a moment's notice.

The N.B.W.A. is housed in a squat, modern office building in Alexandria, Virginia. Its 24-person staff is directed by Ron Sarasin, a genial, polished, tanned-in-winter ex-congressman from Connecticut and former chief lobbyist for the National Restaurant Association. When Sarasin became president of the wholesalers, in 1990, it was a sleepy organization with little political influence. Just how little became clear a few months after Sarasin took over, when Congress, seeking to reduce the Federal deficit, voted to double the excise tax on beer, to $18 a barrel. It was the first such increase in 40 years, and while it did not begin to make up for inflation over that period, the industry felt it was taking a hit. Intent on boosting the beer wholesalers' presence on Capitol Hill, Sarasin enlisted the services of political lobbyist David Rehr. . . .

He certainly had his work cut out for him. "On a scale of 1 to 10, the N.B.W.A. was at a 3," Rehr recalled. "My job was to take it to 7.5 and eventually to 10." We were talking in a conference room at the association's headquarters, a building whose interior is so spotless that it feels like a museum. With his smooth face, thick brown hair, crisp white shirt and tasseled loafers buffed to a military shine, the 38-year-old Rehr seemed spotless, too. Unlike many lobbyists who shun the limelight, he is expansive about his efforts to promote beer—efforts that, he quickly noted, differed sharply from tobacco's.

> *"The Clinton Administration has not proposed a single new tax or advertising restriction on beer or alcohol generally."*

"The tobacco industry had the attitude of an elephant hiding behind a telephone pole," he said. As an example, he cited Duke University: it was founded with tobacco money, but industry executives, fearing negative publicity, don't mention this. In contrast, Rehr said: "Our view as beer wholesalers is that we're proud of our product—we're going to put the elephant on the street. We have to make sure we remind people that beer is an integral part of our culture."

That philosophy guided Rehr as he set about remaking the N.B.W.A. His first task was to devise a catchy slogan that summed up the work of beer wholesalers. From his time on the Hill, he knew that when meeting members, "you don't have 15 minutes to explain who you are." Batting around ideas with a friend, he eventually hit on "Family Businesses Distributing America's Beverage." The phrase evoked beer's association with baseball, picnics and the Fourth of July, and everything subsequently sent to the Hill would bear it.

Step 2 was increasing the N.B.W.A.'s visibility. An early opportunity came in January 1993. With President Clinton preparing his health-care-reform package, there was talk of financing it in part by another tax hike on alcohol, beer included. Rehr immediately sent out faxes to the association's members, urging them to call the White House and express their opposition. The phone lines were soon jammed, and the proposed increase was quickly dropped. Encouraged, Rehr set up a "blast fax" capacity at his office, enabling him to send out action alerts to N.B.W.A. members, as well as to members of Congress, when urgent issues arise.

## Buying Influence Through Six PAC

To lend weight to those appeals, Rehr moved to expand the N.B.W.A.'s political action committee. Prior to his arrival, Six PAC, as it is informally called, was spending about $430,000 per two-year election cycle. Under Rehr's prodding, that figure quickly jumped to $1.5 million—more than even the A.F.L.-C.I.O. could muster through its PAC. Convinced that the best way to promote the wholesalers' interests was to elect a pro-business Congress, Rehr bestowed most of that money on Republicans. He also made a point of giving to candidates in close races, thus increasing their sense of indebtedness. The N.B.W.A.'s money helped engineer the Republican takeover of the House in 1994, an event that gave the association many powerful friends in Congress.

Those friends have been eager to show their gratitude. Every spring, for instance, the association holds a legislative conference in Washington, bringing in wholesalers and brewers from around the country to lobby on key issues. For the 1997 meeting, more than 800 showed up. They were addressed by a number of congressmen, including Republican leaders as well as Dick Gephardt, who praised Anheuser-Busch and expressed support for

> *"Owing to beer industry pressure . . . Congress passed up a major opportunity to investigate the issue of alcohol ads on television."*

House Resolution 158, an N.B.W.A.-inspired bill to roll back the 1991 beer-tax increase.

When it was first introduced, H.R. 158 was given little chance. But the N.B.W.A. made it a top legislative priority, and at the spring conference, Rehr roused the troops with a stirring description of all the jobs and sales that the earlier hike had cost the industry. Soon after, the wholesalers descended like an angry pack on Congress, seeking out their individual representatives and urging them to support H.R. 158. It now has more than 80 co-sponsors. [As of October 1999, there has been no change in the federal beer excise tax.]

## The Controversy over Liquor Ads on Television

In some cases, Rehr has worked hard to make sure Congress does not act. A good example occurred in 1996, after Seagram, breaking a 48-year-old voluntary ban on hard-liquor television ads, decided to begin running commercials for Crown Royal whisky and other products. With public protest flaring, subcommittees in both the House and Senate scheduled hearings on the issue. Rehr—worried that beer's own right to advertise would be called into question—met

> *"Like tobacco, alcohol imposes enormous costs on society. . . . The question is, Is the industry doing enough to reduce these costs or to compensate society for them?"*

with several Senate staff members to express his concern. "I made the case that we have been responsible in our advertising," he said. "We didn't want the hearing to become a circus. They'd bring in all the 'neo-prohibitionists' and let them go crazy. And they'd bring in the spirits people, who would dump all over us."

With Anheuser-Busch and the Beer Institute also weighing in, the hearings were postponed several times, then dropped altogether. Owing to beer industry pressure, then, Congress passed up a major opportunity to investigate the issue of alcohol ads on television. . . .

## The Anti-Alcohol Lobby Is Far Less Powerful

For most of the last 15 years, George Hacker has run the alcohol-policies project of the Center for Science in the Public Interest, and perhaps more than anyone in Washington, he understands how good Big Alcohol is at what it does. Courteous and soft-spoken, with gray-flecked dark hair, small-frame glasses and a slight build, Hacker in person seems unassuming, but he is the undisputed general of the nation's alcohol-control forces. As Hacker hastens to assert, he is no Carrie Nation; last year, he ordered a case of Champagne to celebrate his 50th birthday. He does, however, believe that alcohol is too readily available at too low a price, and at his office near Dupont Circle he is forever working to change that.

"Like tobacco, alcohol imposes enormous costs on society," Hacker said. "The question is, Is the industry doing enough to reduce these costs or to compensate society for them?" Big Alcohol, he added, "likes to look just at the individual. That's the point of its messages to 'drink responsibly' and 'know when to say when.' But it's not simply a matter of individual responsibility. Because this is an addictive substance. And because it can be purchased 24 hours a day and is sold in colorfully packaged containers that appeal to kids. These are the kinds of things that we're trying to target, much as in the tobacco debate."

Yet as Hacker is the first to admit, alcohol is a far more formidable adversary than tobacco. "Alcohol has been a lot smarter than tobacco," he grudgingly noted. "It's been forced to because of the experience of Prohibition. The industry knows what can happen if it's not careful."

Hacker's struggles are compounded by his lack of resources. He has a staff of just seven and a budget of $500,000. He cannot afford to take anyone to lunch. And his organization has no political action committee to make contributions to members of Congress. As a result, he is constantly being outmaneuvered by the industry. "Everything takes place behind closed doors," he lamented. . . .

## The Legal Battle over Alcohol Continues in Louisiana

In March 1998, the Louisiana legislature is to begin a special session devoted to fiscal matters. The Governor, though, can introduce a few non-fiscal bills of pressing importance. With the memory of Benjamin Wynne still fresh, and his own task force taking such a strong stand, alcohol-control advocates regarded it as foregone that Governor Foster would include the loophole-closing bill in his package. Yet more than two months after the task force's vote, he had yet to make a decision. "We, like any other state—and probably more so, because of the culture here—have problems with alcohol," Foster explained in an interview. "But I've got some major things I need to get done, and since it's a short session, we want to keep controversial things out."

> *"In terms of money, influence and connections, the public-health forces simply can't compete [with the alcohol industry]."*

On March 12, Foster did finally decide to go ahead and introduce the bill. Its prospects in the Legislature remain uncertain, however, and even if the measure does carry, the alcohol-control movement has no other item on its agenda, like tax hikes or advertising restrictions, that would further challenge the industry. For all the new activism in Louisiana, the liquor lobby there remains firmly in command.

The same is generally true elsewhere. The new push by community groups has been met by an equally vigorous counterpush by the industry. And in terms of money, influence and connections, the public-health forces simply can't compete. From Baton Rouge to Washington, Big Alcohol seems unassailable.

## Big Tobacco Once Seemed Invincible, Too

Of course, that's what was once said of Big Tobacco. As recently as [1993], Philip Morris, R.J. Reynolds and the rest of that industry seemed politically invincible. Then came a series of unforeseen developments—the leak of sensitive documents, the emergence of a whistle-blower, the public relations debacle of tobacco executives testifying under oath in Congress and, finally, the election of a President ready to take on the industry—and the walls that Big Tobacco had so carefully erected came tumbling down. Big Alcohol, having so intently studied tobacco's fortunes, knows that it could suffer the same fate. Industry executives, in fact, live in constant dread that some event—a celebrity killed by a drunken driver, say—will ignite a blaze of public indignation that they will not be able to put out.

But David Rehr, George Brown and all the rest are working hard to make sure that their business does not go up in smoke.

# Chapter 5

# How Can Alcohol-Related Problems Be Prevented?

# Chapter Preface

Alcoholism is just one of the many problems associated with alcohol abuse. Approximately 17,000 Americans are killed in alcohol-related automobile accidents each year, and hundreds more die from alcohol poisoning. Alcohol has also been linked to crime, domestic violence, and child abuse. Obviously, public policy experts are always seeking ways to help reduce these alcohol-related problems.

One novel approach was suggested in a 1994 *Newsweek* editorial by writer and chemical-dependency treatment counselor Mike Brake. He believes that individuals should be required to obtain a "license to drink," just as they must do in order to drive or own a gun, and to show these licenses when purchasing alcohol. Individuals would lose their licenses if convicted of an alcohol-related crime, and "from that point on," he says, "attempting to buy or possess alcohol or being found with a detectable blood level of booze would subject them to a misdemeanor charge." "A commonly accepted canon of civilized society," explains Brake, "is that when the public health is threatened, privacy rights must be compromised."

Brake's suggestion can be characterized as restrictive: It seeks to reduce alcohol-related problems by limiting individuals' access to alcohol. High taxes on alcoholic beverages, regulations on what types of stores may sell alcohol, and minimum-age drinking laws also seek to curb alcohol-related problems by reducing alcohol availability.

Advocates of a less restrictive approach believe that limiting people's access to alcohol is unfair and ineffective. In particular, they believe that forbidding young people from drinking is counterproductive. Alcohol-related problems could be reduced, they argue, if people were instead taught to drink responsibly.

In parallel to Brake's concept of drinking permits, Roderic B. Park, a professor at the University of Colorado, believes that young people should be issued "learner's permits" for drinking, so that they can begin to learn to drink responsibly without breaking age-21 laws. "With parental or guardian permission," he says, "a person under the age of 21 might apply for such a 'license' which allowed limited use of beverage alcohol." Park maintains that "the way people become most responsible is by giving them responsibility."

Park's plan is based on a more permissive philosophy, while Brake's is more restrictive—however, this does not mean the two approaches are mutually exclusive. While none have done so, any state could, in theory, issue "learner's permits" to young people while also revoking "drinking licenses" from those who abuse alcohol. And in real life, most state governments use a combination of restrictive and permissive alcohol policies. The authors in the following chapter debate how effective these various approaches are in reducing alcohol-related problems.

# Raising Taxes on Alcoholic Beverages Would Reduce Alcohol-Related Problems

## by Center for Science in the Public Interest

**About the author:** *The Center for Science in the Public Interest is a nonprofit education and advocacy organization that seeks to reduce the damage caused by alcoholic beverages.*

Three main rationales have been advanced to support increases in alcohol excise taxes:
- raising revenue
- reducing alcohol consumption and related problems
- providing funding for key government programs

Historically, the first has attracted more interest, and remains an important factor today, particularly in light of recent federal budget cuts in social programs and growing state needs.

Recently, however, interest in the public health benefits of raising excise taxes has increased. Numerous studies indicate that boosting alcohol taxes can be an effective means of deterring and reducing youth alcohol use, reducing alcohol-related motor vehicle accident mortality and morbidity among young people, improving college completion rates, and ameliorating some of the other problems associated with excessive drinking, including alcohol-related violence and liver cirrhosis.

### Raising Alcohol Taxes Reduces Alcohol Consumption

Research by Michael Grossman and Douglas Coate of the National Bureau of Economic Research, and Gregory Arluck of the New York Telephone Company concluded that even modest price increases—30 cents for a bottle of liquor and 10 cents for a six-pack of beer—would decrease drinking among young people as much as raising the drinking age by one year. Other studies by Coate and

Grossman indicate "that if beer taxes had kept pace with inflation since 1951, and if taxes on beer and spirits had been set at equivalent levels, the number of youths who drink beer four to seven times a week would have declined by 32 percent and the number of youths who drink beer one to three times per week would have declined by 24 percent." A good review of alcohol tax issues in the context of public health appears in *Research Monograph - 25, Economics and the Prevention of Alcohol-Related Problems*, a 1993 publication of the National Institute on Alcohol Abuse and Alcoholism. Although many research questions still need to be addressed, there is little doubt that increasing alcohol taxes and prices will reduce demand and consumption and help reduce the carnage and costs related to drinking.

## The Revenue Generated by Alcohol Taxation . . .

Alcohol taxes most often flow into states' general funds; however, some states have earmarked alcohol tax revenue specifically to combat alcohol problems through treatment, prevention, and law enforcement. Other states earmark part or all of the revenue for programs such as alcohol research, alcoholic-beverage control offices, local governments, state building construction, pension relief, transportation and, ironically, the state grape industry (Arkansas, Ohio, Oregon, Washington).

For example, a 1993 alcohol excise tax increase in New Mexico generates approximately $15 million annually in new revenue. About one-third of this money went toward alcohol prevention and treatment activities at the local level.

> *"Even modest price increases—30 cents for a bottle of liquor and 10 cents for a six-pack of beer—would decrease drinking among young people as much as raising the drinking age by one year."*

Arizona earmarks more than one-third of its liquor tax revenue for the state corrections fund. Approximately the same percentage of Michigan's revenue from liquor taxes goes to convention promotion, with an equal share dedicated to school aid. Idaho, Nevada, New Jersey, Ohio, and Texas are among those states that provide a portion of alcohol revenues for alcohol education and prevention programs.

The revenue collected from all federal, state and local alcoholic beverage sources in 1995 totaled $17 billion. This included excise and other alcohol-specific taxes, import duties, license fees and general state sales taxes.

## . . . Is Less than the Societal Costs of Alcohol Consumption

Based on estimates for previous years, the annual national economic costs of alcohol consumption for 1995 topped $100 billion. These costs were due to loss of productivity, property damage, and medical expenses. States also recognize the economic costs. In a comprehensive report released in October 1995, the state of Minnesota estimated the 1991 economic cost of alcohol-related problems in the state to be $1.74 billion, or nearly $400 for every resident of the state. In contrast, Minnesota's per capita revenue from state alcoholic-beverage collections for that year totaled $12.61 (state collections equaled $55.9 million—$38.6 million from distilled spirits, $14 million from beer, and $3.3 from wine).

Raising alcohol excise taxes would help reduce the vast discrepancy between alcohol-related costs and revenues, while requiring drinkers to contribute more in proportion to the amount they drink.

> *"Most of the money [from increased alcohol taxes] would be raised from heavy drinkers, who consume most of the alcohol and cause or suffer a disproportionate share of alcohol problems."*

If taxes were raised, the 40 percent of Americans who say they abstain from alcoholic beverages would continue to pay no alcohol taxes. Most of the money would be raised from heavy drinkers, who consume most of the alcohol and cause or suffer a disproportionate share of alcohol problems.

In addition, increases in alcohol tax rates often lead to higher prices, which in turn reduce demand and sales. Even a small increase in taxes has been associated with lower consumption and reduced mortality, potentially saving states, employers, and taxpayers millions of dollars. . . .

## Price Elasticity

Almost all analysts agree that a price increase will reduce alcoholic-beverage sales and consumption. Many individuals will drink less frequently; switch to (cheaper) lower-proof liquor, soft drinks and other non-alcoholic beverages; or drink less on each drinking occasion.

Some consumers, of course, will "evade" the price hikes by buying less expensive brands of their favorite drinks and will continue to drink as much as ever. Indeed, the alcoholic-beverage industry has claimed that if prices rise sharply, bootleg beverages might replace a small fraction of legally produced products.

The effect of price on consumption is referred to as "price elasticity." An elasticity of –1.0 means that for every 10 percent increase in price, consumption would decline by 10 percent. Most studies indicate a –0.3 to –0.4 elasticity for beer (meaning that a 10 percent rise in prices would cause a 3 to 4 percent drop in sales), with slightly higher elasticities for wine and liquor.

Elasticities as high as –1.0 or –2.0 seem less likely: Drinking is a deeply ingrained habit, and some 8 million Americans are addicted to alcohol. Consequently, projections in this guide are based on a conservative price-elasticity of –0.35, meaning that a 10 percent rise in price would cause a 3.5 percent drop in sales.

## Predicting the Effects of Higher Alcohol Taxes

Predictions of the effect of reduced consumption on alcohol problems vary widely. Industry claims that higher taxes will deter drinking by moderate consumers, but will fail to discourage drinking by those who abuse alcohol. Thus, alcohol problems will not abate. However, a National Academy of Sciences panel found that light and moderate drinkers—about 90 percent of all drinkers—account for about half of all damage related to alcohol. Therefore, reductions in drinking among this group should also decrease problems. Furthermore, other studies demonstrate a link between state liquor tax increases and reductions in liver cirrhosis mortality. These findings indicate that heavier drinkers are responsive to tax-induced price increases.

Opponents of tax increases argue that higher prices would discourage only light and moderate drinkers from buying, while alcoholics and other heavy drinkers would maintain their consumption. Other experts assert that wealthy people—regardless of how heavily they drink—would maintain their level of consumption, while young and low-income people would decrease their consumption. Still others maintain that the most straightforward assumption is that alcohol problems would decrease in rough proportion to declines in overall consumption.

Past studies on the effects of state alcohol tax increases by Phillip Cook of Duke University reveal that even relatively modest tax hikes were associated with reductions in liver cirrhosis mortality and traffic crash deaths. These findings suggest that even heavy drinkers react to alcohol tax increases by drinking less.

Higher prices may also help delay and reduce drinking among price-sensitive young people. Today's low taxes on beer—the alcoholic beverage of choice among young people—position beer in their price range. For example, a 1995 Labor Day weekend promotion in Northern Virginia grocery stores offered 12-packs of brand-name beer for $3.49, a cost of just $.29 per beer. In many states, aggressive discounting and rebating regularly bring the cost down even lower. In California, with a coupon and rebate, the cost of a 6-pack sometimes falls as low as $.70.

> *"[If alcohol taxes are raised,] many individuals will drink less frequently; switch to (cheaper) lower-proof liquor, soft drinks and other non-alcoholic beverages; or drink less on each drinking occasion."*

Economists have established that even moderate price increases can reduce alcoholic beverage consumption among youth. This would be a welcome step forward, considering that junior and senior high school students drank 35 percent of the wine coolers sold in the United States and 1.1 billion cans of beer in 1991.

## As Alcohol Consumption Declines, So Do Alcohol-Related Problems

Predicting the effect that reduced drinking would have on alcohol problems and costs cannot be done with absolute precision. However, we can reasonably assume that problems would decline, and that specific problems and costs would be affected differently, depending on drinking patterns and the characteristics of population sub-groups. We will assume that alcohol problems would decrease in direct proportion to decreases in alcohol consumption.

# Law Enforcement Strategies Can Help Reduce Underage Drinking

## by Bobby Little and Mike Bishop

**About the authors:** *Bobby Little and Mike Bishop are contributors to* FBI Law Enforcement Bulletin, *in which the following viewpoint was originally published.*

Several sophisticated criminological research projects have confirmed empirically something that law enforcement practitioners have known for a long time: many officers simply do not make teenage alcohol use an enforcement priority. One study surveyed a sample of police personnel and found that many officers rate this type of enforcement activity among the lowest of police responsibilities. A second study revealed that some of the reasons police offered for assigning a low priority to this type of crime included perceived legal obstacles associated with processing juveniles and the unpleasant paperwork and special detention procedures required for minors. Officers also cited such reasons as a lack of juvenile detention facilities or inadequate space inside existing centers, the lack of significant punishment for teen alcohol use, and disagreement with some of the laws regulating underage drinking, especially the illegality of alcohol consumption by adults ages 18 through 20. Although some of these objections represent legitimate concerns, many valid reasons exist for making enforcement of underage alcohol use a higher priority. A factually based rationale for making alcohol violations a priority combined with proven strategies for deterring the illegal purchase, possession, and consumption of alcohol by minors stands the best chance of addressing this growing concern.

## The Factual Rationale

Most adults remember taking their first drink at a young age; for some, getting drunk was a rite of passage. To these individuals, underage drinking is a harmless activity, a victimless crime. Yet, the fact remains: underage drinking

Reprinted from Bobby Little and Mike Bishop, "Minor Drinker/Major Consequences: Enforcement Strategies for Underage Alcoholic Beverage Law Violators," *FBI Law Enforcement Bulletin*, June 1, 1998. (Endnotes in the original have been omitted in this reprint.)

can have devastating consequences and demands serious attention.

*Death and Destruction.* More teens die in alcohol-related motor vehicle crashes than from any other cause. Alcohol use also contributes to a significant proportion of other types of teenage deaths, such as drownings, suicides, and recreational fatalities. Teenage alcoholism is alarmingly high in the United States and is associated with crimes ranging from petty larceny to homicide. The economic losses alone from alcohol-related property damage, lost productivity, and other detrimental consequences associated with alcohol abuse cost society tens of billions of dollars per year.

In addition to the death toll, property damage, and economic losses, tens of thousands of people are injured seriously in alcohol-related mishaps every year. These accidents occur on the job, around the home, and during social activities.

*Adverse Health Effects.* Medical studies have documented the detrimental effects of alcohol on the human liver, stomach, pancreas, and other internal organs. Chronic alcohol abuse can lead to alcoholism, exacerbating the toll on the body. Young female alcoholics put their unborn children at risk for fetal alcohol syndrome.

*Public Demand for Police Attention.* Finally, the public wants the police to address the problem of underage drinking. In many states, legislatures have passed or are considering passing tougher laws associated with both adult drunk driving and alcohol use by minors. Examples include raising the legal drinking age, lowering the blood-alcohol content (BAC) for legally defined levels of intoxication, enacting stiffer penalties for drunk driving, suspending the driver's licenses of youths caught purchasing or possessing alcohol, and prohibiting licensed, juvenile drivers from operating motor vehicles during certain hours, such as midnight to 5 A.M.

In short, the loss of life, property damage, economic costs, and negative health effects associated with underage drinking, as well as public outcry for police attention, provide sufficient reasons to make the illegal use of alcohol by teens a greater concern among police agencies. To do so, law enforcement agencies can employ a number of tactics.

## Investigative Strategies

*Undercover Stings.* About 90 percent of high school students have tried alcohol, and approximately 60 percent of both high school and college students drink regularly. Forty percent of college students regularly "binge-drink," defined as consuming five or more drinks consecutively; 4 percent of students drink every day.

Unfortunately, the ease with which underage drinkers can purchase alcohol represents a national problem. In an effort to combat this problem, many police agencies supplement surveillance activities with sting operations, during which a minor operative attempts to purchase alcohol from various licensed establishments, such as convenience stores, restaurants, and bars.

Agencies need to take precautions prior to such operations. The commander of the agency should interview and assess the suitability of minors prior to approving their use for paid employment or volunteer work. In some states, additional legal guidelines apply. In Alabama, for example, the minor's parent or guardian must sign a consent form and provide the law enforcement agency with a copy of the child's birth certificate, driver's license, and a recent photograph. In addition, agency policies may require that personnel conducting a sting provide a supervisor with a proposed operational plan for approval prior to action. Further, the attempted purchase should be audio- or videotaped, and money used in the operation should be marked and retrieved whenever possible. When the operative is used in an on-premise location, such as a restaurant, lounge, or club, an undercover officer or agent should take a position inside the establishment to observe the potential sale.

> *"The public wants the police to address the problem of underage drinking."*

All law enforcement agencies using minor operatives should consider adopting such guidelines as standard operating procedure. Still, officers should contact the local prosecutor or judicial authority before using an operative. In some states, using minors as operatives may present the potential for legal challenge by the defense counsel or may not be legal at all.

Despite the inherent difficulties in using a minor operative, such sting operations have met with success. When Alabama Alcoholic Beverage Control (ABC) officers initiated this technique, approximately 70 percent of the establishments sold alcohol to the underage operative. Following several years of making cases using this technique, the proportion of establishments selling to minor operatives dropped to about 25 percent.

*Cops 'N Shops.* The Cops 'N Shops program is popular with alcohol merchants in many states, and it produces some deterrent effect on youths trying to purchase alcoholic beverages. The purpose of the program is threefold: to curb the purchase of alcoholic beverages by minors, to assist retail licensees in their efforts to operate their establishments within legal guidelines, and to lower the number of minors who drink and drive. Cops 'N Shops differs from undercover stings in that it focuses on the violator, rather than the alcoholic beverage retail industry. Individuals of legal drinking age who purchase alcohol to sell or give to minors represent a secondary target for this type of operation.

Traditionally, an agent or officer poses as an employee or a customer in a retail establishment, waiting to arrest any minor attempting to purchase alcohol. Sometimes, illegal transactions take place in the parking lot between individuals who legally purchase the alcohol to give to minors waiting outside. Placing a backup officer outside nets these offenders.

Attempts to deter unlawful buyers include special signs to scare those contemplating the offense. These Cops 'N Shops signs, placed at all entrances, notify everyone entering the store that agents may pose as employees and warn that any person violating the law will be prosecuted. Though retailers are sometimes reluctant to participate in the program, Cops 'N Shops has become a viable enforcement strategy in many states.

*Party Patrols.* Another enforcement strategy involves the use of party patrols. These patrols appear to be the easiest way to make a large number of arrests for underage drinking. Typically, informants at local high schools and universities tip off law enforcement to underage drinkers planning a party. Undercover operatives can attend such gatherings, or officers acting alone can surveil the location and make arrests. A weekend drunk driving and party patrol program in Oregon increased the arrest of minors for possession from 60 to 1,000 in 1 year. There also was a corresponding decrease of 35 percent in underage and young adult automobile crashes. When not hunting teenage parties and citing underage drinkers, the officers operated sobriety checkpoints and conducted drunk driving enforcement patrols.

*Walk-throughs.* The walk-through is a method of observing activity inside alcoholic beverage retail outlets such as bars and restaurants. Officers may enter such public places either covertly, in plain clothes, or overtly, in uniform. The obvious advantage of covert entry is that it lets the officer observe alcohol violations without evoking the suspicion of customers or employees. This technique enables officers to spot violations by customers, including attempts to illegally purchase or consume alcoholic beverages or to provide alcohol to underage drinkers. Walk-throughs also allow officers to scrutinize bartenders and other employees who may be serving underage patrons.

In Alabama, the alcoholic beverage industry is considered heavily regulated, and as a result, law enforcement officers with proper jurisdiction may conduct administrative searches or inspections of licensed premises without search warrants. The law in other states may not condone an intensive search without a warrant, but it may allow a walk-through to look for violations. Officers should check with their local prosecutors before employing these techniques.

> *"Oregon increased the arrest of minors for possession from 60 to 1,000 in 1 year. There was also a corresponding decrease of 35 percent in underage and young adult automobile crashes."*

*Legislative Action.* Certain legislative and policy actions may effectively deter teenage alcohol use and reduce the number of alcohol-related crashes among young drivers. Many states have lowered the legally acceptable levels of blood-alcohol content for drivers under 21. In Alabama, for example, a youth under age 21 caught operating a motor vehicle with .02 BAC or above is charged with driving under the influence. Two other legislative proposals include laws prohibiting driving by young, novice drivers between certain times, especially midnight to 5 A.M., and a 90-day license suspension for youths convicted of possessing alcoholic beverages or using a false driver's license to purchase alcohol.

## A Problem That Demands Action

Simply put, underage drinking is against the law. Yet, in a culture that views alcohol consumption as a part of growing up, even those tasked with enforcing the law may overlook violations. The many consequences of irresponsible drinking, by youths and adults alike, demand action.

During a time of increasing attention to other drugs of abuse, such as marijuana and cocaine, police administrators who must operate with limited financial resources may have difficulty allocating the necessary staff to combat the underage drinking problem. Yet, with help from policy makers, retailers, and the public, agencies can implement innovative enforcement strategies to curb underage drinking.

# The Government Should Lower the Legal Threshold for Drunk Driving

## by the National Highway Traffic Safety Administration

**About the author:** *Part of the federal Department of Transportation, the National Highway Traffic Safety Administration is charged with developing regulations and programs that reduce the deaths, injuries, and economic losses resulting from motor vehicle crashes.*

On March 3, 1998, more than 150 representatives of national organizations and highway safety partners convened at the White House to witness President Clinton address the nation on setting new standards to prevent impaired driving. The President encouraged all Americans to do more to prevent the many tragic and unnecessary alcohol-related deaths and injuries that occur on our nation's roads. The President called for the promotion of a national legal limit, under which it would be illegal *per se* to operate a motor vehicle with a blood alcohol content (BAC) of .08 or higher, across the country, including on federal property. . . .

## Drunk Driving Kills Thousands Each Year

Impaired driving is the most frequently committed violent crime in America. Every 30 minutes, someone in this country dies in an alcohol-related crash. In the time it takes you to read through this plan, someone else will die needlessly and violently on a street or highway.

For many years, we have made good progress. Due to the tireless efforts of many organizations and citizens around the country, alcohol-related traffic deaths have decreased significantly. In the last decade, alcohol-related fatalities dropped from 24,050 in 1986 to 16,189 in 1997, according to the National Highway Traffic Safety Administration (NHTSA). This 32% drop in alcohol-related deaths is generally attributed to: 1) stronger laws; 2) tougher enforcement and adjudication; and 3) more effective public education.

Excerpted from the National Highway Traffic Safety Administration publication "Presidential Initiative for Making .08 BAC the National Legal Limit" (1998), published at www.nhtsa.dot.gov/people/injury/alcohol/limit.08/PresInit/index.html.

Americans understand the impaired driving problem, societal norms have changed, fewer people are driving after drinking, and more are getting caught when they do. And equally important, Americans support the enforcement of these laws and swift and fair sentencing for offenders.

Unfortunately, significant reductions must be reached to achieve the year 2005 goal of reducing alcohol-related fatalities to 11,000. Fatalities in alcohol-related crashes rose by 4% from 1994 to 1995, the first increase in a decade. In 1997, 38.6% of the 42,065 motor vehicle crash deaths were attributed to alcohol use. . . .

Alcohol is the single greatest factor in motor vehicle deaths and injuries, and it's a deadly involvement. Only 4% of all crashes involve the use of alcohol, but 39% of fatal crashes do. With 16,189 deaths in one year, there are thousands too many grieving families. In addition to these tragic deaths, one million people are injured in alcohol-related traffic crashes annually. . . .

## Measuring Impairment

The amount of alcohol in a person's body is measured by the weight of the alcohol in a certain volume of blood. This is called the blood alcohol concentration or BAC. BAC measurements provide an objective way to identify levels of impairment, because alcohol concentration in the body is directly related to impairment.

The BAC measurement is expressed as grams per deciliter (g/dl) of blood, and in most states a person is considered legally intoxicated if his or her BAC is .10 g/dl or greater. Breath testing is the primary method used by law enforcement agencies for measuring BACs. At the time of the first face-to-face contact with a suspected impaired driver, techniques for detecting whether alcohol is present or absent can be performed easily by law enforcement officers during roadside stops using hand-held passive alcohol sensors. Use of these devices is non-invasive and can even be performed while the person is still in his or her vehicle. . . .

## The Effect of Alcohol on Driving Ability

With each drink consumed, a person's blood alcohol concentration increases. Although outward appearances vary, virtually all drivers are substantially impaired at .08 BAC. Laboratory and on-road research shows that the vast majority of drivers, even experienced drivers, are significantly impaired at .08 with regard to critical driving tasks such as braking, steering, lane changing, judgment and divided attention. Decrements in performance for drivers at .08 BAC are on the order of 40–60% worse than when they are at .00 BAC. Research findings suggest that the most crucial aspect of impairment is the reduction in the ability to handle several tasks at once. This skill is precisely what driving a motor vehicle requires.

The risk of being in a motor vehicle crash also increases as the BAC level rises. The risk of being in a crash rises gradually with each BAC level, but then rises very rapidly after a driver reaches or exceeds .08 BAC compared to drivers with no alcohol in their system. Research by the Insurance Institute for Highway Safety indicates that the relative risk of being killed in a single vehicle crash for drivers at BACs between .05 and .09 is 11 times that of drivers with no alcohol in their system.

## The Science Behind the Case for .08

Setting the BAC limit at .08 is a reasonable response to the problem of impaired driving. The effect of California's .08 law was analyzed by NHTSA. The agency found that 81% of the driving population knew that the BAC limit was stricter (from a successful public education effort). The state experienced a 12% reduction in alcohol-related fatalities, although some of this can be credited to the new administrative license revocation law, which was enacted during the year that the BAC standard was lowered. The state also experienced an increase in driving under the influence (DUI) arrests.

A multi-state analysis of the effect of lowering BAC levels to .08 was conducted by Boston University's School of Public Health. The results of that study were reported in the September 1996 issue of the *American Journal of Public Health*, a peer-reviewed journal.

The Boston University study compared the first five states to lower their BAC limit to .08 (California, Maine, Oregon, Utah, and Vermont) with five nearby states that retained the .10 limit. The results of this study suggest .08 laws, particularly in combination with administrative license revocation, reduce the proportion of fatal crashes involving drivers and fatally injured drivers at blood alcohol levels of .08 and higher by 16% and those at BAC of .15 and greater by 18%.

*"Impaired driving is the most frequently committed violent crime in America."*

The immediate significance of these findings is that, not only did the .08 BAC laws, particularly in combination with administrative license revocation, reduce the overall incidence of alcohol fatalities, but they also reduced fatalities at the higher BAC levels. The effect on the number of extremely impaired drivers was even greater than the overall effect.

The study concluded that if all states lowered their BAC limits to .08, alcohol-related highway deaths would decrease by 500–600 per year which would result in an economic cost savings of about $1.5 billion. Reducing deaths by 500 each year to the year 2005 would result in a decrease in alcohol-related fatalities to about 13,200, just by passing .08 laws. . . .

All of the published studies so far on the effects of .08 show significant decreases in alcohol-related fatalities using various measures. The public supports a .08 BAC level. NHTSA surveys all show that most people would not drive after consuming two or three drinks in an hour. Three recent scientific telephone polls indicate that 2 out of every 3 Americans think the BAC standard should be lowered to .08.

Most other industrialized nations have set BAC limits at .08 or lower and have had these laws in place for many years. For example, Canada, Great Britain, Austria, Germany, New Zealand, and Switzerland each have adopted a legal limit of .08 BAC. All of the states in Australia have a limit of .05 BAC, along with countries such as France and Belgium. Sweden set its limit at .02 BAC. The European Union is urging all of its 18 member countries to adopt a uniform .05 BAC limit. . . .

## Responding to the Critics of .08 Laws

Question: *Doesn't a .08 law target "social drinkers" instead of the high-BAC alcohol abuser?*

Answer: .08 is not social drinking. It takes quite a bit of alcohol for one to reach a .08 BAC—over 4 cans of beer consumed in one hour on an empty stomach for a typical 170 lb male; 3 beers for a 137 lb female.

Studies also show that .08 BAC laws affect all drinking drivers, both those who reach very high BACs (.15 BAC or greater) and those who reach lower BACs.

*Under a .08 law, wouldn't a 120 lb woman who has two glasses of wine in a two hour period reach .08 BAC and be subject to arrest, fines, jail, higher insurance rates and license revocation if pulled over at a "sobriety checkpoint?"*

It is possible, but not probable. The two glasses of wine referred to would be 6 oz of wine with 13% alcohol. This is equivalent to almost three cans of regular beer with 5% alcohol. This would be on an empty stomach. If this woman is eating or has food in her stomach, it would take more drinks to reach .08 BAC. But, no matter how many drinks it takes to reach .08 BAC, everyone is impaired with regard to critical driving tasks at this level—even experienced drinkers. These include braking, steering, lane changing, judgment and divided attention.

*Won't a .08 BAC law diminish efforts to deal with the real problem—the hard core drinking drivers with very high BACs?*

> *"The vast majority of drivers, even experienced drivers, are significantly impaired at .08 [BAC] with regard to critical driving tasks."*

While .08 BAC laws result in a slight increase in DWI arrests, there is no evidence that .08 BAC laws overburden the police or clog up the courts with driving while intoxicated (DWI) cases.

NHTSA continues to attack the impaired driving problem from all angles. A .08 BAC law is just one of many laws and programs that NHTSA is encouraging states to adopt.

Other legislation that NHTSA promotes include zero tolerance (.02 BAC) laws for drivers under age 21, administrative license revocation laws to ensure swift punishment for DWI, graduated licensing programs for new drivers, and various vehicle sanctions for repeat DWI offenders.

In the area of enforcement, NHTSA promotes the use of sobriety checkpoints and saturation patrols to catch impaired drivers, training for police on standardized field sobriety testing, and increased enforcement of underage drinking and driving.

NHTSA also encourages responsible alcohol service programs, which have the potential of preventing intoxicated patrons from driving.

NHTSA spends substantial time and energy promoting all of the above.

*Instead of lowering the illegal BAC limit from .10 BAC to .08 BAC, why not adopt more severe sanctions for drivers with high BAC levels (e.g. those at .15 or .20 and higher)? These are the majority of drinking drivers arrested and involved in fatal crashes.*

Some states, such as Florida, use both systems. Florida lowered its per se BAC limit to .08 on January 1, 1994. For many years, Florida has had mandatory minimum jail sentences and fines for drivers convicted of DWI at BAC = .15 or greater. These "mandatory minimums" do not apply to drivers under .15 BAC. Both laws are rational and make sense.

> *"If all states lowered their BAC limits to .08, alcohol-related highway deaths would decrease by 500–600 per year."*

It should not be "one or the other," but can be both. There is evidence that a .08 standard reduces alcohol-related fatalities and affects drivers at all BAC levels. It also appears that various vehicle sanctions (immobilization, impoundment, forfeiture) may be effective on the alcohol abusing repeat DWI offenders.

*Isn't .08 BAC just the first step in a process to lower the illegal limit even further?*

NHTSA believes that a .08 limit is practical, rational and acceptable to the public. Until there is substantial new evidence, NHTSA has no plans to recommend limits lower than .08 for adults, except for commercial drivers (where the national standard is already .04) and for drivers under age 21 where NHTSA recommends zero tolerance (.02 or lower).

# Restrictive Alcohol Policies Are Ineffective

## by David J. Hanson

**About the author:** *David J. Hanson is a professor of sociology at the State University of New York at Potsdam and the author of* Alcohol Education *and* Preventing Alcohol Abuse.

*What can we do to reduce alcohol abuse?*

People have different ideas about what kind of laws and policies might reduce alcohol abuse. The prohibitionists said we should eliminate all alcohol beverages, but that didn't—and won't—work. Prohibition actually leads to even more problems, such as the growth of organized crime, increased disrespect for law, unregulated and dangerous beverages, increased violence, the loss of tax revenue, corruption of law enforcement and other public officials, increases in binge drinking, and many other serious problems.

## The Prohibitionist Approach

*What do today's prohibitionists believe?*

Because of the clear failure of prohibition, today's prohibitionists and other reduction-of-consumption advocates now typically call for a variety of laws and other measures to reduce rather than completely prohibit consumption. They tend to believe that:

- The substance of alcohol is, in and of itself, the cause of all drinking problems.
- The availability of alcohol determines the extent to which it will be consumed; availability causes people to drink more.
- The quantity of alcohol consumed (rather than the speed with which it is consumed, the purpose for which it is consumed, the social environment in which it is consumed, etc.) determines the extent of drinking problems.
- Educational efforts should stress the problems that alcohol consumption can cause and should promote abstinence.

*What do they advocate?*

These beliefs lead reduction-of-consumptionists (often called neo-

Reprinted from David J. Hanson, "Alcohol Law and Policy," published at www2.potsdam.edu/alcohol-info, by permission of the author.

prohibitionists, neo-drys, or neo-Victorians) to call for such measures as:
- Increasing taxes on alcohol beverages
- Limiting or reducing the number of sales outlets
- Limiting the alcohol content of drinks
- Prohibiting or limiting advertising
- Requiring warning messages with all advertisements
- Expanding the warning labels on all alcohol beverage containers
- Expanding the display of warning signs in establishments that sell or serve alcohol beverages
- Limiting the days or hours during which alcohol beverages can be sold
- Increasing server liability for subsequent problems associated with consumption
- Limiting the sale of alcohol beverages to people of specific ages
- Decreasing the legal blood alcohol content level for driving vehicles
- Eliminating the tax deductibility of alcohol beverages as a business expense

## Research Does Not Support Reduction-of-Consumption Policies

*What's the evidence?*

Many reduction-of-consumption policies and proposals are currently very popular, but what does research tell us?

*Limiting or prohibiting advertising of alcohol beverages.* This is one of the most extensively studied issues and the evidence regarding it is very clear: There is virtually no evidence that advertising has any significant impact on consumption levels. More importantly, it has "no impact on either experimentation with alcohol or abuse of it," according to a recent definitive review of worldwide evidence [by researcher Joseph C. Fisher] and supported by other reviews of the research. On the other hand, there is evidence that advertising can increase a brand's market share, a finding consistent with the experience and actions of advertisers.

*Increasing taxes on alcohol beverages.* Wouldn't increasing the cost of alcohol beverages reduce the consumption and, thereby, their abuse? This reasonable question is based on two assumptions: (1) that higher alcohol prices will reduce demand and (2) that reducing consumption will reduce abuse.

The evidence suggests that rapid price increases tend to have a temporary effect on reducing the purchase of alcohol, primarily among moderate drinkers. But, price is only one of numerous factors affecting the consumption of alcohol beverages. For example, problem drinkers tend not to let cost deter them while a third of the population wouldn't drink if alcohol beverages were free. Other research evidence indicates that overall consumption levels in a population are not related to abuse. This fact is relevant to the following proposals.

*Limiting or reducing the number of sales outlets and limiting the days or hours during which alcohol beverages can be sold.* Numerous studies, including analyses of behavior following actual changes in state and provincial laws, fail to find any evidence supporting these proposals. In fact, some investigators have found that the tougher the controls over availability, the greater the alcohol abuse. For example, where taverns and other on-premise outlets are fewer and more geographically dispersed, the incidence of driving while intoxicated tends to be higher. Others have found that lower availability is associated with less frequent but very heavy drinking and other problems.

> *"[Prohibitionists tend to believe that] the substance of alcohol is, in and of itself, the cause of all drinking problems."*

The experience of New Zealand is instructive. Since deregulation of the industry in 1989, the number of alcohol sales outlets has more than doubled, but the overall alcohol consumption continues to fall. There is no connection between increased availability and increased alcohol consumption.

The evidence from studies around the world suggests that neither limiting the number of outlets nor the days/hours of sale would be effective in reducing alcohol problems. To the contrary, it might increase problems or create new ones. For example, Australian laws closing bars at six o'clock got the working men out of the establishments and possibly home to their families in time for dinner. However, they also produced the undesirable custom known as the six o'clock swill, which involves consuming as much alcohol as possible between the end of work and the six o'clock closing time.

Similarly, restricting the availability of alcohol can increase serious harm to some drinkers. For example, when restrictions were placed on the hours during which alcohol beverages could be sold in some urban areas, the consumption of such hazardous, often lethal, substances as rubbing alcohol and sterno fuel increased. Following this tragic discovery, restrictions were lifted and hours were extended in order to decrease consumption of toxic forms of alcohol.

## More Harm than Good

*Requiring warning messages with all advertisements, expanding the warning labels on all alcohol beverage containers, and expanding the display of warning signs in establishments that sell or serve alcohol beverages.* Studies specifically of alcohol beverage container warnings have demonstrated that they have virtually no impact on drinking behavior, and absolutely none on drinking problems. This is consistent with a review of 400 studies on the effectiveness of product warnings, which concluded that they have no impact on behavior.

Studies reporting awareness of warnings are highly suspect. For example, thirty-one percent of a large sample of women reported seeing the warning label in June of 1989, which was five months before it appeared on beverage containers. And those who are most at risk of alcohol abuse appear to be the ones who are most strongly resistant to warnings.

Warning labels on advertising may actually be counterproductive, doing more harm than good. Some researchers have found that drinkers appear to consume more after viewing warning labels in a form of defiance or unconscious effort to assert their freedom and autonomy by doing what they are, in essence, told not to do. The "forbidden fruit" phenomenon has been extensively documented with regard to alcohol and other products.

*Limiting the sale of alcohol beverages to people of specific ages.* Legislation that is intended to prohibit drinking customs that are embedded in a group risks failure, as did national prohibition in countries around the world, such as Iceland, Russia, Finland, and the United States.

Not surprisingly, age-specific prohibition appears to be ineffective in reducing either the proportion of drinkers or their drinking problems. [According to researcher James F. Mosher,] "Statistics show that underaged persons increased their use of alcohol steadily from the 1930s to the 1960s, when legislation to curtail sales was most active." Then, following the reduction of the drinking age in the 1970s, the proportion of collegians who drank trended downward. *In short, legislation has little impact on the drinking behaviors of young people.*

Unfortunately, minimum age legislation sometimes backfires. For example, as one student observed [in a survey in the *International Journal of Addictions*], it "might be easier to hide a little pot in my room than a six pack of beer." Perhaps more importantly, higher minimum age legislation tends to force young people to drink "underground," in unsupervised locations in which they learn undesirable alcohol attitudes and behaviors. And it may lead them to drink or to drink more: the forbidden fruit. This is important because problem drinkers appear to begin their drinking at a later age than others, to have their first drinking experience outside the home, to become intoxicated the first time they drink, and to drink as an act of rebellion (open or secret) against authority.

> *"Lower [alcohol] availability is associated with less frequent but very heavy drinking."*

*Increased server liability for subsequent problems associated with consumption.* Does making a public or private server of alcohol financially responsible for damage caused by serving alcohol to an intoxicated person lead to more responsible serving practices?

This question has been virtually ignored by investigators. However, one study [by Alexander C. Wagenaar and Harold D. Holder] examined the effects of two server liability cases in Texas during the 1980s. Before the lawsuits, Texans had very little liability for the consequences of their alcohol serving practices. The study found that after these two highly publicized and very controversial cases, single-vehicle nighttime crashes in Texas declined 6.5% in 1983 and 5.3% in 1994. The researchers may be correct in assuming that these declines were due to the effects of the dramatic and sudden change in the law rather than any other factors. Additional research is needed to determine if increasing server liability is effective in reducing alcohol abuse, especially in the long term.

*Decreasing the legal blood alcohol content level for driving vehicles.* The effects of lowering the legal blood alcohol content (BAC) for drivers are unclear. However, the average BAC among fatally injured drivers is .17 and about half have a BAC of .20 or higher (which is twice the legal limit in most states). Thus, the problem is primarily among very heavy drinkers, who tend to be male, aged 25–35, have a history of driving while intoxicated (DWI) convictions, and be polydrug users.

Automatic license revocation may be the single most effective measure to reduce drunk driving. But the problem is not simple and it resists simplistic solutions. . . .

## The Misleading "Gateway Theory"

*What's the "Gateway Theory"?*

Advocates of the reduction-of-consumption theory commonly promote the idea that alcohol is a "gateway" substance that leads people to use marijuana, which supposedly leads them on to use cocaine and other hard drugs. The New York State Division of Alcoholism and Alcohol Abuse presents this questionable theory as established fact by titling one of its publications *Alcohol: The Gateway Drug*. The "evidence" is that most people who use illegal drugs drank alcohol first. Of course, most people who use illicit drugs also drank milk, ate candy bars, and drank cola first. But only a very few of those who consume alcohol ever continue on to use cocaine or heroin. On the other hand, about a quarter of hard core drug abusers in New York City have never consumed alcohol. The theory is clearly wrong, but that doesn't stop it from being promoted as truth and as a basis for the public policy of zero tolerance for youthful alcohol use.

Recent research casts further doubt on the gateway theory. Following their examination of the scientific evidence, researchers Stanton Peele and Archie Brodsky point out that the best predictors of abusive substance use are social, family, and psychological depredations that occur independent of supposed gateway linkages.

> *"Both research and common sense tell that the young people least likely to drink disruptively are those who are introduced to alcohol by moderate-drinking parents, rather than being initiated into drinking by their peers."*

Rather than promoting the misleading gateway theory, they suggest that "What makes far more sense is to acknowledge the obvious to children—that there is healthy and unhealthy drinking," and explain that "both research and common sense tell that the young people least likely to drink disruptively are those who are introduced to alcohol by moderate-drinking parents, rather than being initiated into drinking by their peers." The researchers explain that an exaggerated focus on alcohol as a supposed gateway to illegal drugs ignores the reality of responsible, moderate consumption and re-directs attention from effective measures to reduce alcohol abuse. The impact of the theory is, therefore, negative.

It appears that risk-takers may be more likely to skip school, to drink at an early age, to drive too fast, to engage in unprotected sex, and to use illegal drugs. In that case, preventing people from engaging in the "gateway" behavior of drinking, or skipping school, or driving too fast will not prevent a risk-taker from taking drugs. Any policy based on the "gateway" theory can be expected to fail.

## There Is a Better Way

Based on the experience of societies around the world, advocates of the moderation approach to reducing alcohol problems tend to assume that:
• The misuse of alcohol, not alcohol itself, is the source of drinking problems.
• It is important to distinguish between drinking and abuse.
• Abuse can be reduced by educating people to make one of two decisions—abstinence or responsible (moderate) drinking.
• Knowledge of what is acceptable and unacceptable drinking behavior should be clear.
• The abuse of alcohol should not be tolerated under any circumstance.
• People who are going to drink as adults should gradually learn how to drink responsibly and in moderation.

Because of this, most moderationists propose that we:
• Abandon the current negative reduction-of-consumption attack upon alcohol and moderate drinking. There is much evidence that this negative approach to alcohol is based on questionable assumptions, that its policies fail to achieve their objectives, and that its policies may be counterproductive.
• Stop stigmatizing alcohol as a "dirty drug," as a poison, as inherently harmful, or a substance to be abhorred and shunned. Alcohol is neither a poison nor a magic elixir capable of solving life's problems.

Stigmatizing alcohol serves no practical purpose, contributes to undesirable emotionalism and ambivalence, and increases the problems it seeks to solve. In stigmatizing alcohol, reductionists may unintentionally trivialize the use of illegal drugs and thereby encourage their use. Or, especially among younger students, they create the false impression that parents who use alcohol in moderation are drug abusers whose good example they should reject. Thus, their misguided effort to equate alcohol use with illicit drugs is likely to be counterproductive.

> *"Stigmatizing alcohol serves no practical purpose . . . and increases the problems it seeks to solve."*

• Begin new policies that place the alternative of responsible (moderate) drinking on an equal level to the alternative of abstinence. Federal and state agencies should not unfairly promote one of these alternatives over the other; both are equally acceptable.

• Make systematic efforts to clarify and promote the distinctions between acceptable and unacceptable drinking. [As researcher Thomas F. Plaut explains,] "The absurdity of defining only 'bad' drinking is analogous to teaching a youngster how to drive only by pointing out what not to do. . . ."

• Firmly penalize unacceptable drinking behaviors, both legally and socially. Intoxication must never be accepted as an excuse for otherwise unacceptable behavior. While the criminal justice system has an important role to play, the most important role must be played by individual peers—friends, relatives, loved ones, co-workers, and other significant others—who assume personal responsibility.

• Permit parents to serve alcohol to their offspring of any age, not only in the home, but in restaurants, parks and other locations, under their direct supervision. If parents wish their children to abstain as adults, they need to serve as appropriate role models and teach them the attitudes and skills they will need in a predominately drinking society. However, if they wish their children to drink in moderation as adults, then they, too, need to serve as appropriate role models and teach their children pertinent attitudes and skills for drinking in moderation.

> *"Research clearly does not support the theory that restrictive legislation is the answer to solving the problem of alcohol abuse."*

• Promote educational efforts to encourage moderate use of alcohol among those who choose to drink. Moderate drinking and abstinence should be presented as equally acceptable or appropriate choices. Those who choose to drink should not force drinking upon abstainers and those who choose not to drink should have comparable respect for those who do.

## Restrictive Legislation Is Not the Answer

Research clearly does not support the theory that restrictive legislation is the answer to solving the problem of alcohol abuse.

Alcohol problems will be reduced primarily to the extent that we, as individuals, take personal responsibility for our own drinking. They will also be reduced further to the degree that we effectively promote either moderation or abstinence among those with whom we interact.

# Age-21 Drinking Laws Exacerbate Alcohol-Related Problems

by **Ruth Engs**

**About the author:** *Ruth Engs is a professor of Applied Health Sciences at Indiana University and the author of the books* Alcohol and Other Drugs: Self Responsibility *and* Controversies in the Addiction Field.

As the University of Vermont and other universities work to address student alcohol abuse, one of the greatest hindrances they face is the fact that the legal drinking age is set at twenty-one, an age most college students won't reach until their junior or senior years.

This perspective is built upon more than two decades studying college student drinking patterns and the history of alcohol use in this country and other cultures. My research has led me to believe strongly that perhaps the simplest and most dramatic action we could take to create more responsible alcohol consumption among college students would be to lower the legal drinking age to eighteen or nineteen. Young adults could be allowed to drink in controlled environments such as restaurants, taverns, pubs and official school and university functions. In these situations—where mature and sensible drinking would be expected—responsible alcohol consumption could be taught through role modeling and educational programs.

## Alcohol Prohibition Does Not Work

Although the legal purchase age is twenty-one years, a majority of college students under this age consume alcohol—certainly not a surprise to anyone. When they have the opportunity to drink, they do so in an irresponsible manner because drinking by these youth is seen as an enticing "forbidden fruit," a "badge of rebellion against authority" and a symbol of "adulthood." As a nation we have tried prohibition legislation twice in the past for controlling irre-

Reprinted from Ruth Engs, "Forbidden Fruit," *Vermont Quarterly*, Winter 1999, by permission of the author. (The interested reader is directed to Prof. Engs's website for further information and for sources used in this article: www.indiana.edu/~engs.)

sponsible drinking problems, during National Prohibition in the 1920s and state prohibition during the 1850s. Because they were unenforceable and because the backlash towards them caused other social problems, these laws were finally repealed.

Prohibition did not work then and prohibition for young people under the age of twenty-one is not working now.

The flaunting of the current laws is readily seen among our nation's university students. Those under the age of twenty-one are more likely to be heavy—sometimes called "binge"—drinkers (consuming more than five drinks at least once a week). For example, 22% of all students under twenty-one compared to 18% over twenty-one years of age are heavy drinkers. Among drinkers only, 32% of under age compared to 24% of legal age are heavy drinkers.

Research from the early 1980s until the present has shown a continuous decrease in drinking and driving related variables which has paralleled the nation's, and also university students', decrease in per capita consumption. However, these declines started in 1980 before the national 1987 law which mandated states to set the legal purchase age at twenty-one.

The decrease in drinking and driving problems are the result of many factors and not just the rise in purchase age or the decreased per capita consumption. These include: education concerning drunk driving, designated driver programs, increased seat belt and air bag usage, safer automobiles, lower speed limits, free taxi services from drinking establishments, etc.

> *"The simplest and most dramatic action we could take to create more responsible alcohol consumption among college students would be to lower the legal drinking age to eighteen or nineteen."*

While there has been a decrease in per capita consumption and motor vehicle crashes, unfortunately, during this same time period there has been an increase in other problems related to heavy and irresponsible drinking among college age youth. Most of these reported behaviors showed little change until after the legal age was mandated at twenty-one in 1987. For example, from 1982 until 1987 about 46% of students reported "vomiting after drinking." This jumped to over 50% after the law change.

Significant increases were also found for other variables: "cutting class after drinking" jumped from 9% to almost 12%; "missing class because of hangover" went from 26% to 28%; "getting lower grades because of drinking" rose from 5% to 7%; and "been in a fight after drinking" increased from 12% to 17%.

This increase in abusive drinking behavior is due to "underground drinking" outside of adult supervision in student rooms and apartments where same-age individuals come together in the 1990s collegiate reincarnation of the speakeasy.

*Chapter 5*

## Normalizing Drinking but Not Drunkenness

Based upon the fact that our current prohibition laws are not working, alternative approaches taken from the experience of cultures who do not have these problems need to be tried. In Europe, two different drinking cultures developed in antiquity. In the Mediterranean regions, wine consumption with meals by all members of the culture evolved, along with a norm of moderation. In the more northern and eastern regions of Europe, drinking to intoxication of grain-based beverages at feasts emerged, along with ambivalence towards alcohol.

Groups such as Italians, Greeks, Chinese, and Jews, who have few drinking related problems, tend to share some common characteristics. Alcohol is neither seen as a poison or a magic potent, there is little or no social pressure to drink, irresponsible behavior is never tolerated, young people learn at home from their parents and from other adults how to handle alcohol in a responsible manner, and there is societal consensus on what constitutes responsible drinking.

We can learn from this. Because the twenty-one-year-old drinking age law is not working, and is counterproductive, it behooves us as a nation to change our current prohibition law and to teach responsible drinking techniques for those who choose to consume alcoholic beverages.

# The Government Should Not Lower the Legal Threshold for Drunk Driving

## by Richard Berman

**About the author:** *Richard Berman is general counsel of the American Beverage Institute, an association of restaurant operators that serve alcohol.*

Say you and your neighbors are fed up with a few speeders who continue to race through your neighborhood. While most drivers obey the posted 25 mph speed limit, a couple of reckless fools consistently drive 50 mph or more, especially on weekend nights. Two solutions are proposed at the next neighborhood meeting: Either demand better police enforcement of the posted limit or drop the limit from 25 mph to 20 mph. Which would you choose?

## A Misguided Approach

That is the essence of the traffic-safety debate now being played out in Congress about the drunk-driving problem. In an effort to reduce drunk-driving deaths, two Democrats, Rep. Nita Lowey of New York and Sen. Frank Lautenberg of New Jersey, proposed redefining the problem to include responsible social drinking—the legislative equivalent of dropping the speed limit to catch people who ignore current limits.

With the backing of Mothers Against Drunk Driving, or MADD, the lawmakers want to lower the blood-alcohol content, or BAC, limit from .10 percent BAC to .08 percent BAC. If they succeed, a 120-pound woman will be considered legally drunk if she drinks two 6-ounce glasses of wine during a two-hour period, according to National Highway Traffic Safety Administration, or NHTSA, data. If apprehended, this woman will face arrest, fines, jail, higher insurance rates and license revocation for behavior that is not part of the drunk-driving problem.

Meanwhile, the real problem of product abusers who drive goes unabated. According to the Department of Transportation, or DOT, the average blood-alcohol content of fatally injured drunk drivers comes in at an incredible .18 percent—more than twice the level of drinking targeted by the legislation Congress is considering. Even MADD's national president recently lamented that the problem is down to a hardened core of alcoholics who do not respond to public appeals. So why target currently legal drinkers?

Ironically, proposals to redefine drunkenness actually will hurt the fight against drunk driving. By diluting the definition of a drunk driver to include social drinkers, lawmakers automatically will increase the pool of drunks by more than 50 percent without increasing the resources to fight it. This will have a debilitating effect on the already underfunded law-enforcement efforts to stop truly drunk drivers.

## Lowering the BAC Threshold Does Not Save Lives

But the worst part about the proposal to lower the BAC threshold is that it won't work.

In the 14 years since the first of 15 states lowered their BAC thresholds to .08, not one government study has been able to show that lower BAC levels save lives. In fact, the only study in existence to make such a bold claim is a highly disputed four-page report written by antialcohol researcher Ralph Hingson (who, incidentally, sits on MADD's board of directors).

The study, which compares five .08 BAC states with five nearby .10 BAC states, concludes that 500 to 600 lives could be saved each year if all 50 states adopted a .08 BAC arrest threshold.

Independent analysis of the Hingson research by Data Nexus Inc. found that the conclusion of that study is not supported by the evidence. Hingson's results, they found, depend upon which states were chosen to be compared with the .08-percent-law states. In other words, if you change the comparison states, the study falls apart.

The DOT did its own, much larger, study of the same five .08 percent states and couldn't verify Hingson's conclusion.

So if, as government data prove, alcohol abusers with high BAC levels cause most drunk-driving deaths and no credible research has shown that .08 percent BAC laws save lives, why does MADD insist on criminalizing social drinkers? The answer is simple: self-preservation.

## A New Crusade

Having succeeded in its original mission to reduce drunk-driving deaths by educating the public and strengthening laws, MADD has declined to declare victory. Instead, it has taken on a new crusade, one which keeps it in business:

the de facto criminalization of social drinking.

Rather than relentlessly pursuing drunk drivers, MADD has charged into the Prohibitionist ranks, changing its motto from "Don't Drive Drunk" to "Impairment Begins With the First Drink." And, lest anyone miss the message, MADD president-elect Karolyn Nunnallee appeared on NBC's *Today* show (Oct. 12, 1996) to lay down her marker: "We will not tolerate drinking and driving—period."

Here is what that means in real life: If you have one or two beers with a slice of pizza prior to driving home, MADD wants you arrested. Social drinking at a tavern would be made nearly impossible for most customers, save for those with chauffeurs. Those who drink a julep or two at the racetrack had better plan on departing on horseback. It seems that this once reasonable organization hopes to launch America into a new era of solitary drinking.

This, of course, is being done for our own good.

## MADD's Primary Concern Is Self-Preservation

Or is it? A look at the organization's tax records makes it clear that securing the public good may not be the only motivation for this profound mission switch. MADD has become a big business. Like any successful firm, MADD has recognized an iron rule: Revenue must exceed expenses.

The tale of the tape is unmistakable: MADD enjoyed a cash flow of $45.5 million in 1994. Its salary and benefits picture was in excess of $8 million. Professional fund-raisers also have a stake in its longevity: They took in $4.3 million in fees. Four million dollars went to postage, with much of that spent to raise more money. More than $2 million was spent on travel and conventions.

> *"MADD has charged into the Prohibitionist ranks, changing its motto from 'Don't Drive Drunk' to 'Impairment Begins With the First Drink.'"*

That's not insignificant. There are a lot of people depending on MADD to stay in business. Despite a huge drop in drunk-driving fatalities (in 1993 the United States already had reached its goal for the year 2000), there is much to lose by declaring victory.

More eye-opening is the fact that of the $183 million MADD spent from 1991 to 1994 inclusive, a mere $332,000 was spent on direct lobbying and $304,000 on grass-roots lobbying, according to their filing with the IRS. That's .348 percent. Not much for an organization dedicated to changing laws, though completely in line with an organization committed to fund-raising and self-perpetuation.

If MADD only were interested in keeping its shingle aloft, that would make little difference. Unfortunately, they have embraced vintage self-preservation tactics that many Americans will find disturbing, including overstating the threat and relying on misleading anecdotes.

## Misleading the Public

MADD insists that drunk driving is on the rise again—by 4 percent between 1994 and 1995, according to its press releases. What it fails to point out is that all highway fatalities increased by that amount, as Americans drove 55 billion more miles in 1995 than the year before. (Alcohol-related fatalities as a percentage of all fatalities stayed the same.)

MADD tells us that alcohol standards for intoxication and arrest in many other industrialized nations are lower than in the United States but fails to mention that the alcohol-related fatality rates of these countries are higher than that of the United States.

MADD continually suggests that every person killed in drunk-driving accidents is a victim. There are victims in this area to be sure. And one is one too many. Yet, according to the DOT, drunk drivers themselves account for more than half of all alcohol-related fatalities, and drunk pedestrians who walk in front of cars represent another 11 percent.

In characterizing every suicide as a homicide, MADD deliberately is inflating people's fears that they, too, will become victims, logically expecting the heightened fear to transfer into heightened financial support.

Though disheartening, there is nothing unusual about the practice of exaggerating a threat to enhance the support of the organization claiming to fight it. Stephen Schneider, once an apostle of the coming ice age and now a global-warming enthusiast, admitted that "scientists should consider stretching the truth to get some broad-based support, to capture the public's imagination. . . . Each of us has to decide what the right balance is between being effective and being honest."

## Two Types of Drinkers

Training and experience make those of us in the restaurant and bar industry acute observers of Americans' drinking habits. Our servers and bartenders are workday social scientists whose data field comes with names, faces and highly visible types of alcohol-related behavior both normal and abusive.

We see the mainly responsible customers who enjoy a few drinks over conversation or food, get up from the table and drive safely home. We see the few problem drinkers who—if we permitted—would tie on a hellbender, then stagger out to their cars to menace the same highways traveled by our friends, families and loyal customers. Most important, we recognize the difference between these two types of drinkers. So should the law. So should MADD.

But isn't the restaurant and bar industry resisting a lower arrest threshold for its own selfish reasons, to sell one more drink to obviously impaired patrons as MADD accuses?

Hardly. Ringing up a few extra highballs isn't worth the risk that drunk drivers pose to our shared communities, and it's bad business to boot. In fact, the downside costs of overserving (litigation, obnoxious drunks, police scrutiny) far outweigh the profit on humoring the occasional drunk with more product.

And in the 44 states with dramshop laws, businesses who push drinks at customers can be held liable for millions of dollars in damages when those customers cause traffic injuries to themselves and others. And restaurants or bars that gain a name as kennels for booze hounds forfeit the business of a broader client base even as they draw the gaze of police and licensing boards.

Our industry would like to pick up the torch that MADD has dropped and hold it to the feet of the drunk driver. Does MADD remember that fellow? He was at one time their prime target. The organization did heroic work in yanking him from the driver's seat.

> *"MADD's efforts to criminalize social drinking have gone too far."*

Brian O'Neill, president of the Insurance Institute for Highway Safety and no apologist for drunks, says of the .08 BAC crusade, "What [politicians] ought to be doing is to provide more resources to vigorously enforce the laws on the books, and they'll save many more lives."

That's the goal of the restaurant industry. And it should be the goal of MADD, with whom we would gladly work to enforce—indeed, stiffen—laws against truly drunk drivers.

We in the industry are well-positioned to spot and deter the alcohol abuser—or any customer who overindulges. We know when people have gone too far and we know when to cut them off. MADD's efforts to criminalize social drinking have gone too far. It's time to cut them off.

# Bibliography

**Books**

Dick B.      *The Good Book and the Big Book: A.A.'s Roots in the Bible.* Paradise Research Publications, 1997.

Edward Behr      *Prohibition: Thirteen Years That Changed America.* New York: Arcade Publishing, 1996.

Charles Bufe      *Alcoholics Anonymous: Cult or Cure?* Tucson, AZ: See Sharp Press, 1998.

Morris E. Chafetz      *Drink Moderately and Live Longer: Understanding The Good of Alcohol.* Lanham, MD: Scarborough House, 1995.

Morris E. Chafetz      *The Tyranny of Experts: Blowing the Whistle on the Cult of Expertise.* Lanham, MD: Madison, 1996.

Timothy E. Donohue      *In the Open: Diary of a Homeless Alcoholic.* Chicago: University of Chicago Press, 1996.

Jerry Dorsman      *How to Quit Drinking Without AA: A Complete Self-Help Guide.* Rocklin, CA: Prima Publishing, 1998.

James Graham      *The Secret History of Alcoholism: The Story of Famous Alcoholics and Their Destructive Behavior.* Boston: Element, 1996.

Pete Hamill      *A Drinking Life: A Memoir.* Boston: Little, Brown, 1995.

David J. Hanson      *Alcohol Education: What We Must Do.* Westport, CT: Praeger, 1996.

David J. Hanson      *Preventing Alcohol Abuse.* Westport, CT: Praeger, 1995.

Raymond V. Haring      *Shattering Myths and Mysteries of Alcohol: Insights and Answers to Drinking, Smoking, and Drug Use.* Healthspan Communications, 1998.

Jonathan Harris      *This Drinking Nation.* New York: Simon & Schuster, 1994.

Hazelden Foundation      *The Twelve Steps of Alcoholics Anonymous.* Center City, MN: Hazelden Information Education, 1996.

Mark Gauvreau Judge      *Wasted: Tales of a Gen X Drunk.* Center City, MN: Hazelden Information Education, 1997.

Audrey Kishline    *Moderate Drinking: The Moderation Management Guide for People Who Want to Reduce Their Drinking*. New York: Crown, 1994.

Caroline Knapp    *Drinking: A Love Story*. New York: Dial Press, 1996.

George McGovern    *Terry: My Daughter's Life-and-Death Struggle with Alcoholism*. New York: Plume, 1997.

Hank Nuwer    *Wrongs of Passage: Fraternities, Sororities, Hazing, and Binge Drinking*. Bloomington: Indiana University Press, 1999.

Robert M. O'Neil    *Alcohol Advertising on the Air: Beyond the Reach of Government?* Washington, DC: The Media Institute, 1997.

Edmund B. O'Reilly    *Sobering Tales: Narratives of Alcoholism and Recovery*. Amherst: University of Massachusetts Press, 1997.

Stanton Peele    *The Diseasing of America: How We Allowed Recovery Zealots and the Treatment Industry to Convince Us We Are Out of Control*. San Francisco: Jossey-Bass, 1999.

Laurence Pringle    *Drinking: A Risky Business*. New York: William Morrow, 1997.

Ken Ragge    *The Real AA: Behind the Myth of 12-Step Recovery*. Tucson, AZ: See Sharp Press, 1998.

Ronald L. Rogers et al.    *Freeing Someone You Love from Alcohol and Other Drugs: A Step-by-Step Plan Starting Today!* New York: Perigee, 1992.

Marc Alan Schuckit    *Educating Yourself About Alcohol and Drugs : A People's Primer*. New York: Plenum Press, 1998.

Jacob Sullum    *For Your Own Good: The Anti-Smoking Crusade and the Tyranny of Public Health*. New York: Free Press, 1998.

Jack Trimpey    *Rational Recovery: The New Cure for Substance Abuse Addiction*. New York: Pocket Books, 1996.

George E. Vaillant    *The Natural History of Alcoholism Revisited*. Cambridge: Harvard University Press, 1995.

**Periodicals**

Mike Brake    "Needed: A License to Drink," *Newsweek*, March 14, 1994.

Jane E. Brody    "Intervening with Someone Who Drinks Too Much," *New York Times*, April 12, 1995.

Neil J. Carr    "Liberating Spirituality: 60 Years of AA," *America*, June 17–24, 1995.

Center for Media Education    "ABSOLUTe Web: Tobacco and Alcohol Industries Launch into Cyberspace," *Infoactive Kids,* Winter 1997. Available from http://www.cme.org.

*CQ Researcher*    "Alcohol Advertising," March 14, 1997. Available from 1414 22nd St. NW, Washington, DC 20037.

# Bibliography

| | |
|---|---|
| *CQ Researcher* | "Drinking on Campus," March 20, 1998. Available from 1414 22nd St. NW, Washington, DC 20037. |
| Tiffany Danitz | "Will One Less for the Road Impair U.S. Civil Liberties?" *Insight on the News*, May 19, 1997. Available from 3600 New York Ave. NE, Washington, DC 20001. |
| Andrew Delbanco and Thomas Delbanco | "A.A. at the Crossroads," *New Yorker*, March 20, 1995. |
| John J. DiIulio Jr. | "Broken Bottles: Alcohol, Disorder, and Crime," *Brookings Review*, Spring 1996. |
| Rodger Doyle | "Deaths Caused by Alcohol," *Scientific American*, December 1996. |
| Susan Gilbert | "Why Some Light Drinkers at 20 May Still Be on Track to Alcoholism," *New York Times*, March 13, 1996. |
| James K. Glassman | "Next Target: Liquor Companies?" *U.S. News & World Report*, July 7, 1997. |
| Christine Gorman | "Can a Drunk Learn Moderation?" *Time*, July 10, 1995. |
| Dianne R. Hales | "A Drink Is What Gets Me Through," *Good Housekeeping*, November 1997. |
| Constance Holden | "New Clues to Alcoholism Risk," *Science*, May 29, 1998. |
| *Issues and Controversies On File* | "Alcohol Issues," February 20, 1998. |
| *Journal of the American Medical Association* | "Benefits and Dangers of Alcohol," January 6, 1999. Available from PO Box 10945, Chicago, IL 60610. |
| Audrey Kishline | "A Toast to Moderation," *Psychology Today*, January/February 1996. |
| Charles Krauthammer | "The New Prohibitionism," *Time*, October 6, 1997. |
| Laurie Leiber and Morris E. Chafetz | "Should the Government Restrict Advertising of Alcoholic Beverages?" *Priorities*, vol. 9, no. 3, 1997. Available from 1995 Broadway, 2nd Floor, New York, NY 10023-5860. |
| David Leonhardt | "How Big Liquor Takes Aim at Teens," *Business Week*, May 19, 1997. |
| Frank D. McConnell | "The Elephant in the Room," *Commonweal*, March 27, 1998. |
| Per Ola and Emily d'Aulaire | "I Can Quit Whenever I Want," *Reader's Digest*, June 1997. |
| Walter Olson | "Life, Liberty, and the Pursuit of a Good Beer: How the ADA Has Turned Alcoholism into a Right," *Washington Monthly*, September 1997. |
| Brian O'Reilly | "In a Dry Era You Can Still Be Trapped by Drinking," *Fortune*, March 6, 1995. |

# Alcoholism

Stanton Peele and
Albert Lowenfels
"Should Doctors Recommend Alcohol to Their Patients?" *Priorities*, no. 1, 1996. Available from 1995 Broadway, 2nd Floor, New York, NY 10023-5860.

Joyce Howard Price
"New Battle About Evil Spirits," *Insight on the News*, February 1, 1999. Available from 3600 New York Ave. NE, Washington, DC 20001.

Susan Quick
"Five Half-Truths About Alcohol—and the Surprising Whole Truths," *Glamour*, May 1997.

Frank Reismann and
David Carroll
"A New View of Addiction: Simple and Complex," *Social Policy*, Winter 1996. Available from 25 W. 43rd St., Room 620, New York, NY 10036.

Joann Ellison Rodgers
"Addiction: A Whole New View," *Psychology Today*, September 1, 1994.

Sally L. Satel
"The Fallacies of No-Fault Addiction," *Public Interest*, January 15, 1999.

Dave Shiflett
"Here's to Your Health," *American Spectator*, October 1996.

Nancy Shute
"The Drinking Dilemma," *U.S. News & World Report*, September 8, 1997.

Norman Solomon
"The Partnership for a Candor-Free America," *Humanist*, May/June 1997.

Jacob Sullum
"Bottle Battle," *Reason*, February 10, 1999.

Elizabeth M. Whelan
"Perils of Prohibition: Why We Should Lower the Drinking Age to 18," *Newsweek,* May 29, 1995.

# Organizations to Contact

The editors have compiled the following list of organizations concerned with the issues debated in this book. The descriptions are derived from materials provided by the organizations. All have publications or information available for interested readers. The list was compiled on the date of publication of the present volume; the information provided here may change. Be aware that many organizations take several weeks or longer to respond to inquiries, so allow as much time as possible.

**Al-Anon Family Groups Headquarters**
1600 Corporate Landing Parkway, Virginia Beach, VA 23454-5617
(757) 563-1600 • fax: (757) 563-1655
e-mail: WSO@al-anon.org • website: http://www.al-anon.alateen.org

Al-Anon is a fellowship of men, women, and children whose lives have been affected by an alcoholic family member or friend. Members share their experience, strength, and hope to help each other and perhaps to aid in the recovery of the alcoholic. Al-Anon provides information on its local chapters and on its affiliated organization, Alateen. Its publications include the monthly magazine *The Forum*, the semiannual *Al-Anon Speaks Out*, the bimonthly *Alateen Talk*, and several books and pamphlets.

**Alcoholics Anonymous (AA)**
Grand Central Station, PO Box 459, New York, NY 10163
(212) 870-3400 • fax: (212) 870-3003
website: http://www.aa.org

Alcoholics Anonymous is a worldwide fellowship of sober alcoholics, whose recovery is based on Twelve Steps. AA requires no dues or fees and accepts no outside funds. It is self-supporting through voluntary contributions of members. It is not affiliated with any other organization. AA's primary purpose is to carry the AA message to the alcoholic who still suffers. Its catalog of publications include the pamphlets *A Brief Guide to Alcoholics Anonymous*, *Young People and AA*, and *Is AA for You?*

**American Beverage Institute (ABI)**
1775 Pennsylvania Ave. NW, Suite 1200, Washington, DC 20006
(202) 463-7110 • fax: (202) 463-7107
e-mail: abi@abionline.org • website: http://www.abionline.org

The American Beverage Institute is a coalition of restaurants and on-premise retailers committed to the responsible serving of alcoholic beverages. ABI is involved in research, consumer education, and legislative outreach. It publishes the monthly *ABI Newsletter*, legislative alerts, and the report ".08% Debate: What's the Harm?"

**The Beer Institute**
122 C St. NW, Suite 750, Washington, DC 20001-2150
(202) 737-2337
e-mail: beer@mail1.mnsinc.com • website: http://www.beerinst.org

The Beer Institute is the official trade association for the American brewing industry. It promotes drinking in moderation and has implemented programs such as alcohol awareness curricula in schools and public service announcements to combat underage drinking and drunk driving. *Focus on Underage Drinking* and *Guarding Against Drug and Alcohol Abuse in the Nineties* are among its many publications.

### Bureau of Alcohol, Tobacco and Firearms
Office of Liaison and Public Information
650 Massachusetts Ave. NW, Room 8290, Washington, DC 20226
(202) 927-8500 • fax: (202) 927-8868
e-mail: alcohol/tobacco@atfhq.atf.treas.gov • website: http://www.atf.treas.gov

The Bureau regulates the qualification and operations of distilleries, wineries, and breweries, as well as importers and wholesalers in the industry. It prevents unlawful practices—such as tax fraud, label fraud, commercial bribery, and smuggling—in the alcohol beverage marketplace. It publishes the monthly *Alcohol and Tobacco Newsletter*.

### Canadian Centre on Substance Abuse (CCSA)
75 Albert St., Suite 300, Ottawa, ON K1P 5E7 CANADA
(613) 235-4048 ext. 222 • fax: (613) 235-8108
e-mail: info@ccsa.ca • website: http://www.ccsa.ca

A Canadian clearinghouse on substance abuse, the CCSA works to disseminate information on the nature, extent, and consequences of substance abuse and to support and assist organizations involved in substance abuse treatment, prevention, and educational programming. The CCSA publishes several books, including *Canadian Profile: Alcohol, Tobacco, and Other Drugs*, as well as reports, policy documents, brochures, research papers, and the newsletter *Action News*.

### Center for Science in the Public Interest (CSPI)—Alcohol Policies Project
1875 Connecticut Ave. NW, Suite 300, Washington, DC 20009
(202) 332-9110 • fax: (202) 265-4954
e-mail: cspi@cspinet.org • website: http://www.cspinet.org/booze

CSPI launched the Alcohol Policies Project to reduce the devastating health and social consequences of drinking. The project's prevention-oriented policy strategy is aimed at curbing alcohol-related problems by advocating advertising reforms, increased excise taxes, and expanded warning requirements. Its publications include the quarterly newsletter *BoozeNews* and *Mad at the Ads! A Citizens' Guide to Challenging Alcohol Advertising Practices*.

### Distilled Spirits Council of the United States (DISCUS)
1250 Eye St. NW, Suite 400, Washington, DC 20005
(202) 628-3544 • fax: (202) 682-8888
website: http://www.discus.health.org

The Distilled Spirits Council of the United States is the national trade association representing producers and marketers of distilled spirits sold in the United States. It seeks to ensure the responsible advertising and marketing of distilled spirits to adult consumers and to prevent such advertising and marketing from targeting individuals below the legal purchase age. DISCUS fact sheets and pamphlets, including *The Drunk Driving Prevention Act*, are available at its website.

### Hazelden Institute
PO Box 176, 15251 Pleasant Valley Rd., Center City, MN 55012-9640
(800) 329-9000 • fax: (651) 213-4590
e-mail: info@hazelden.org • website: http://www.hazelden.org

Hazelden is a nonprofit organization dedicated to helping people recover from alcoholism and other addictions. It provides residential and outpatient treatment for adults and young people, programs for families affected by chemical dependency, and training for a variety of professionals. The institute publishes the quarterly newsletter *Hazelden Voice*, the bimonthly newspaper column *Alive & Free*, books, press releases, research reports, and public policy papers.

**Moderation Management (MM)**
PO Box 1752, Woodinville, WA 98072
(888) 561-9834
e-mail: mm@moderation.org • website: http://www.moderation.org

Moderation Management is a recovery program and national support network for people who have made the decision to reduce their drinking and make other positive lifestyle changes. MM empowers individuals to accept personal responsibility for choosing and maintaining their own recovery path, whether through moderation or abstinence. They offer the book *Moderate Drinking: The Moderation Management Guide for People Who Want to Reduce Their Drinking*, as well as additional suggested reading material, books, pamphlets, and guidelines regarding drinking in moderation.

**Mothers Against Drunk Driving (MADD)**
511 E. John Carpenter Frwy., #700, Irving, TX 75062
(800) 438-6233
e-mail: info@madd.org • website: http://www.madd.org

Mothers Against Drunk Driving seeks to act as the voice of victims of drunk driving accidents by speaking on their behalf to communities, businesses, and educational groups and by providing materials for use in medical facilities and health and driver education programs. MADD publishes *Driven* magazine and the newsletter *MADD in Action* as well as a variety of brochures and other materials on drunk driving.

**National Association for Children of Alcoholics (NACoA)**
11426 Rockville Pike, Suite 100, Rockville, MD 20852
(888) 554-COAS (554-2627) • fax: (301) 468-0987
e-mail: nacoa@erols.com • website: http://www.health.org/nacoa

NACoA is the only national nonprofit membership organization working on behalf of children of alcoholics. Its mission is to advocate for all children and families affected by alcoholism and other drug dependencies. The association publishes books, pamphlets, videos, educational kits, and the bimonthly *NACoA Network Newsletter*.

**National Center on Addiction and Substance Abuse (CASA)**
Columbia University, 152 West 57th St., New York, NY 10019
(212) 841-5200 • fax: (212) 956-8020
website: http://www.casacolumbia.org

The National Center on Addiction and Substance Abuse brings together all professional disciplines needed to study and combat substance abuse. CASA informs Americans about the economic and social costs of substance abuse; assesses what works in prevention, treatment, and law enforcement; and removes the stigma of substance abuse. Publications include the reports "No Safe Haven: Children of Substance-Abusing Parents," and "Cigarettes, Alcohol, Marijuana: Gateways to Illicit Drug Use."

**National Council on Alcoholism and Drug Dependence (NCADD)**
12 West 21st St., New York, NY 10010
(212) 206-6770 • fax: (212) 645-1690
e-mail: national@ncadd.org • website: http://www.ncadd.org

NCADD is a volunteer health organization that helps individuals overcome addictions, advises the federal government on drug and alcohol policies, and develops substance abuse prevention and education programs for youth. It publishes the quarterly news-letter *NCADD Amethyst*, the monthly newsletter *NCADD Washington Report*, fact sheets, and brochures.

**National Institute on Alcohol Abuse and Alcoholism (NIAAA)**
Willco Building, 6000 Executive Blvd., Bethesda, MD 20892-7003
(301) 496-4000
e-mail: niaaaweb-r@exchange.nih.gov • website: http://www.niaaa.nih.gov

NIAAA supports and conducts biomedical and behavioral research on the causes, con-sequences, treatment, and prevention of alcoholism and alcohol-related problems. NIAAA also provides leadership in the national effort to reduce the severe and often fatal consequences of these problems. It publishes the quarterly journal *Alcohol Health & Research World, Alcohol Alert* bulletins, reports, and pamphlets.

**National Organization on Fetal Alcohol Syndrome (NOFAS)**
418 C St. NE, Washington, DC 20002
(202) 785-4585 • fax: (202) 466-6456
e-mail: nofas@erols.com • website: http://www.nofas.com

NOFAS is a nonprofit organization dedicated to raising public awareness of Fetal Alco-hol Syndrome, and to developing and implementing innovative ideas in prevention, education, intervention, and advocacy in communities throughout the nation. It publish-es the *NOFAS Newsletter*.

**Rational Recovery**
Box 800, Lotus, CA 95651
(530) 621-2667 • fax: (530) 622-4296
e-mail: icc@rational.org • website: http://www.rational.org/recovery

Rational Recovery is a national self-help organization that offers a cognitive rather than spiritual approach to recovery from alcoholism. Its philosophy holds that alcoholics can attain sobriety without depending on other people or a "higher power." It publishes materials about the organization and its use of rational-emotive therapy.

**SMART Recovery**
24000 Mercantile Road, Suite 11, Beachwood, OH 44122
(216) 292-0220 • fax: (216) 831-3776
e-mail: srmail1@aol.com • website: http://www.smartrecovery.org

SMART Recovery is an abstinence-based, not-for-profit organization offering a cognitive-behavioral based self-help program for people with addictive problems. Its publications include the quarterly newsletter *SMART Recovery News & Views* and *Alco-hol: How To Give It Up and Be Glad You Did*.

**The Wine Institute**
425 Market St., Suite 1000, San Francisco, CA 94105
(415) 512-0151 • fax: (415) 442-0742
e-mail: communications@wineinstitute.org • website: http://www.wineinstitute.org

The Wine Institute introduces and advocates public policy measures to enhance the environment for the responsible consumption and enjoyment of wine. It publishes the monthly newsletter *NewsFlash* and the reports "American Heart Association Advisory Acknowledges 'Potentially Sizable Health Benefit' of Alcohol" and "Study Finds Bet-ter Brain Functioning Among Moderate Alcohol Consuming Women."

**Internet Resources**

**Alcohol: Problems and Solutions Website**
website: http://www2.potsdam.edu/alcohol-info

This website describes alcohol use and abuse along with effective ways to reduce or eliminate drinking problems such as underage drinking, drinking and driving, and binge drinking. The *In Their Own Words* section contains interviews with experts on a wide variety of alcohol-related issues, *In the News* provides current news articles for downloading, and *In My Opinion* offers essays including "It's Better to Teach Safe Use of Alcohol."

**The Stanton Peele Addiction Website**
website: http://peele.sas.nl

Stanton Peele has been researching and writing about addiction for thirty years. His controversial approach negates the American medical model of addiction as a disease. Instead, he views it as a behavior which can be overcome through maturity, improved coping skills, and better self-management and self-esteem. His website includes an "Ask Stanton" question and answer section and an extensive virtual library of articles available for viewing. Peele has also authored several books, including *The Truth About Addiction and Recovery* and *Diseasing of America*, which may be ordered from the website.

# Index

Abel, Ernest, 48
accidents, 24
  *see also* automobile accidents
addiction
  and compulsive behavior, 85, 88
  disease model of, 69–72, 76–77
  and emotional disorders, 22
  and genetics, 71
*Addiction Counselling World*
  (magazine), 110
adolescents. *See* teenagers
*Adult Children of Alcoholics* (Woititz),
  105
advertisements
  in broadcast media, 116–17, 135
    for beer, 116, 118, 119, 122,
      134–36, 147
    cost of, 134, 135
    effects of, 29
      are harmful, 135–37
      are not harmful, 122, 123, 126,
        128–29, 173
    reaction to, 117–19
    regulation of
      by government, 120–22, 128,
        137–39
      by industry, 121–22, 124–25, 131,
        133
    public opinion on, 125, 137, 138
  for wine, 116, 118, 119, 122, 135
  counteradvertisements, 139
  on Internet, 119
  in print media, 127, 136
  and smoking, 115, 123
  and Supreme Court, 121, 128
  and warning labels, 138–39, 174–75
*Advertising, Alcohol Consumption, and
  Abuse* (Fisher), 128
African Americans, 22, 23
Al-Anon, 31, 104, 105

*Al-Anon Spoken Here,* 104
Alateen, 31
alcohol
  abuse of, 14
  availability of, 173–74, 175
  beverage equivalence, 122–23
  and family problems, 37
  as gateway drug, 32–33, 35, 176–77
  moral neutrality of, 57–58
  physiological effects of, 20–21, 35
  restriction of
    is effective, 172, 173–75
    is ineffective, 172, 179–80
  universality of, 52–54
*Alcohol and Alcohol Problems*
  (Keller), 53
*Alcohol: The Gateway Drug,* 176
Alcoholics Anonymous (AA), 15–16
  case histories, 97–98, 99
  described, 110–11
  and disease model of alcoholism, 66,
    112
  and economics, 109
  founding of, 103
  growth of, 93–94
  is effective, 90, 92, 97–98
  is harmful, 110, 111–12
  is ineffective, 107–109
  as model for addiction treatment,
    91–92, 103
  organization of, 92–93
  philosophy of, 102–103
  as spiritual movement, 90, 95–100,
    102–103, 111–12
*Alcoholics Anonymous Big Book*
  (Wilson), 91–92, 94, 99, 103
*Alcoholics Anonymous Comes of Age*
  (Wilson), 101
*Alcoholics Anonymous: Cult or Cure?*
  (Bufe), 90, 110

alcoholism
  causes of, 14–15, 20, 68
  costs of, 68, 163
  definition of, 14, 19, 54–56
  extent of, 14, 21, 147
  physiological effects of, 25–26
  public opinion on, 163
  risk factors for, 21–23
  symptoms of, 14, 19–20
  withdrawal symptoms from, 27
American Academy of Child and
  Adolescent Psychiatry, 30
American Heart Association, 131
*American Journal of Public Health,*
  169
American Medical Association, 66
American Temperance Society, 15
Anderson, David, 40
Andrews, Colman, 50
Anheuser-Busch, 149–50, 152
Anti-Saloon League of America, 15
anxiety, 22–23, 28
Asian Americans, 22, 81–82
attention deficit disorder, 23
Australia, 174
automobile accidents, 24, 123, 144
  and blood-alcohol content, 167,
    168–70
  extent of, 167, 168, 180, 185
  and party patrols, 165
  and teenagers, 35, 163
Ayers, Sharron, 144–45

Baker, Sue, 112
Baltz, Leslie Anne, 40
beer industry
  and advertisements, 116, 118, 119,
    122, 134–36, 147
  and beverage alcohol equivalence,
    123
  and market share, 120, 134
  political influence of, 121, 146–47,
    149–52
Beer Institute, 149
behavior
  compulsive, 83–84, 85, 86–88
  model of alcoholism, 67, 74
    is cruel, 77
Berman, Richard, 182
*Beverage Industry* (trade publication),
120
*Big Book* (Wilson), 91–92, 94, 99, 103
binge drinking
  and deaths, 40
  definition of, 39–40, 59–60
  effects of, 40
  extent of, 21, 40, 60–62, 180
  and health, 25
  *see also under* college students;
    teenagers
Bishop, Mike, 162
blood-alcohol content (BAC)
  and driving, 167, 168–69, 176,
    182–83, 186
    public opinion on, 169–70
  and law enforcement, 186
  lowering threshold is effective, 169,
    170–71
  lowering threshold is ineffective, 183
  and teenagers, 165
blood pressure, 25
Bowden, Julie, 105
Brake, Mike, 156
breast cancer, 142
Britain, 46–47
broadcast industry
  and advertisements, 118–19, 134
    code for, 122, 125
  and influence of advertisers, 136–37
Brodsky, Archie, 176–77
Brown, George, 146–47
Buchman, Frank N.D., 102
Bufe, Charles, 90, 110
Bureau of Alcohol, Tobacco and
  Firearms, 130–31
B-vitamins, 26
Byrd, Richard, 147–48

Califano, Joseph A., Jr., 32–33
cancers, 25, 142
Castelli, William, 18
Center for Media Education, 119
Center for Science in the Public
  Interest (CSPI), 32, 118, 131–32,
  152–53, 157
Center on Addiction and Substance
  Abuse at Columbia University
  (CASA), 32–33, 37
Chafetz, Morris E., 122, 126
Chapman, Stephen, 130

children
  and advertisements, 117, 119, 135
  of alcoholics, 80, 105, 106
    behavior of, 31
    emotional problems of, 24, 30–32
    and genetics, 74–75
  extent of drinking among, 134
  and fetal alcohol syndrome, 26
  and television, 136
Chinese Americans, 181
Christopher, James, 90
Clinton, Bill
  and advertising ban, 117, 119, 137
  and blood-alcohol content, 148, 167
Cloninger, Robert, 81, 82
Coate, Douglas, 157–58
codependence, 28–29
  definition of, 108–109
  movements, 105–106
*Codependence Mistreated-
  Misunderstood* (Schaef), 105
Cohen, Fran, 39
College Alcohol Study, 34
college students
  and bars, 144–45
  and binge drinking, 34, 47, 180
    effects of, 38, 39, 40
    extent of, 40, 42, 60, 61
  and drinking
    effects of, 36
    extent of, 38, 61–62, 163, 175
  and school alcohol policies, 38–39,
    40–43
  underground drinking of, 175, 180
*Columbia University College of
  Physicians and Surgeons Complete
  Home Medical Guide, The,* 14
Constitution, U.S.
  Eighteenth Amendment, 15
  First Amendment, 121, 124–25
  Twenty-first Amendment, 15
*Contemporary Drug Problems,*
  105–106
Cops 'N Shops, 164–65
crime, 36
Criqui, Michael, 18

deaths, 14, 23–24, 134, 147, 163
  from automobile accidents, 123
  from binge drinking, 40

from smoking, 147
DeJong, Bill, 41
delirium tremens, 27
DeLuca, John, 148–49
depression, 22–23, 28
dietary guidelines, 46–47, 48, 142
disease
  addiction as, 69–72
  definition of, 69
  model of addiction, 76–77
  model of alcoholism, 64, 112
    and Alcoholics Anonymous (AA),
      66
    and behavior, 83–84
    and genetics, 73, 74–75
    is harmful, 85–88
    and medical profession, 66–67
*Disease Concept of Alcoholism, The*
  (Jellinek), 64, 66
*Diseasing of America, The* (Peele), 67,
  106
distillation, 53
Distilled Spirits Council of the U.S.
  (DISCUS)
  and advertisements
    ban of, 116, 117, 133
    code for, 120
domestic violence, 24, 147
dramshop laws, 186
Dreyfus, Edward A., 83
drinking
  benefits of, 51, 52
  costs of, 134, 158–59
  decrease in, 131, 134
  history of, 15, 16, 45–46
  legal age should be lowered, 179–80
  moderate
    benefits of, 18, 23
    described, 142–43
    and health effects, 141–42
    and tax increase, 160
  problem, 14
  public opinion on, 44, 48–49, 56–57
  social pressure for, 22
  *see also under* college students;
    teenagers
drugs
  alcohol as gateway to, 32–33, 35,
    176–77
  interaction with alcohol, 26

education
for college students, 61–62
for medical professionals, 68
elderly, 21, 22–23, 26
emotional disorders, 22–23, 25–26, 84–85
Engs, Ruth, 61, 179
Eskimos, 82
ethnicity, 22, 47, 64, 81–82, 181

Federal Communications Commission (FCC), 117, 118, 124, 137
Federal Trade Commission (FTC), 118, 122
fermentation, 52–54
fetal alcohol syndrome (FAS), 26, 48
Fingarette, Herbert, 54
Fisher, Joseph C., 128
Foster, M.J., 153
Framingham Heart Study, 18
France, 141
fraternity system, 42–43
"French Paradox, The," 18

Garvin, David A., 121–22
gateway drugs, 32–33, 35, 176–77
genetics
and addiction, 71
and alcoholism
public opinion on, 78–79
and development of disease, 76
and physiological effects of alcohol, 22
and predisposition, 73
and research, 64, 79–81
on adoptees, 74–75
on twins, 74
*Getting Better Inside Alcoholics Anonymous* (Robertson), 102
Goodwin, Donald, 79, 106
Gorski, Terence, 106
Gravitz, Herbert, 105
Greek Americans, 47, 181
Grossman, Michael, 157–58
Guay, Dennis, 41
Gupta, Anil K., 121, 122

Hacker, George A., 133, 152–53
Hammersley, Richard, 112

Hanson, David J., 59, 61, 172
Harvard School of Public Health, 34
"Healing Ourselves and Our Planet" (Room), 105–106
health, 36–37
*see also specific conditions*
heart disease
causes of, 70–71
and drinking, 18, 24–25
moderate, 46, 131, 141–42
*Heavy Drinking: The Myth of Alcoholism as a Disease* (Fingarette), 54
Hemphill, Thomas A., 116
Hester, Reid K., 108
Hingson, Ralph, 183
Hispanic Americans, 22
Hobbs, Thomas R., 65
*How to Stay Sober: Recovery Without Religion* (Christopher), 90
Hundt, Reed E., 117, 118, 137
Hyman, Steven, 90

Institute for Social Research (ISR), 61
International Doctors of Alcoholics Anonymous (IDAA), 67
Irish Americans, 22, 47, 64
Italian Americans, 47, 64, 181
Italy, 59–60

James, Oliver, 111, 112
Jamshid (king of Persia), 53
Jellinek, Elvin M., 64, 66
Jewish Americans, 22, 47, 181
*Journal of the American Medical Association* (*JAMA*), 18, 66, 142

Katz, Solomon H., 53
Keller, Mark, 53
Kendler, Kenneth, 64
Kennard, William, 147
Kennedy, Joseph, II, 117, 138, 147, 148
Kenny, Ursula, 110
Koch, Robert, 148
Krebs, Hans A., 53
Krueger, Scott, 40

Lad, Lawrence J., 121, 122
*Lancet,* 67

Lautenberg, Frank, 182
law enforcement
  and blood-alcohol content, 170, 186
  investigative strategies of, 163–65
  and teenagers, 162
Lee, Philip, 46
legislation
  federal, 138, 147, 151–52, 167
  and political influence of alcohol
    industry, 121
  state, 144–46, 153, 165–66, 186
  on blood-alcohol content, 169, 171
Lemanski, Michael J., 101
Lester, David, 80
licenses to drink, 156
*Life Extension* (Pearson and Shaw),
  78–79
Little, Bobby, 162
liver disorders, 25
Lott, Trent, 117, 137
Lowenfels, Albert B., 18
Lowey, Nita, 182

Makela, Klaus, 92
malnutrition, 26
marijuana, 33, 34
Massing, Michael, 131, 144
Mather, Cotton, 15
Mather, Increase, 45
Matthew, Theobald, 15
May, William W., 95
McGrath, Ray, 149
Miller, William R., 108
Mothers Against Drunk Driving
  (MADD), 118, 182–85
murder, 24, 147
Murray, Robin, 79–80

National Beer Wholesalers Association
  (N.B.W.A.), 150–52
National Center for Health Statistics,
  14
National Highway Traffic Safety
  Administration, 167
National Institute of Drug Abuse, 33
National Institute on Alcohol Abuse
  and Alcoholism (NIAAA), 34–35
National Prohibition Act, 15
Native Americans, 22, 81–82
*Natural History of Alcoholism, The*

  (Vaillant), 107
Nestle, Marion, 46
*Newsweek* (magazine), 156
*New York Times,* 49, 131
New Zealand, 47, 174
Noah, 53
Noble Experiment. *See* Prohibition
*Normal and the Abnormal in
  Adolescent Drinking, The,* 127
Nunnallee, Karolyn, 184

O'Neill, Brian, 186
Oriental flush, 81–82
Oxford Group Movement, 102

Park, Roderic B., 156
party patrols, 165
Pasteur, Louis, 53
Pearson, Durk, 78–79
Peck, M. Scott, 98
Peele, Stanton, 44, 78
  on behavior model of alcoholism, 67
  and gateway theory, 176–77
  and twelve-step programs, 106
  personality traits, 23, 177
PGA (pure grain alcohol), 39
pregnancy, 26, 48
price elasticity, 159
Prohibition, 15, 45, 65–66
*Prohibition: The Era of Excess*
  (Sinclair), 65–66
*Psychology Today* (magazine), 108

Ragge, Ken, 110
*Real AA* (Ragge), 110
*Recovery: A Guide for Adult Children
  of Alcoholics* (Gravitz and Bowden),
  105
Rehr, David, 150–52
religion
  Alcoholics Anonymous as, 90,
    95–100, 102–103, 111–12
  and alcoholism, 98–99
Reno, Janet, 137
Robertson, Nan, 102
Room, Robin, 105–106
Rush, Benjamin, 65

Sarasin, Ron, 150
Schaef, Anne Wilson, 105

Schuckit, Marc Alan, 73, 80–81, 82
Seagram America, 116, 119, 133, 149, 152
senior citizens, 21, 22–23, 26
Sensible Advertising and Family Education Act, 138
Shalala, Donna E., 119
Shaw, Sandra, 78–79
Silkworth, William Duncan, 95, 101
Sinclair, A., 65–66
*60 Minutes* (television show), 18,141
Skipper, Greg, 69
Smith, Robert, 66, 102
smoking, 25, 68
  and advertisements, 115, 123
  and counteradvertisements, 139
  deaths from, 147
  tobacco wars, 115, 130
Soviet Union, 129
Spain, 47
Subby, Robert, 108–109
suicide, 24, 35
Supreme Court
  and ban on advertising prices, 128
  and First Amendment, 121
Sweden, 59
Switzerland, 47

Tapp, Charles, 144–46
taxes
  increase in
    will decrease drinking, 157–58, 159–60
    will not decrease drinking, 173
teenagers
  and abstinence, 127–28
  of alcoholics, 30–31
  and automobile accidents, 35, 163
  and beer, 134–35
  and binge drinking, 24, 34, 47, 60, 134
  and blood-alcohol content (BAC), 165
  and crime, 36
  and drinking
    and advertisements, 126, 128–29, 134–35
    and driving, 123
    effects of, 35–36
    extent of, 21, 32, 33–34, 60, 119, 127, 163
  and drugs, 34

and law enforcement, 162, 163–65
and legislation, 165–66
and licenses to drink, 156
and minimum drinking age, 175
and price increases, 157–58, 160
and suicide, 35
and television, 136
temperance movements
  history of, 15, 65–66
  moderation approach, 177–78
  prohibitionist approach, 172–73
Thompson, J.J., 38
Thurmond, Strom, 141
*Today* (television show), 184
traffic accidents. *See* automobile accidents
treatments
  abstinence, 27–28
  brief interventions, 36–37, 47–48, 68
  effectiveness of, 108
  nonspiritual based, 90, 109
  twelve-step programs, 90
    are effective, 110
    are ineffective, 107–109
    described, 102–106
    and disease model of alcoholism, 85–86
    economics of, 109
    professionals in, 106–107
    *see also* Alcoholics Anonymous (AA)
"Twelve Steps of Recovery" (Wilson), 102–103

undercover stings, 163–64
*Under the Influence* (Milam), 80
United Kingdom, 60
*U.S. News & World Report* (magazine), 38–39, 41, 42

Vaillant, George E.
  and behavior model of alcoholism, 64, 80, 82
  and ethnicity and drinking, 47
  and ineffectiveness of Alcoholics Anonymous, 107
Voigt, Mary M., 53
Volstead Act, 15

Waldo, W., 76

Walsh, Raoul, 67
Wechsler, Henry
  on binge drinking, 39–40, 43
  and binge drinking among college
    students, 61
  on school drinking policies, 41
Wegscheider-Cruse, Sharon, 109
Well-Connected, 19
Wernicke-Korsakoff Syndrome, 26
Wesley, John, 15
Wilson, William Griffith, 66, 101–102
wine industry
  and advertisements, 116, 118, 119,
    122, 134
  and beverage alcohol equivalence, 123
  and heart disease, 131

and market share, 120
  political influence of, 121, 148–49
Woititz, Janet Geringer, 105
Wolin, Steven J., 106
Woman's Christian Temperance Union,
  15
women
  and alcoholism of partners, 24
  and physiological effects of
    alcoholism, 25
  pregnant, 26, 48
  and risk of alcoholism, 21–22
World Health Organization, 47–48
Wynne, Benjamin, 145

Zimmerman, Robert, 91, 141